KICK-ASS 2 PRELUDE:
HIT-GIRL

KICK-ASS 2 PRELUDE: HIT-GIRL. Hardback ISBN: 9781781162651. Contains material originally published in magazine form as *Hit-Girl* #1-5. Published by Titan Books, A division of Titan Publishing Group Ltd., 144 Southwark St., London, SE1 0UP. Copyright © 2012-2013 Millarworld Ltd. and John S. Romita. All Rights Reserved. "HIT-GIRL," "KICK-ASS," "KICK-ASS 2," the Hit-Girl and Kick-Ass logos, and all prominent characters and their likenesses featured herein are trademarks of Millarworld Limited & John S. Romita. "Millarworld" and the Millarworld logo are trademarks of Millarworld Limited. No part of this publication may be reproduced, stored in a retrieval system, or transmitted, in any form or by any means, without the prior written permission of the publisher. Names, characters, places and incidents featured in this publication are either the product of the author's imagination or used fictitiously. Any resemblance to actual persons, living or dead (except for satirical purposes), is entirely coincidental.

A CIP catalogue record for this title is available from the British Library.

First edition: March 2013

3 5 7 9 10 8 6 4 2

Printed in Spain

KICK-ASS 2 PRELUDE:

HIT-GIRL

Writer & Co-Creator
MARK MILLAR

Breakdowns & Co-Creator
JOHN ROMITA JR.

Finishes & Ink Washes
TOM PALMER

Colourist
DEAN WHITE
with MICHAEL KELLEHER

Letterer
CHRIS ELIOPOULOS

Editor
JENNIFER LEE

Collection Editor: **JENNIFER LEE**

Book Designer: **SPRING HOTELING**

SVP of Print & Digital Publishing Sales (Marvel): **DAVID GABRIEL**

SVP of Operations & Procurement, Publishing (Marvel): **DAVID BOGART**

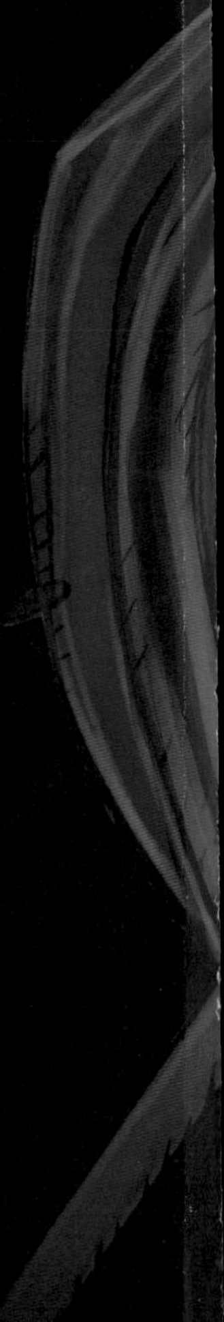

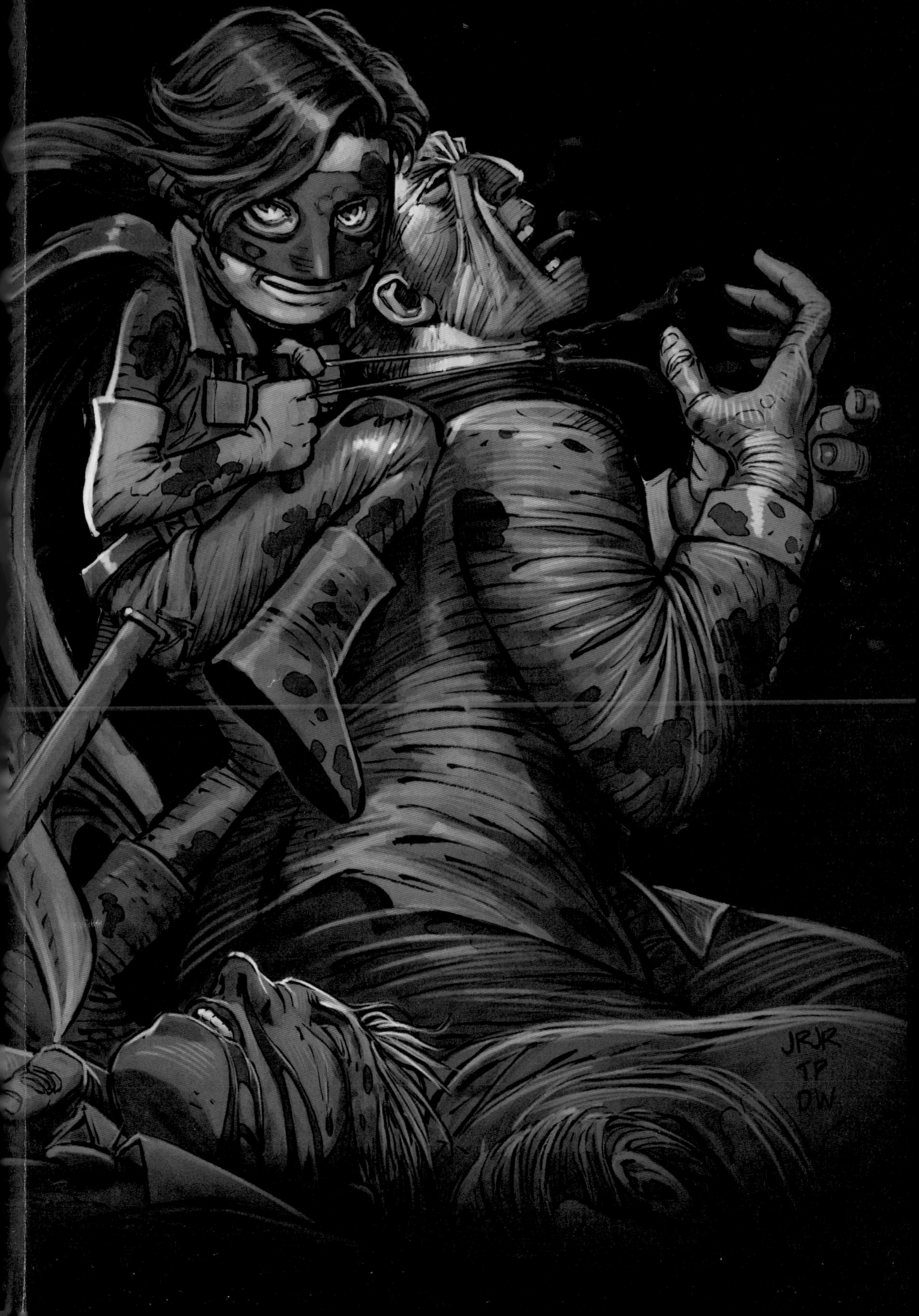
JRJR
TP
DW

INTRODUCTION

I am writing this to you from Mark Millar's dank, Scottish cellar. He says if I don't keep typing, he's going to turn on those jumper cables he's got hooked up to my balls! He went for a pint though, so please, I have seconds, seconds only! Someone send help! Please, I hear him coming bac—

ZZZttt!!!

Aagh!!

So, maybe that's not exactly true. Maybe I'm actually writing this from the comfort of my desk in Long Island. But you'd believe it, right? It's exactly the sort of thing you expect from a man who's written more gut-wrenching ultraviolence, more earth-shaking action than anyone I know. Hell, it's the kind of thing I expected, too, when I first met him.

Which brings me to London, spring 2012. I was there for my first Kapow!Con, and I had barely dropped off my bags when I got a text from Mark, asking me to come meet him for a drink. We had chatted through emails a bit in the weeks leading up to the convention, but I'd never met the man face-to-face. I was nervous. I half expected to walk up to the convention center and see some douchebag come flying through the glass, Mark stepping out after him, swords strapped on, pint in hand, delivering some awesome quip in a growling brogue before chopping the guy's feet off.

But that's not the man I found sitting there at the café by the convention offices. The man I found, Mark Millar, was cradling and feeding his newborn daughter, sipping at a coffee. As soon as he saw me he smiled and waved me over. "Young man!" he said, offering me a seat.

You can probably guess this initial meeting didn't end with the death of untold hundreds. It was really just a great conversation. I have young children myself, and so we got lost for a while, trading stories about these beautiful kids who keep us up all night like fucking maniacs, but whom we love more than the world. Honestly, it surprised me a little, how open and down-to-earth Mark was from go, and above all, how heartfelt his conversation was. Thinking back now, though, I know it shouldn't have surprised me. Because the ugly truth is that at its core, for me, Mark's work has always been about heart.

Now I can hear you out there: "Heart? Fuck off Snyder!" But hear me out...

Because for me, what makes Mark's work beloved by fans around the world isn't really the ball-zapping thrills or the incredible action. It's his love for his characters. It's the way he makes you relate to and care deeply about each of his creations from the first turn of the page. The craftsmanship in each voice, the quirks in each character's thinking—Mark makes his characters' hearts beat for you, makes them live for you in the most immediate, gripping ways. Better than just about anyone. So at the risk of offending you guys (and maybe even you, Mark), I'd say that at the very heart of Mark's work is, well... heart. Yes, this book has the hyper-violent awesomeness you want and expect from Mark (wait 'til you get to the teddy-bear execution!)… but the magic of the book is how Mark brings to life Mindy's everyday problems side-by-side with the badassery. Here, in HIT-GIRL, we see her vulnerable for the first time, really vulnerable. Don't get me wrong, this is the Mindy you know and love—the vigilante, raised to be the toughest, deadliest hero in the world. But it's also Mindy the kid, trying to figure out how to be child, a daughter, a friend… a Mindy I'm sure you'll come to know and love even more.

Now if Mark's writing is the heart of this book, then John Romita Jr.'s storytelling is its soul. After all, what awesome thing is there to say about his work that hasn't been said before? His signature style is here in all its glory, so expressive and dynamic. His storytelling has never been better than it is in HIT-GIRL. And of course, here there's an extra thrill of getting to see him cut loose, shake off the restraints of all things kid-friendly, and get totally down and dirty. You can just tell from the art how much fun he's having, and it makes for an incredible read. And there's no overestimating the contribution of the crew John has with him here. Between Tom Palmer's rich line-work and finishes, Dean White's evocative colors and Chris Eliopoulos' artful lettering, you've got one of the best teams in visual storytelling.

So friends, to finish up, what follows here is a great book, by a great team, featuring the most bad-ass character currently in comics… There's no way you can read this book and not get swept away by the characters, the mindblowing action, and the adoration of comics inherent on every page. Because, like all the KICK-ASS books, this one is also about the transformative power of comics, about their ability to inspire wonder and desires—good and bad. Like I said, it's a book made with much love, and I couldn't be more honored that Mark decided to reach out to me to write this. Savor this book; it's a wonder.

Still, the next time Mark invites me for a drink, he better bring his fucking swords. Swords, Mark!

Scott Snyder is a novelist and the award-winning writer for BATMAN, SWAMP THING, SEVERED, and AMERICAN VAMPIRE.

ONE

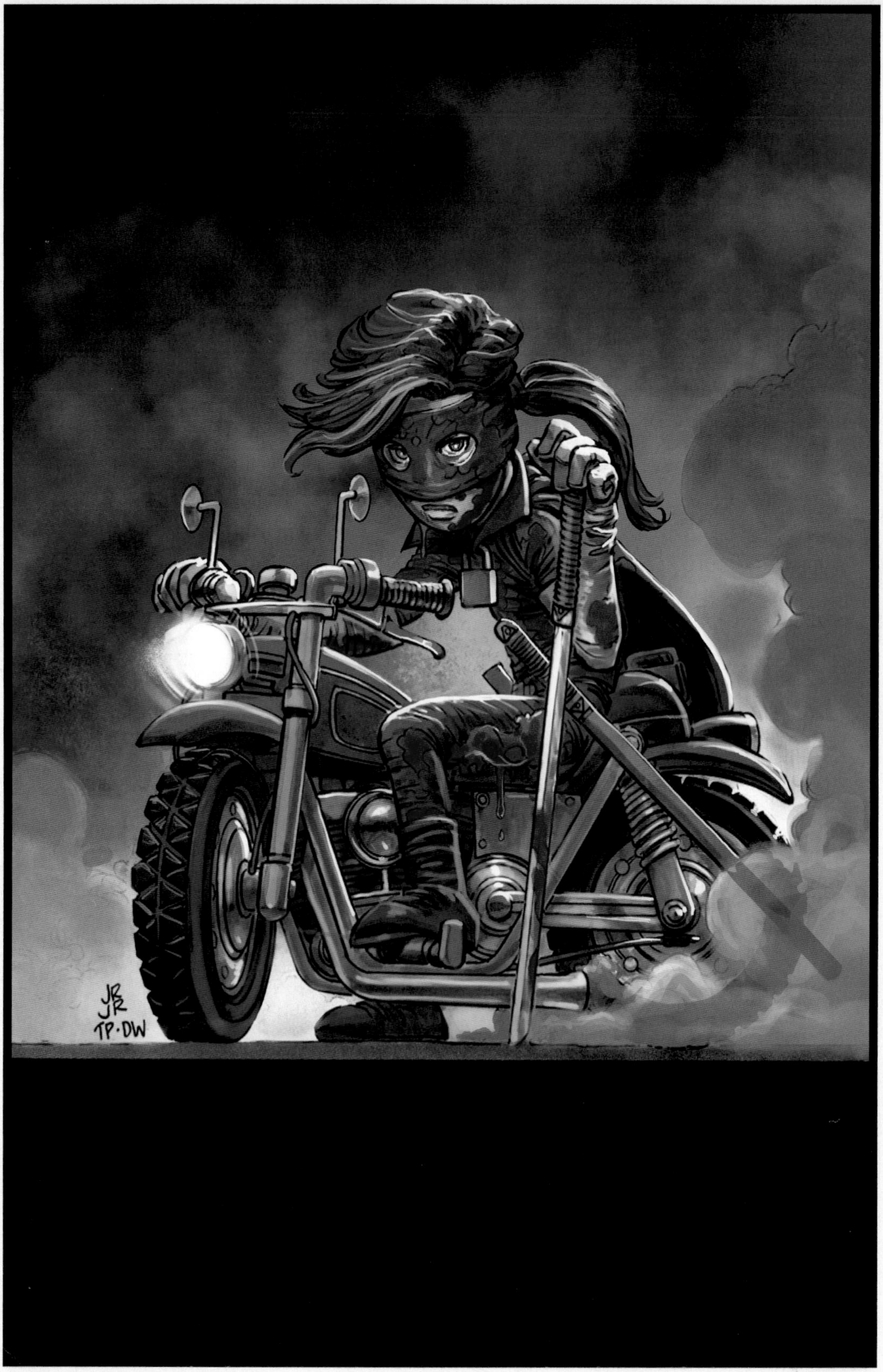
JR JR TP·DW

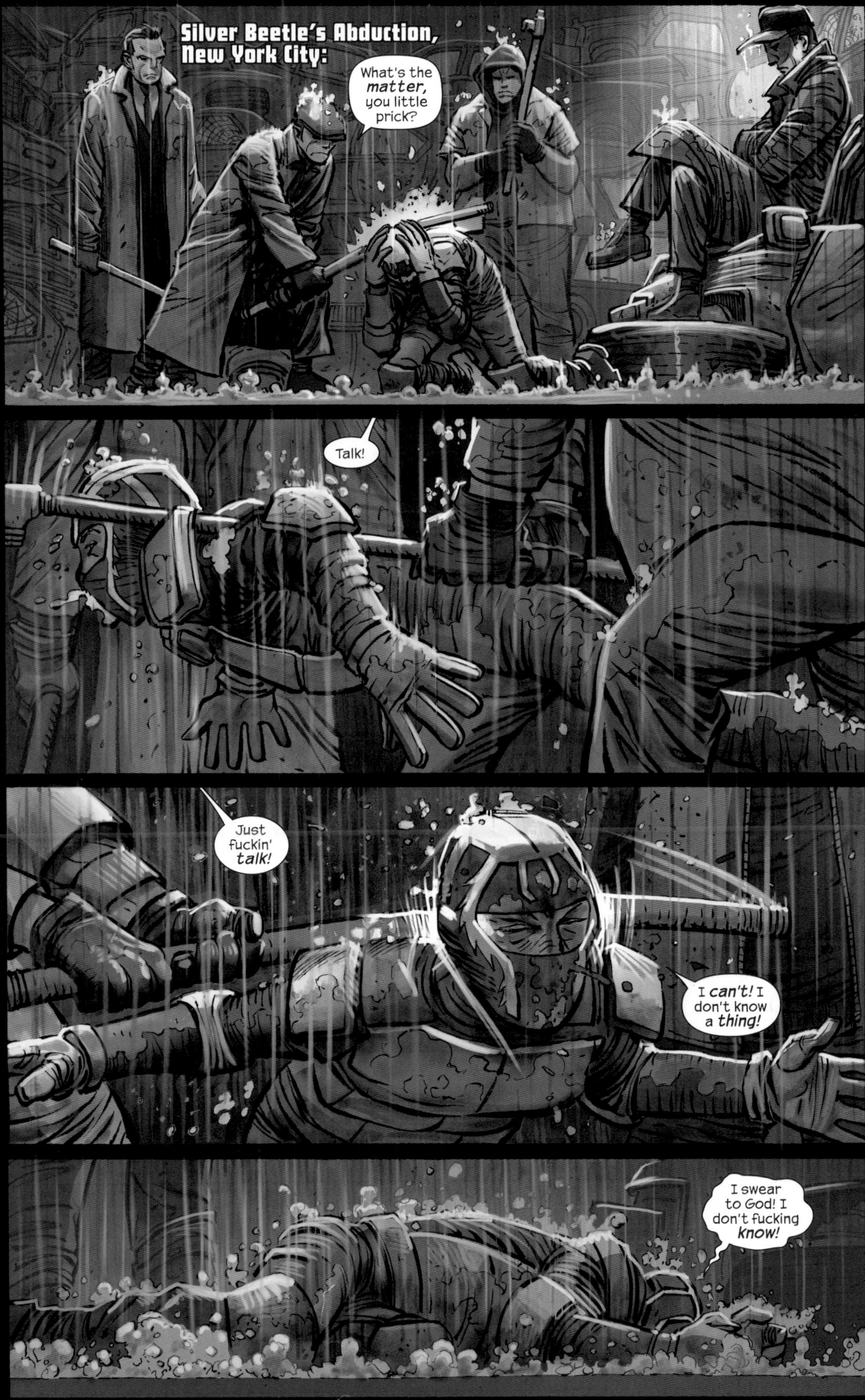
Silver Beetle's Abduction, New York City:
What's the *matter,* you little prick?
Talk!
Just fuckin' *talk!*
I *can't!* I don't know a *thing!*
I swear to God! I don't fucking *know!*

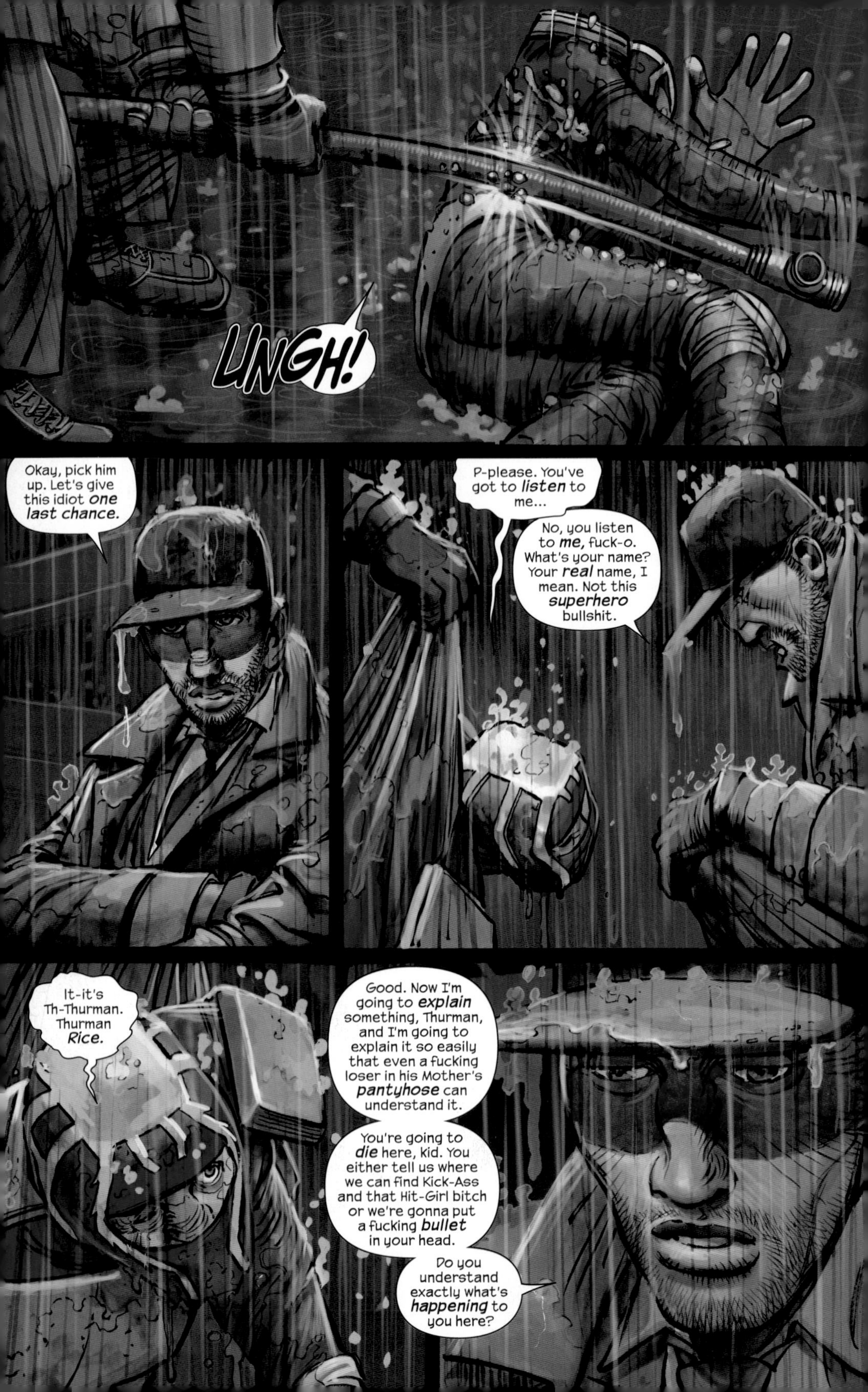
UNGH!
Okay, pick him up. Let's give this idiot *one last chance.*
P-please. You've got to *listen* to me...
No, you listen to *me,* fuck-o. What's your name? Your *real* name, I mean. Not this *superhero* bullshit.
It-it's Th-Thurman. Thurman *Rice.*
Good. Now I'm going to *explain* something, Thurman, and I'm going to explain it so easily that even a fucking loser in his Mother's *pantyhose* can understand it.
You're going to *die* here, kid. You either tell us where we can find Kick-Ass and that Hit-Girl bitch or we're gonna put a fucking *bullet* in your head.
Do you understand exactly what's *happening* to you here?

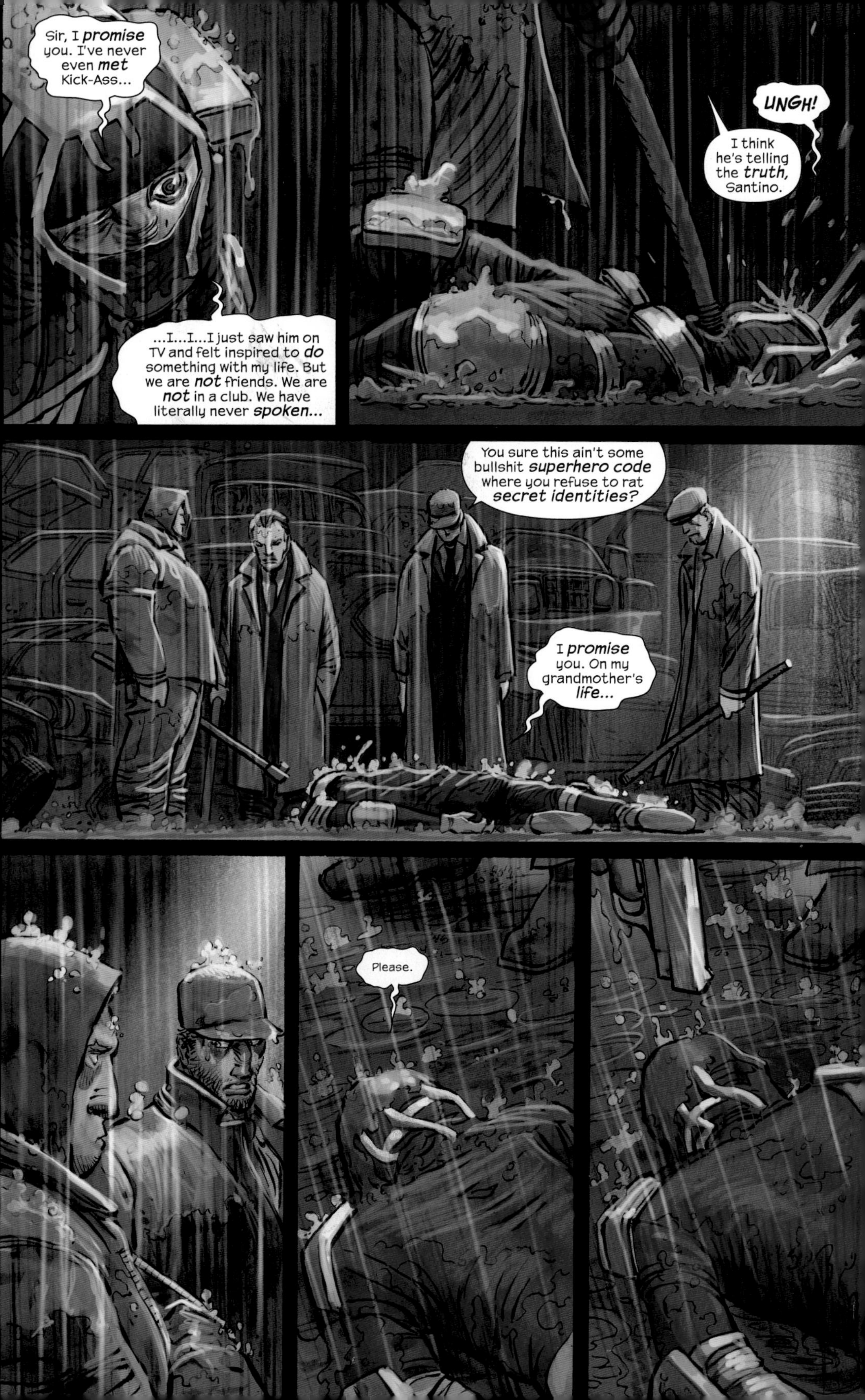
Sir, I *promise* you. I've never even *met* Kick-Ass...
...I...I...I just saw him on TV and felt inspired to *do* something with my life. But we are *not* friends. We are *not* in a club. We have literally never *spoken*...
UNGH!
I think he's telling the *truth,* Santino.
You sure this ain't some bullshit *superhero code* where you refuse to rat *secret identities*?
I *promise* you. On my grandmother's *life*...
Please.

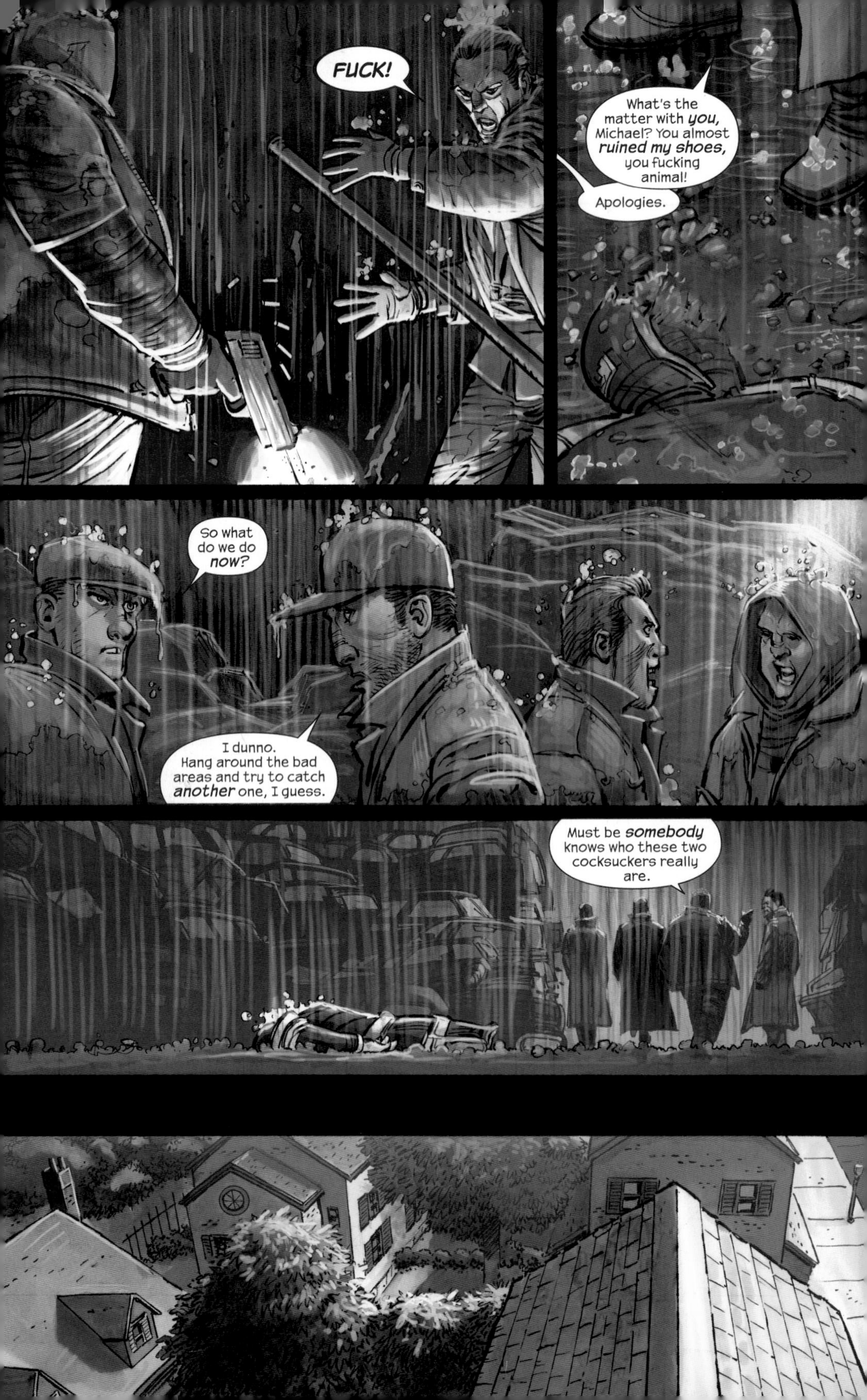
FUCK!
What's the matter with *you,* Michael? You almost *ruined my shoes,* you fucking animal!
Apologies.
So what do we do *now?*
I dunno. Hang around the bad areas and try to catch *another* one, I guess.
Must be *somebody* knows who these two cocksuckers really are.

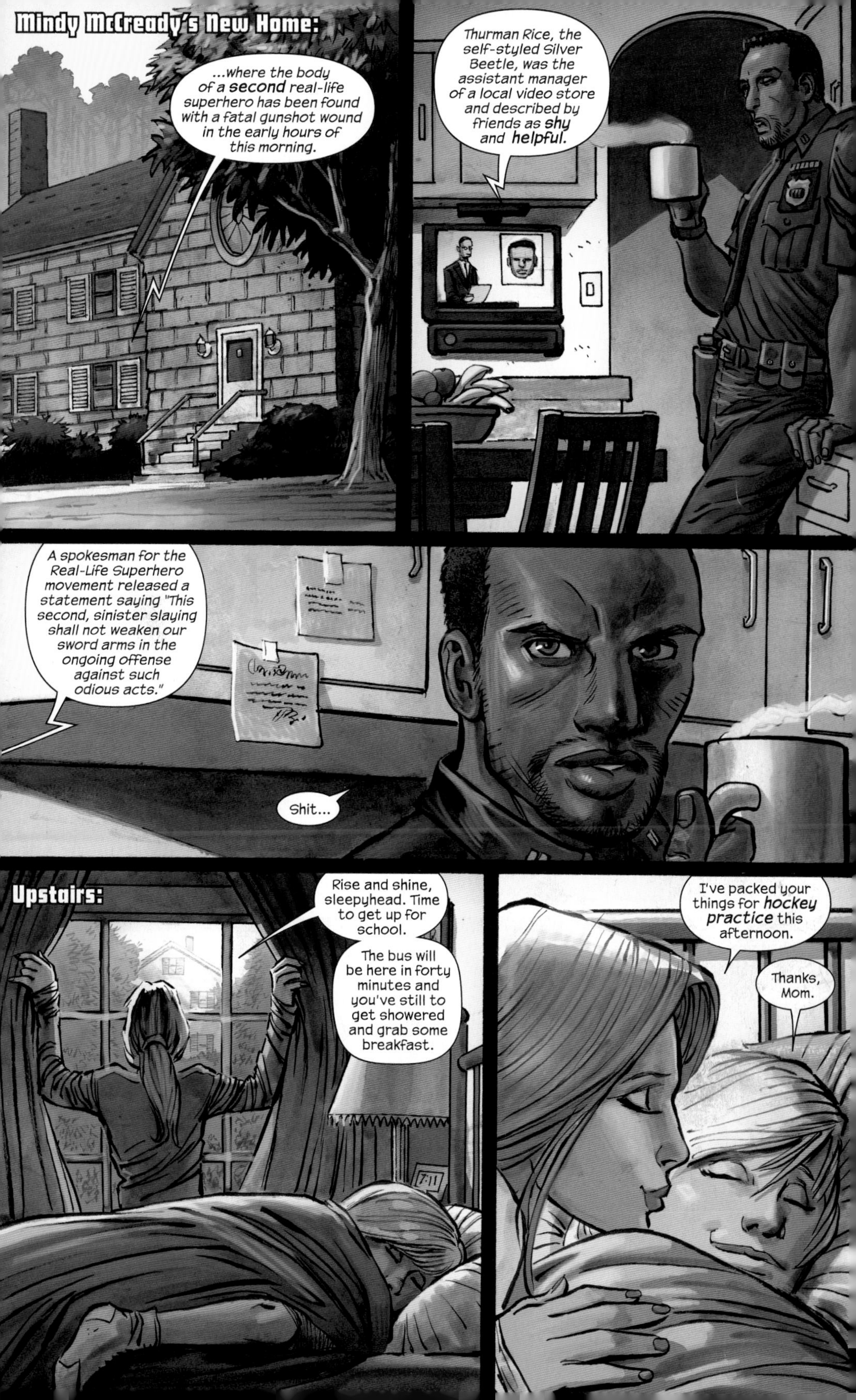
Mindy McCready's New Home:
...where the body of a **second** real-life superhero has been found with a fatal gunshot wound in the early hours of this morning.
Thurman Rice, the self-styled Silver Beetle, was the assistant manager of a local video store and described by friends as **shy** and **helpful**.
A spokesman for the Real-Life Superhero movement released a statement saying "This second, sinister slaying shall not weaken our sword arms in the ongoing offense against such odious acts."
Shit...
Upstairs:
Rise and shine, sleepyhead. Time to get up for school.
The bus will be here in forty minutes and you've still to get showered and grab some breakfast.
7:11
I've packed your things for ***hockey practice*** this afternoon.
Thanks, Mom.

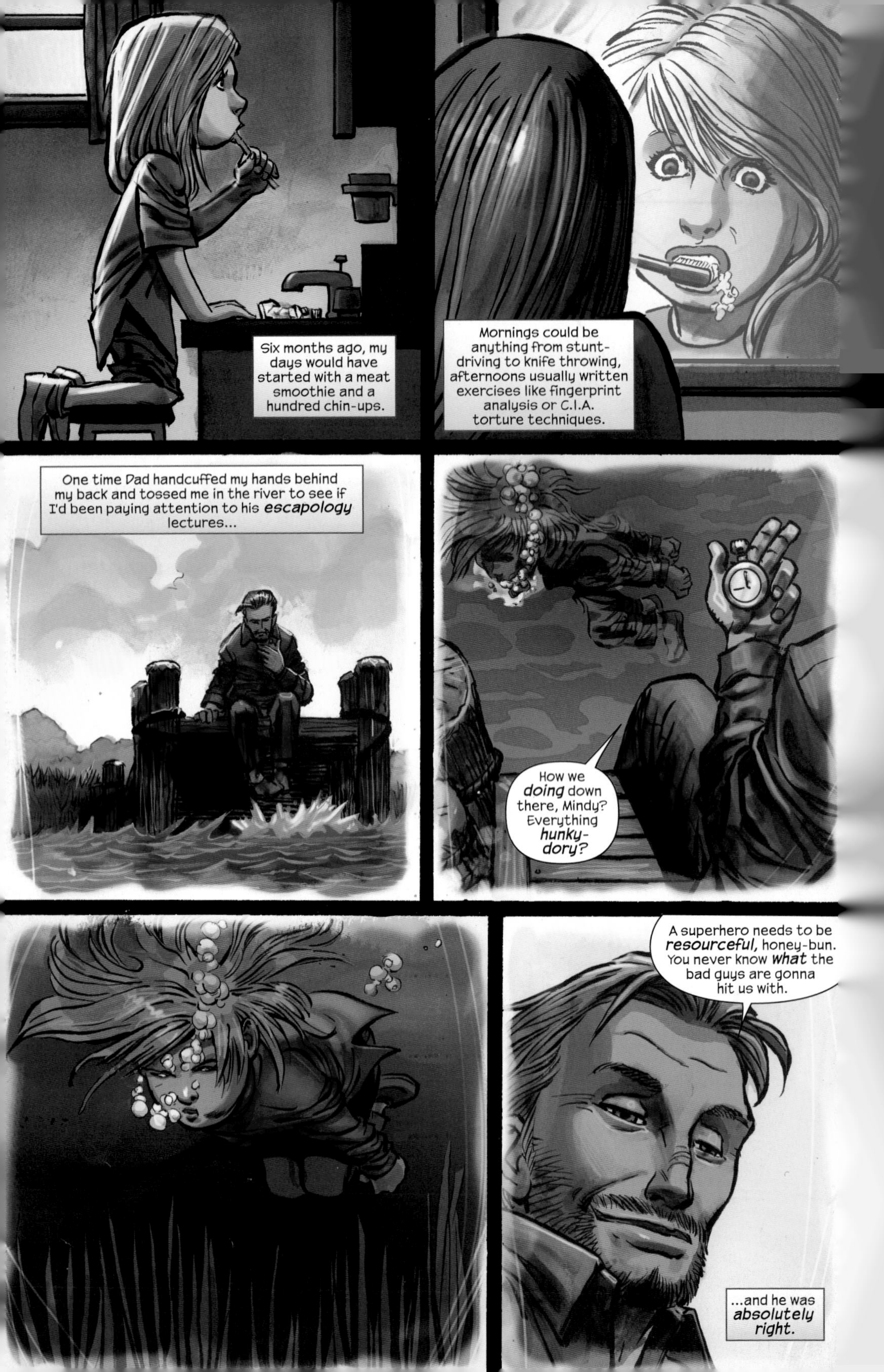
Six months ago, my days would have started with a meat smoothie and a hundred chin-ups.
Mornings could be anything from stunt-driving to knife throwing, afternoons usually written exercises like fingerprint analysis or C.I.A. torture techniques.
One time Dad handcuffed my hands behind my back and tossed me in the river to see if I'd been paying attention to his *escapology* lectures...
How we *doing* down there, Mindy? Everything *hunky-dory?*
A superhero needs to be *resourceful,* honey-bun. You never know *what* the bad guys are gonna hit us with.
...and he was *absolutely right.*

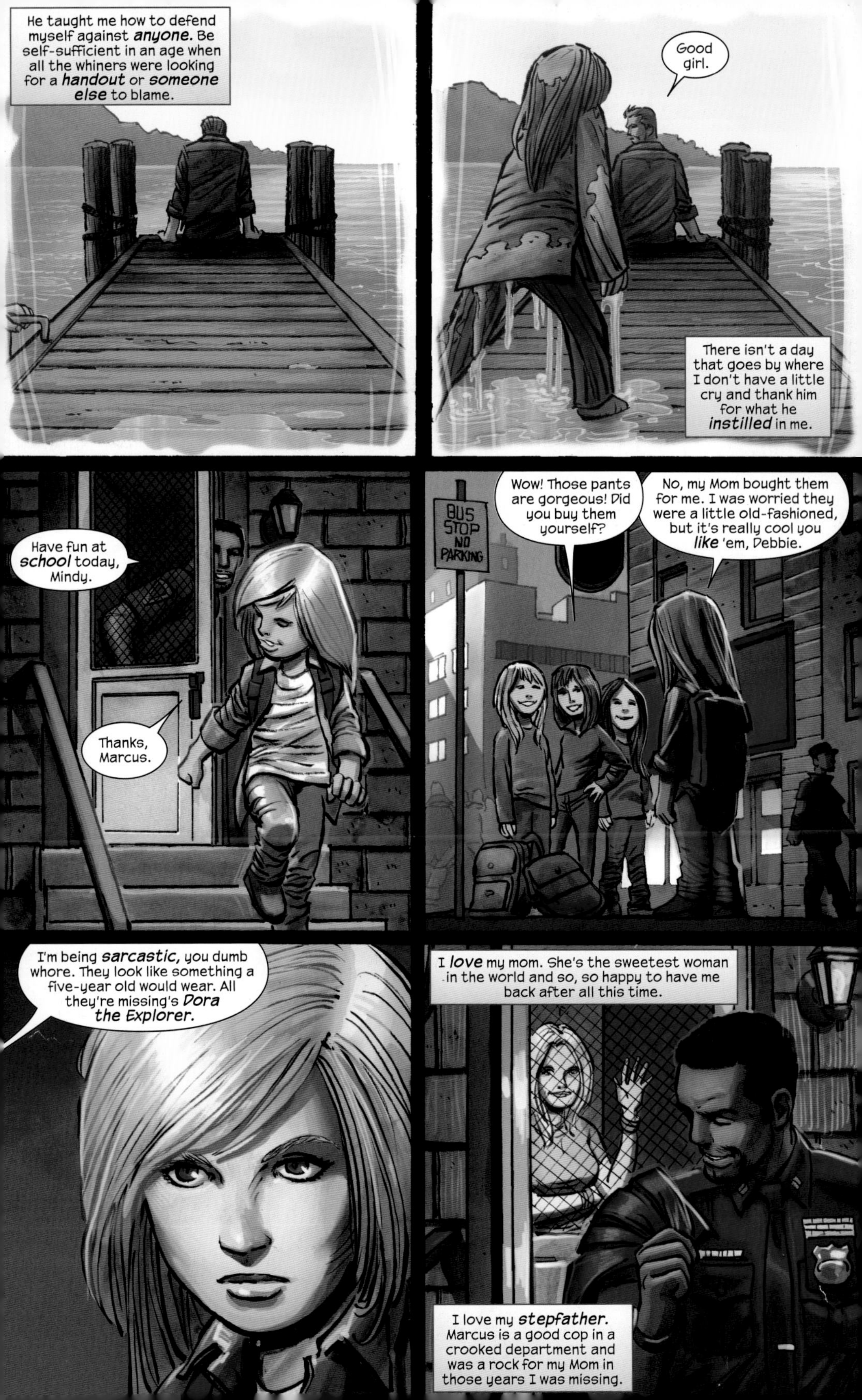
He taught me how to defend myself against *anyone.* Be self-sufficient in an age when all the whiners were looking for a *handout* or *someone else* to blame.
Good girl.
There isn't a day that goes by where I don't have a little cry and thank him for what he *instilled* in me.
Have fun at *school* today, Mindy.
Thanks, Marcus.
BUS STOP NO PARKING
Wow! Those pants are gorgeous! Did you buy them yourself?
No, my Mom bought them for me. I was worried they were a little old-fashioned, but it's really cool you *like* 'em, Debbie.
I'm being *sarcastic,* you dumb whore. They look like something a five-year old would wear. All they're missing's *Dora the Explorer.*
I *love* my mom. She's the sweetest woman in the world and so, so happy to have me back after all this time.
I love my *stepfather.* Marcus is a good cop in a crooked department and was a rock for my Mom in those years I was missing.

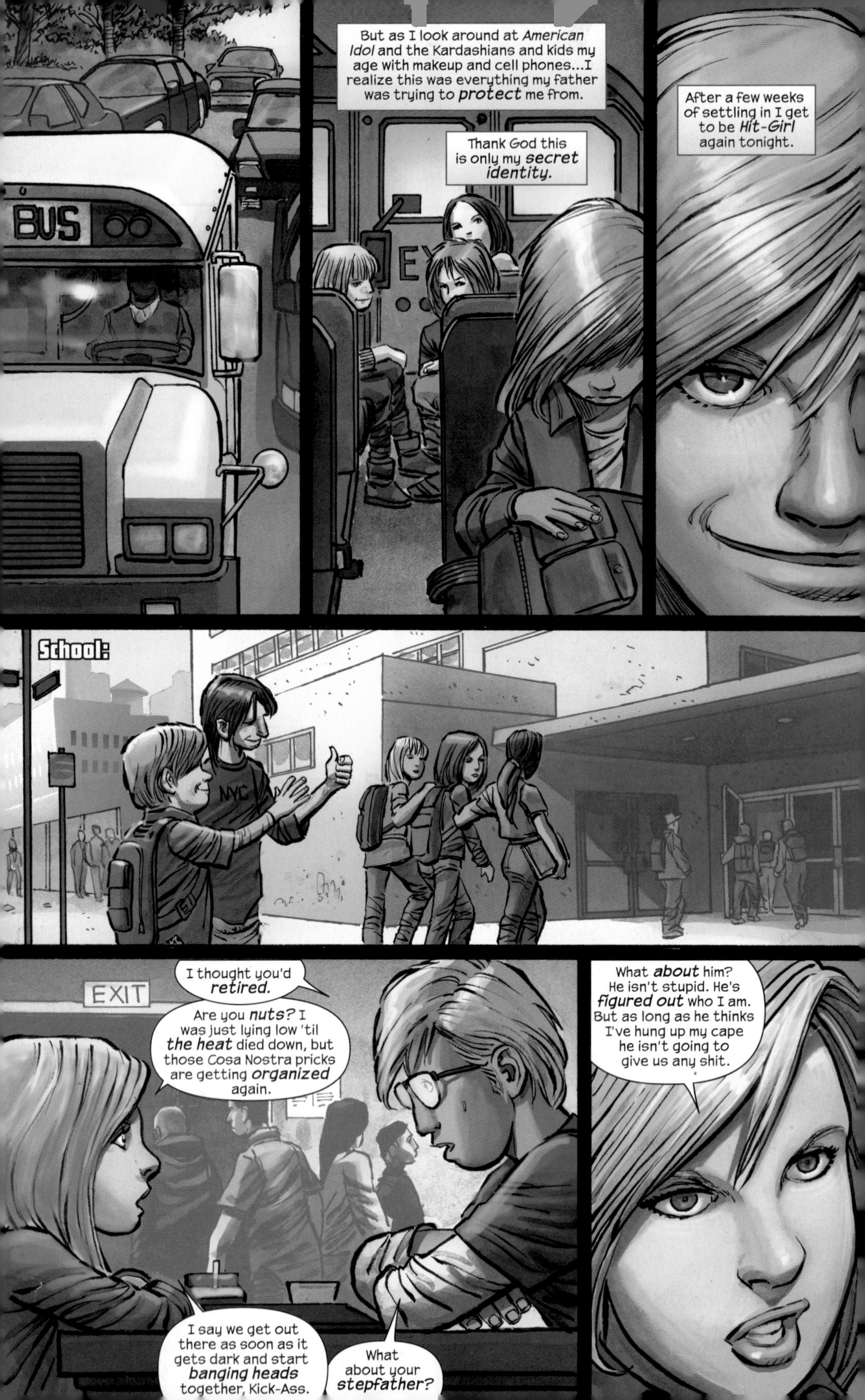
BUS
But as I look around at American Idol and the Kardashians and kids my age with makeup and cell phones...I realize this was everything my father was trying to protect me from.
Thank God this is only my secret identity.
After a few weeks of settling in I get to be Hit-Girl again tonight.
School:
NYC
EXIT
I thought you'd retired.
Are you nuts? I was just lying low 'til the heat died down, but those Cosa Nostra pricks are getting organized again.
I say we get out there as soon as it gets dark and start banging heads together, Kick-Ass.
What about your stepfather?
What about him? He isn't stupid. He's figured out who I am. But as long as he thinks I've hung up my cape he isn't going to give us any shit.

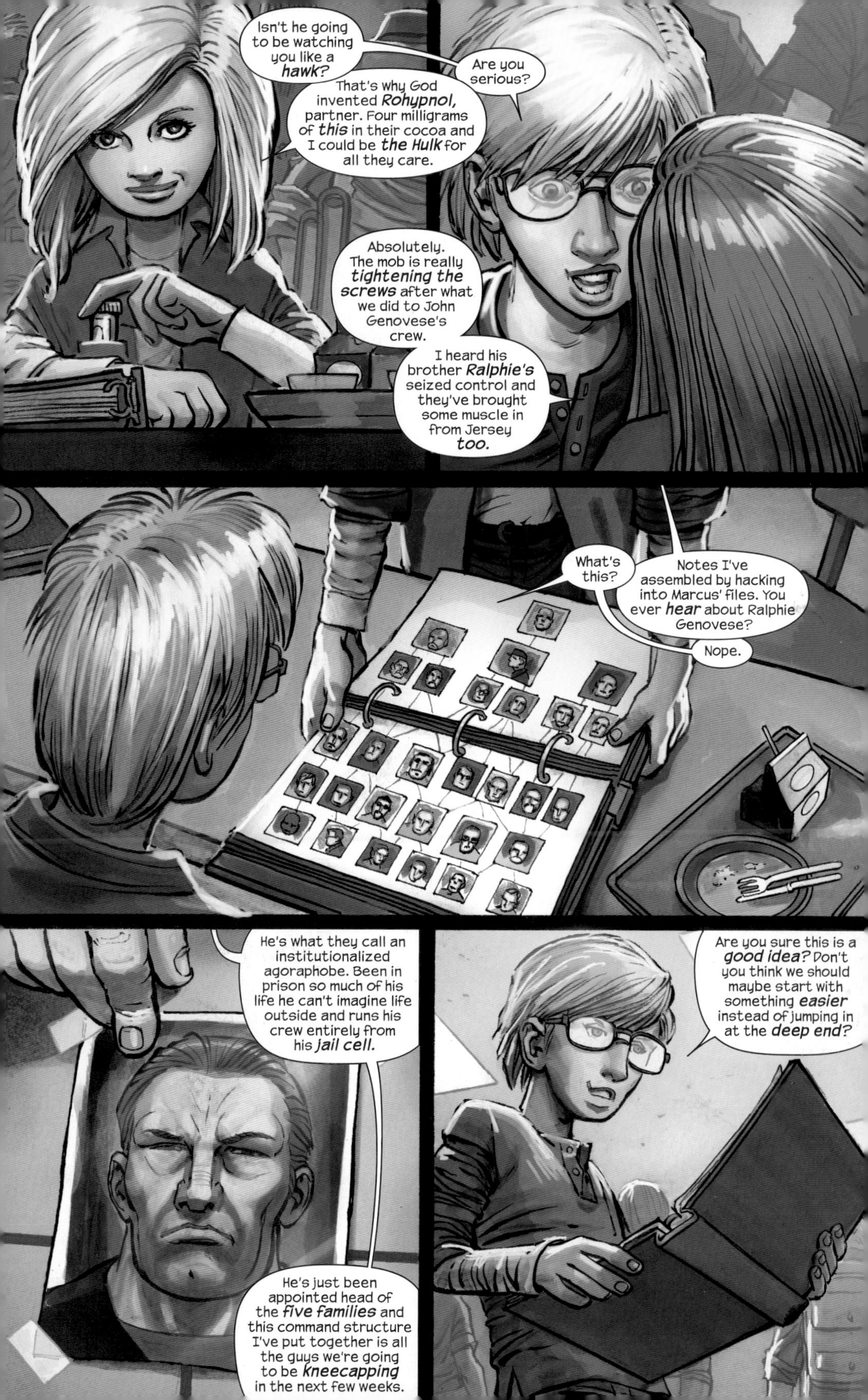
Isn't he going to be watching you like a hawk?
Are you serious?
That's why God invented Rohypnol, partner. Four milligrams of this in their cocoa and I could be the Hulk for all they care.
Absolutely. The mob is really tightening the screws after what we did to John Genovese's crew.
I heard his brother Ralphie's seized control and they've brought some muscle in from Jersey too.
What's this?
Notes I've assembled by hacking into Marcus' files. You ever hear about Ralphie Genovese?
Nope.
He's what they call an institutionalized agoraphobe. Been in prison so much of his life he can't imagine life outside and runs his crew entirely from his jail cell.
He's just been appointed head of the five families and this command structure I've put together is all the guys we're going to be kneecapping in the next few weeks.
Are you sure this is a good idea? Don't you think we should maybe start with something easier instead of jumping in at the deep end?

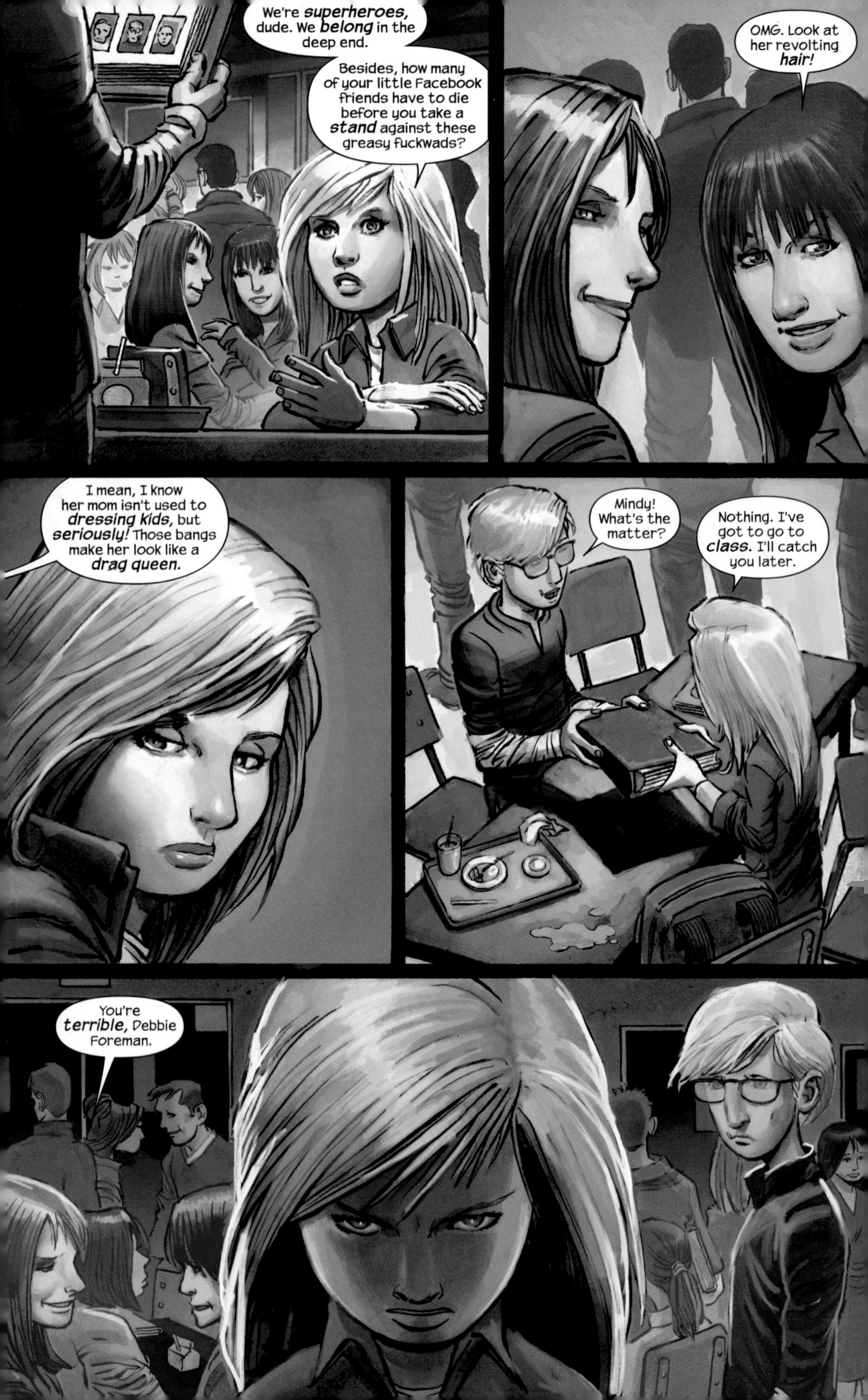
We're superheroes, dude. We belong in the deep end.
Besides, how many of your little Facebook friends have to die before you take a stand against these greasy fuckwads?
OMG. Look at her revolting hair!
I mean, I know her mom isn't used to dressing kids, but seriously! Those bangs make her look like a drag queen.
Mindy! What's the matter?
Nothing. I've got to go to class. I'll catch you later.
You're terrible, Debbie Foreman.

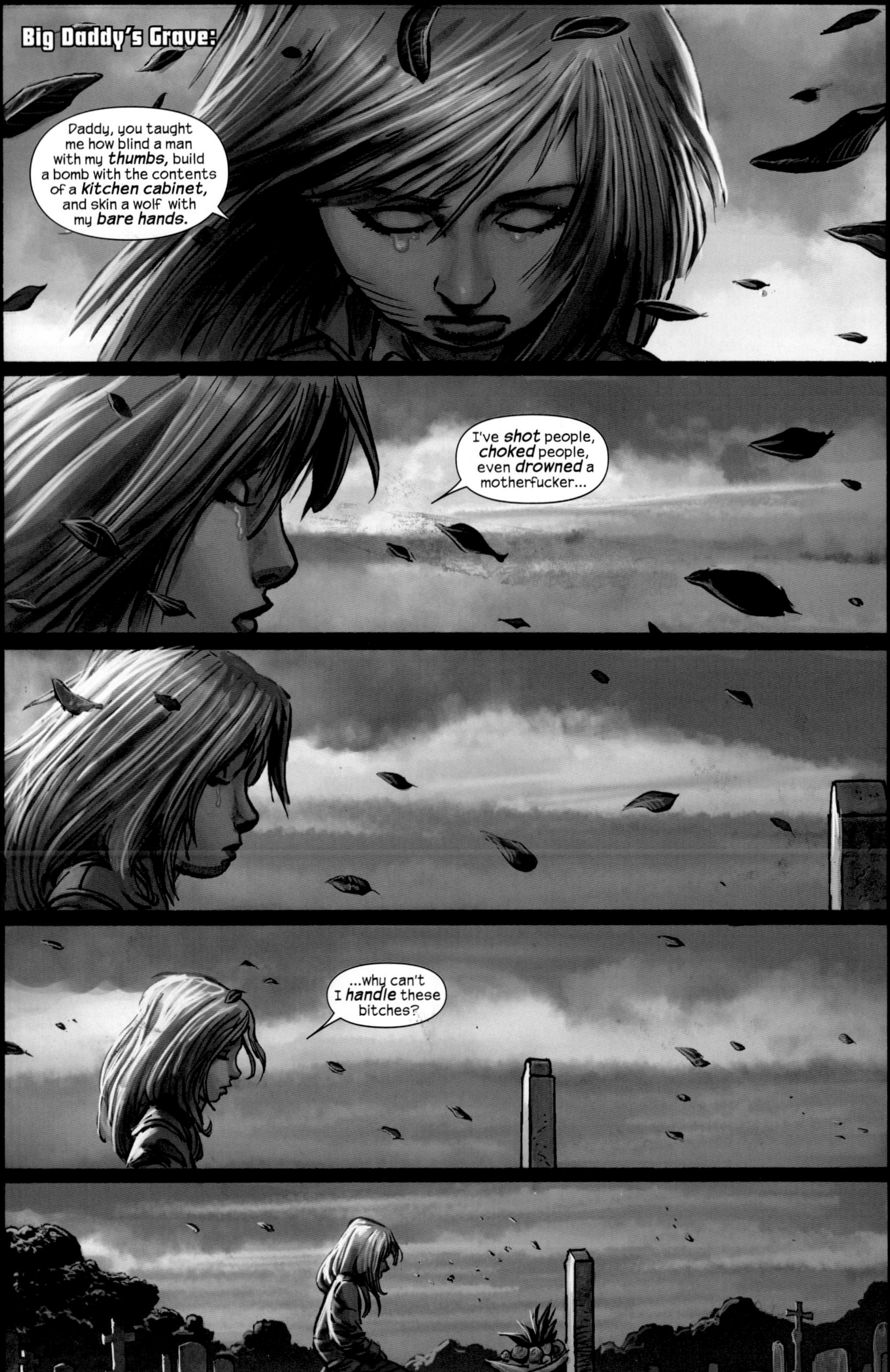
Big Daddy's Grave:
Daddy, you taught me how blind a man with my thumbs, build a bomb with the contents of a kitchen cabinet, and skin a wolf with my bare hands.
I've shot people, choked people, even drowned a motherfucker...
...why can't I handle these bitches?

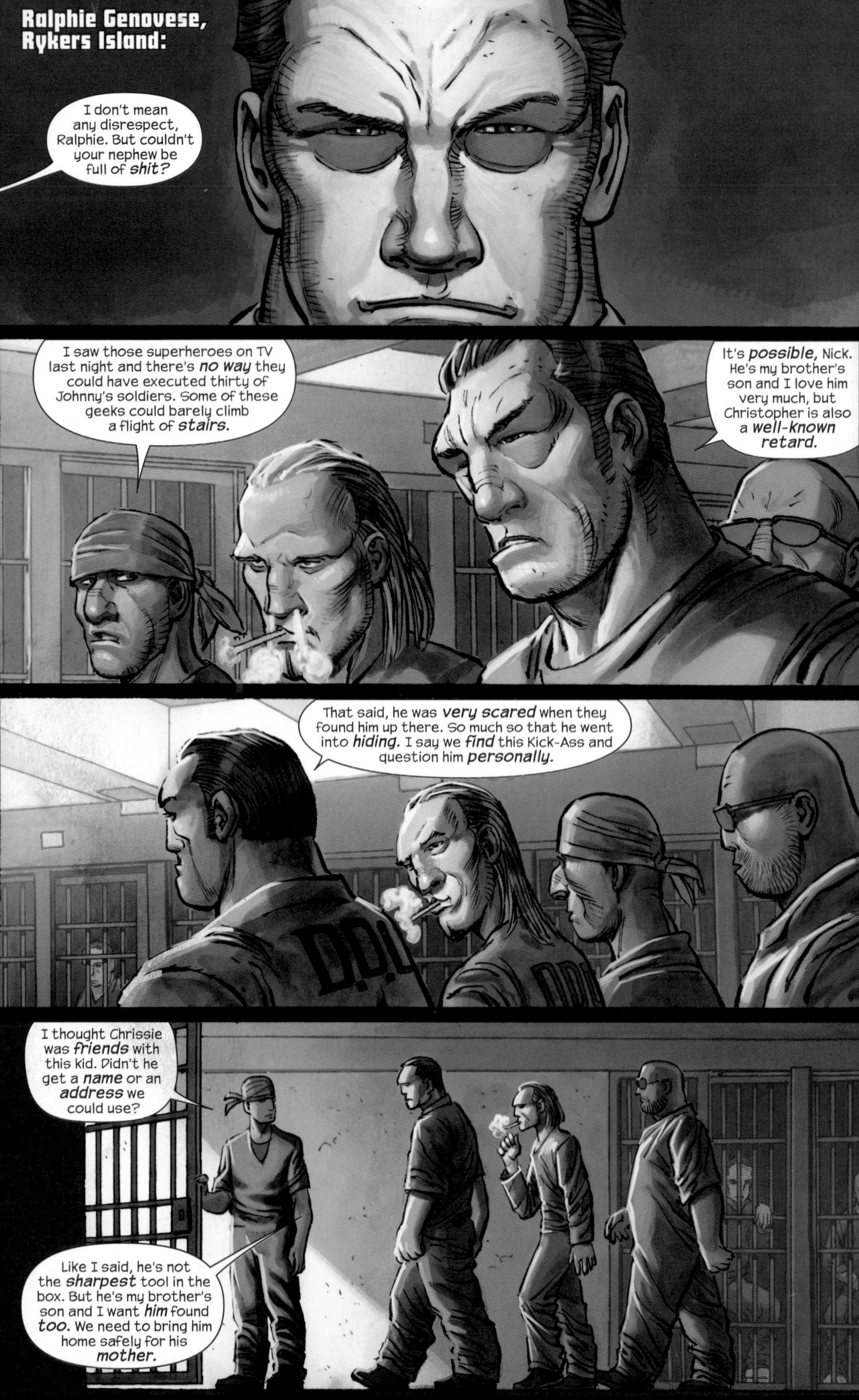
Ralphie Genovese, Rykers Island:
I don't mean any disrespect, Ralphie. But couldn't your nephew be full of shit?
I saw those superheroes on TV last night and there's no way they could have executed thirty of Johnny's soldiers. Some of these geeks could barely climb a flight of stairs.
It's possible, Nick. He's my brother's son and I love him very much, but Christopher is also a well-known retard.
That said, he was very scared when they found him up there. So much so that he went into hiding. I say we find this Kick-Ass and question him personally.
I thought Chrissie was friends with this kid. Didn't he get a name or an address we could use?
Like I said, he's not the sharpest tool in the box. But he's my brother's son and I want him found too. We need to bring him home safely for his mother.

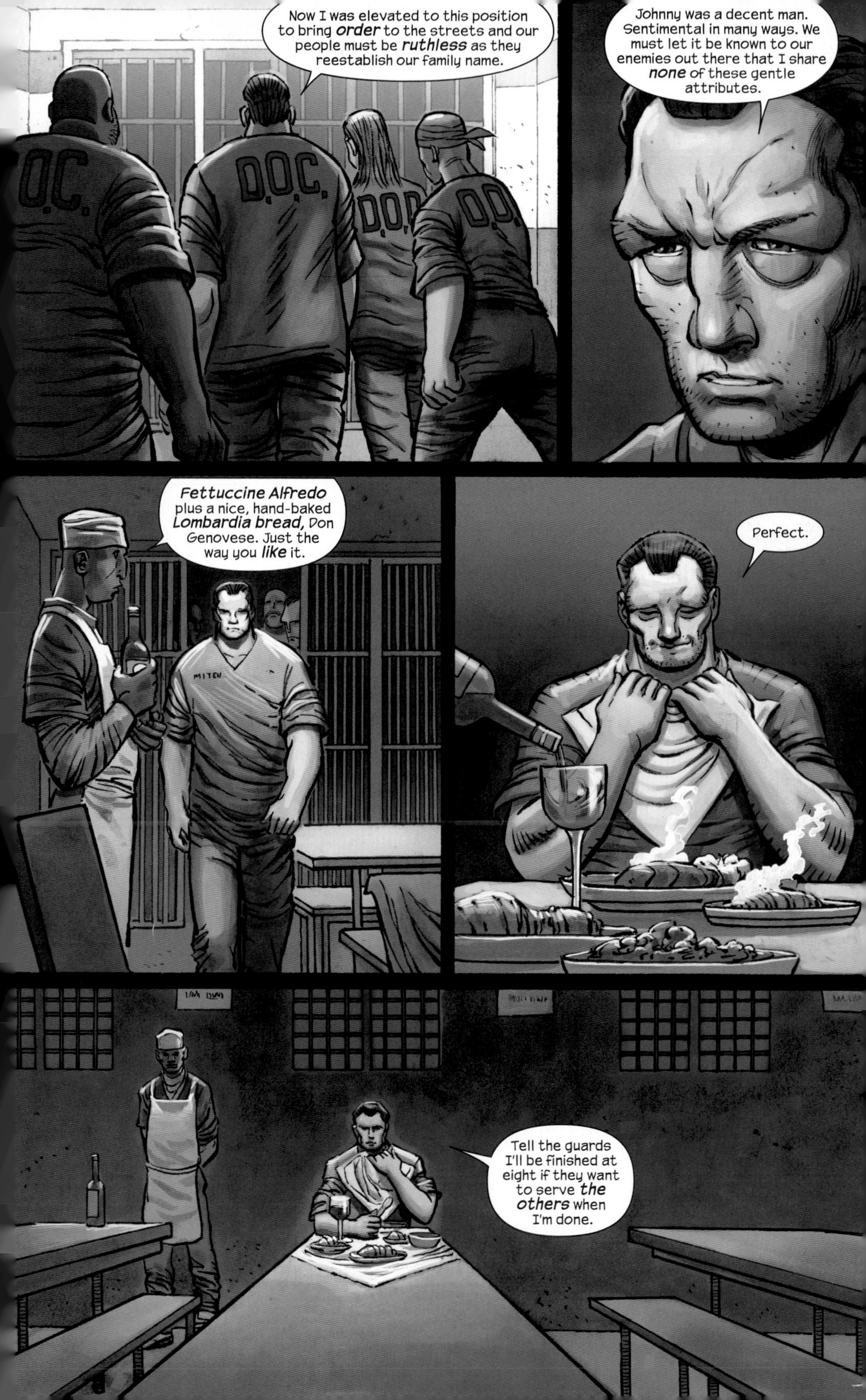

Now I was elevated to this position to bring order to the streets and our people must be ruthless as they reestablish our family name.
Johnny was a decent man. Sentimental in many ways. We must let it be known to our enemies out there that I share none of these gentle attributes.
Fettuccine Alfredo plus a nice, hand-baked Lombardia bread, Don Genovese. Just the way you like it.
Perfect.
Tell the guards I'll be finished at eight if they want to serve the others when I'm done.

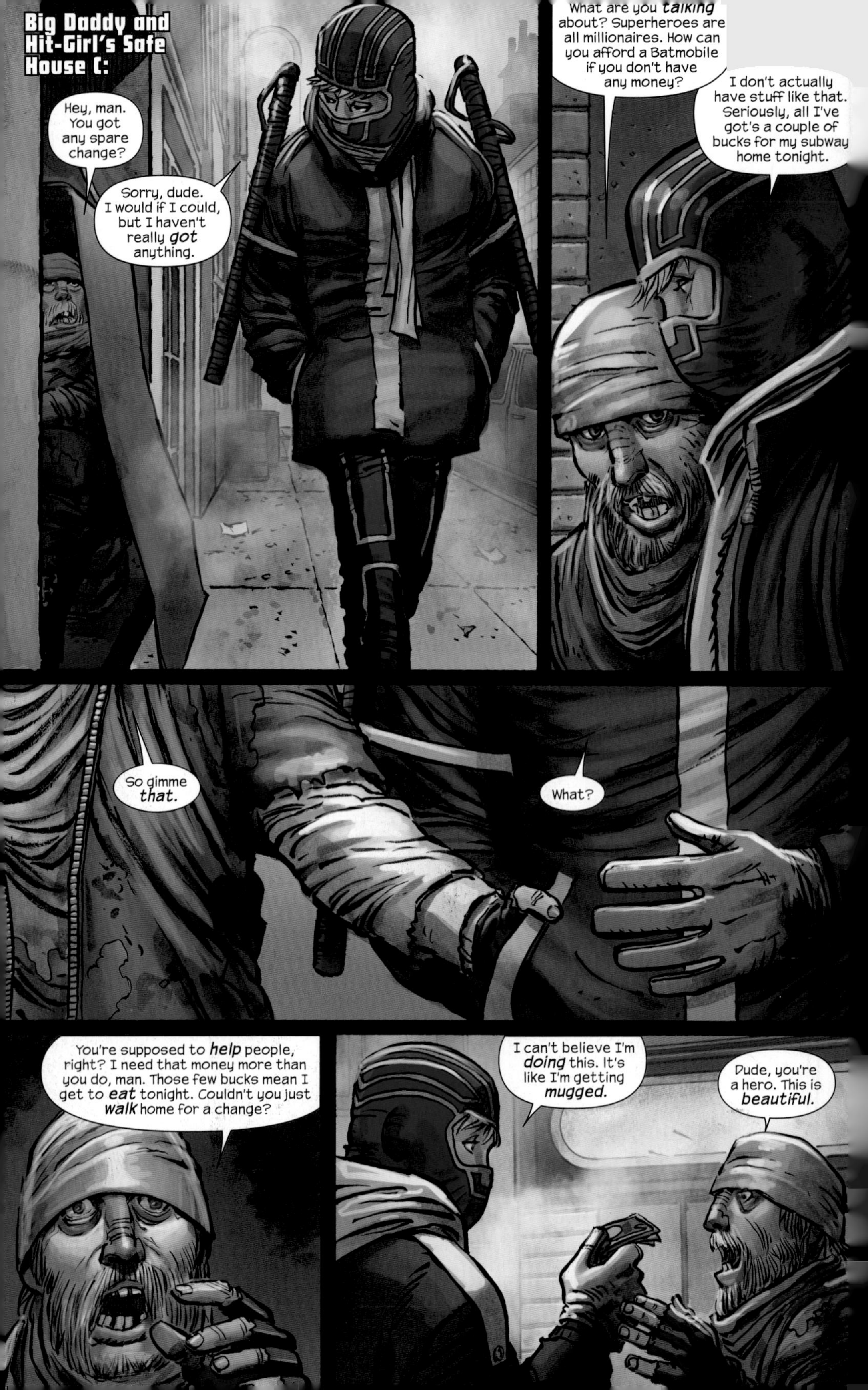
Big Daddy and Hit-Girl's Safe House C:
Hey, man. You got any spare change?
Sorry, dude. I would if I could, but I haven't really got anything.
What are you talking about? Superheroes are all millionaires. How can you afford a Batmobile if you don't have any money?
I don't actually have stuff like that. Seriously, all I've got's a couple of bucks for my subway home tonight.
So gimme that.
What?
You're supposed to help people, right? I need that money more than you do, man. Those few bucks mean I get to eat tonight. Couldn't you just walk home for a change?
I can't believe I'm doing this. It's like I'm getting mugged.
Dude, you're a hero. This is beautiful.

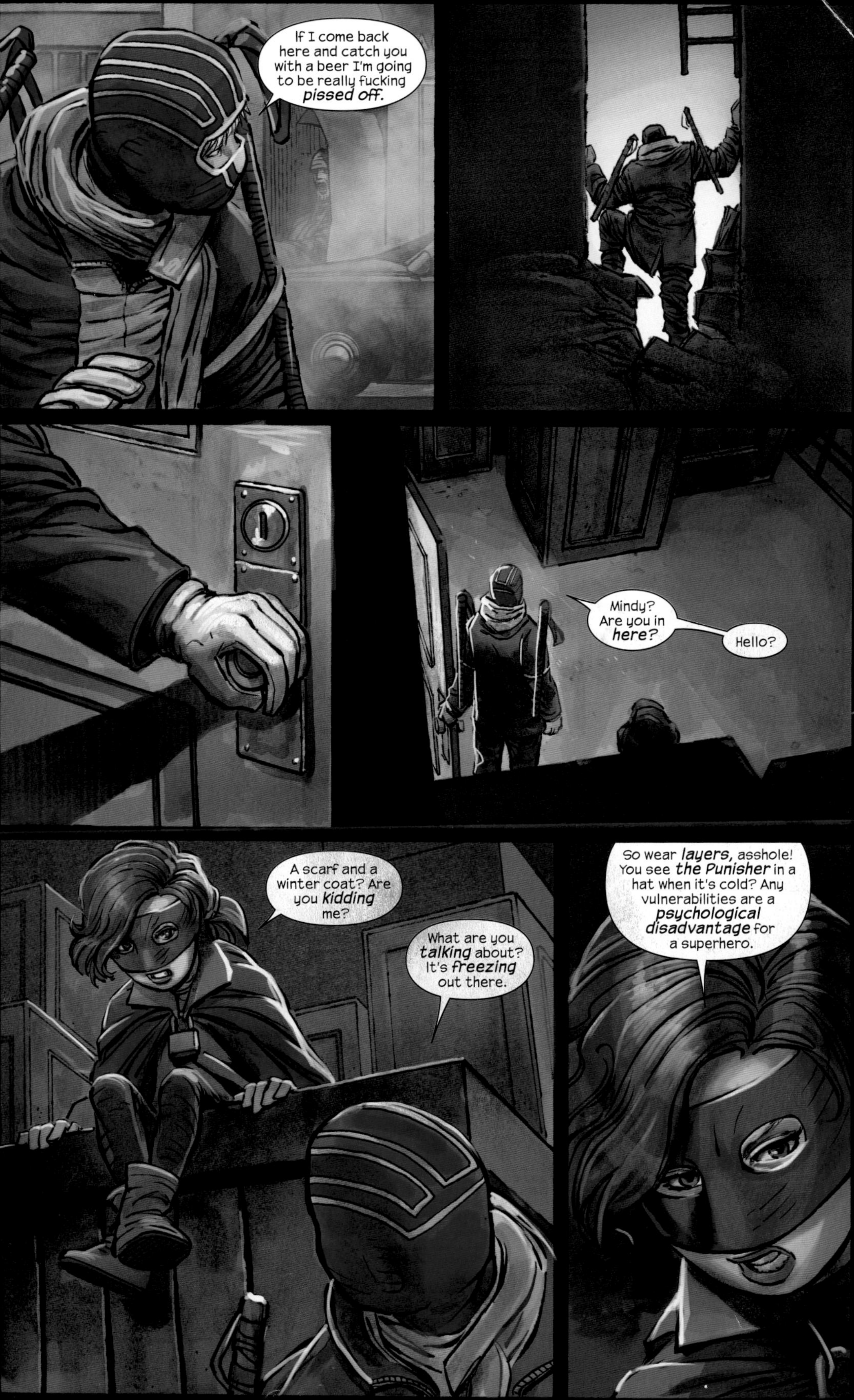
If I come back here and catch you with a beer I'm going to be really fucking pissed off.
Mindy? Are you in here?
Hello?
A scarf and a winter coat? Are you kidding me?
What are you talking about? It's freezing out there.
So wear layers, asshole! You see the Punisher in a hat when it's cold? Any vulnerabilities are a psychological disadvantage for a superhero.

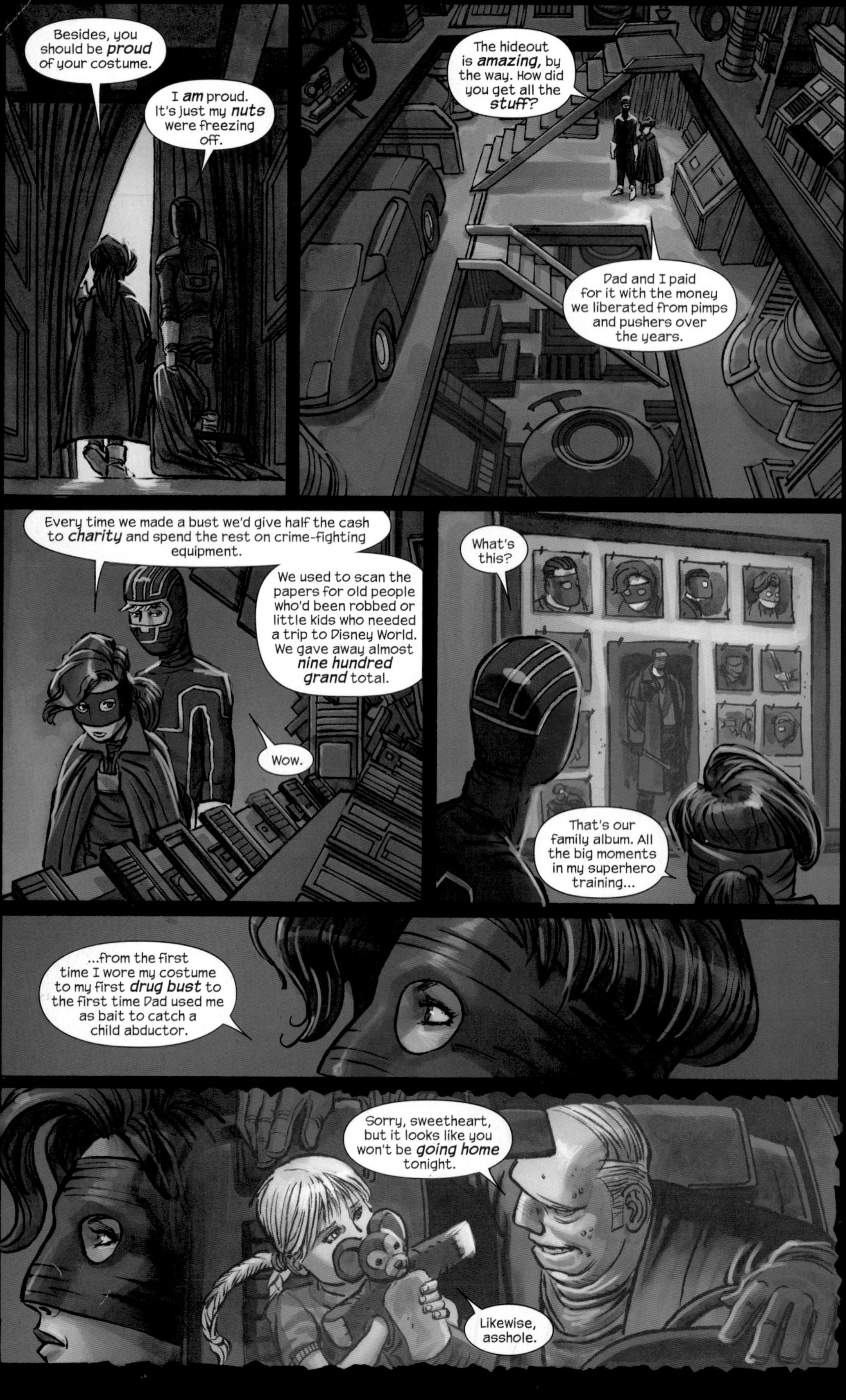
Besides, you should be proud of your costume.
I am proud. It's just my nuts were freezing off.
The hideout is amazing, by the way. How did you get all the stuff?
Dad and I paid for it with the money we liberated from pimps and pushers over the years.
Every time we made a bust we'd give half the cash to charity and spend the rest on crime-fighting equipment.
We used to scan the papers for old people who'd been robbed or little kids who needed a trip to Disney World. We gave away almost nine hundred grand total.
Wow.
What's this?
That's our family album. All the big moments in my superhero training...
...from the first time I wore my costume to my first drug bust to the first time Dad used me as bait to catch a child abductor.
Sorry, sweetheart, but it looks like you won't be going home tonight.
Likewise, asshole.

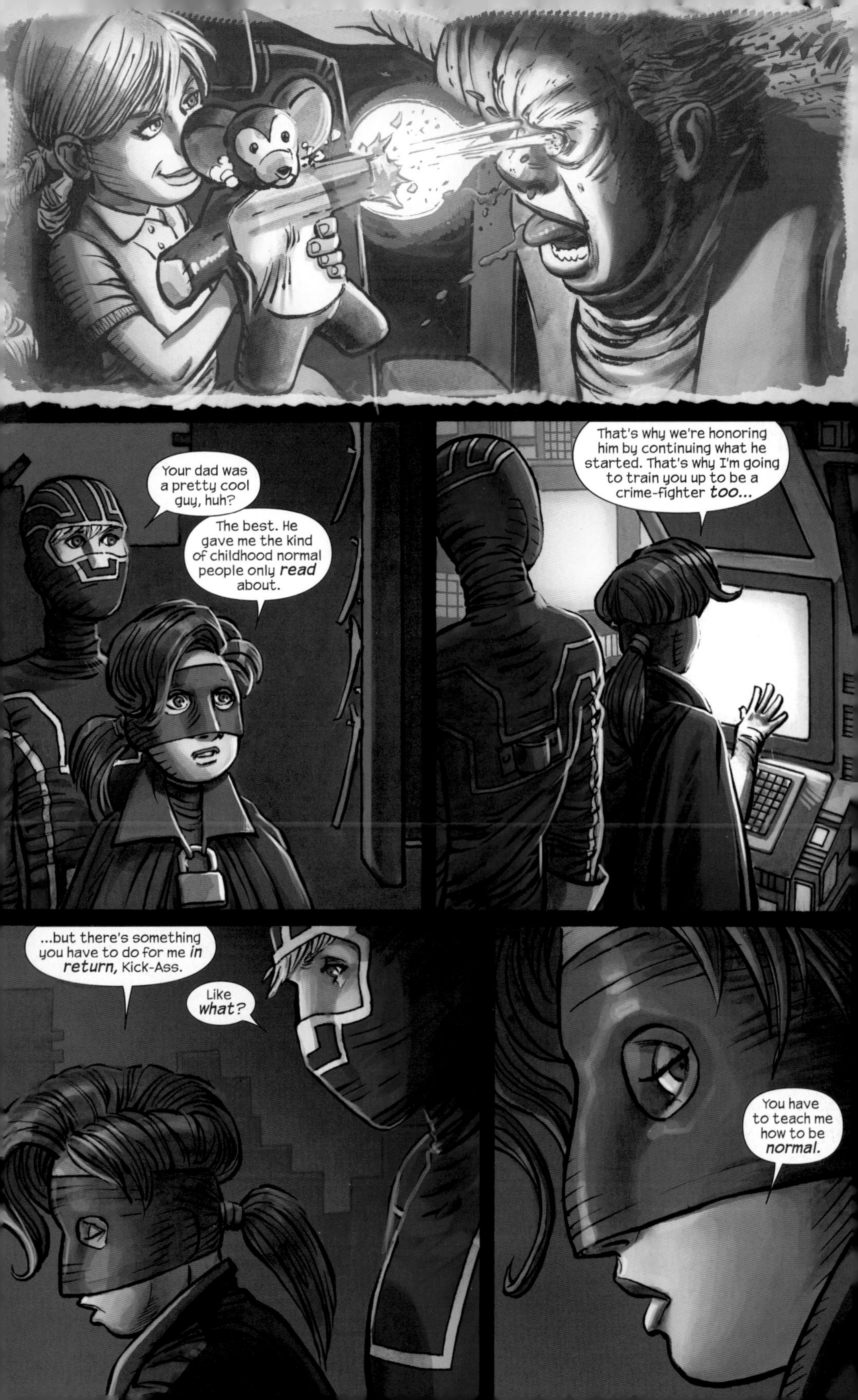
Your dad was a pretty cool guy, huh?
The best. He gave me the kind of childhood normal people only *read* about.
That's why we're honoring him by continuing what he started. That's why I'm going to train you up to be a crime-fighter *too...*
...but there's something you have to do for me *in return,* Kick-Ass.
Like *what?*
You have to teach me how to be *normal.*

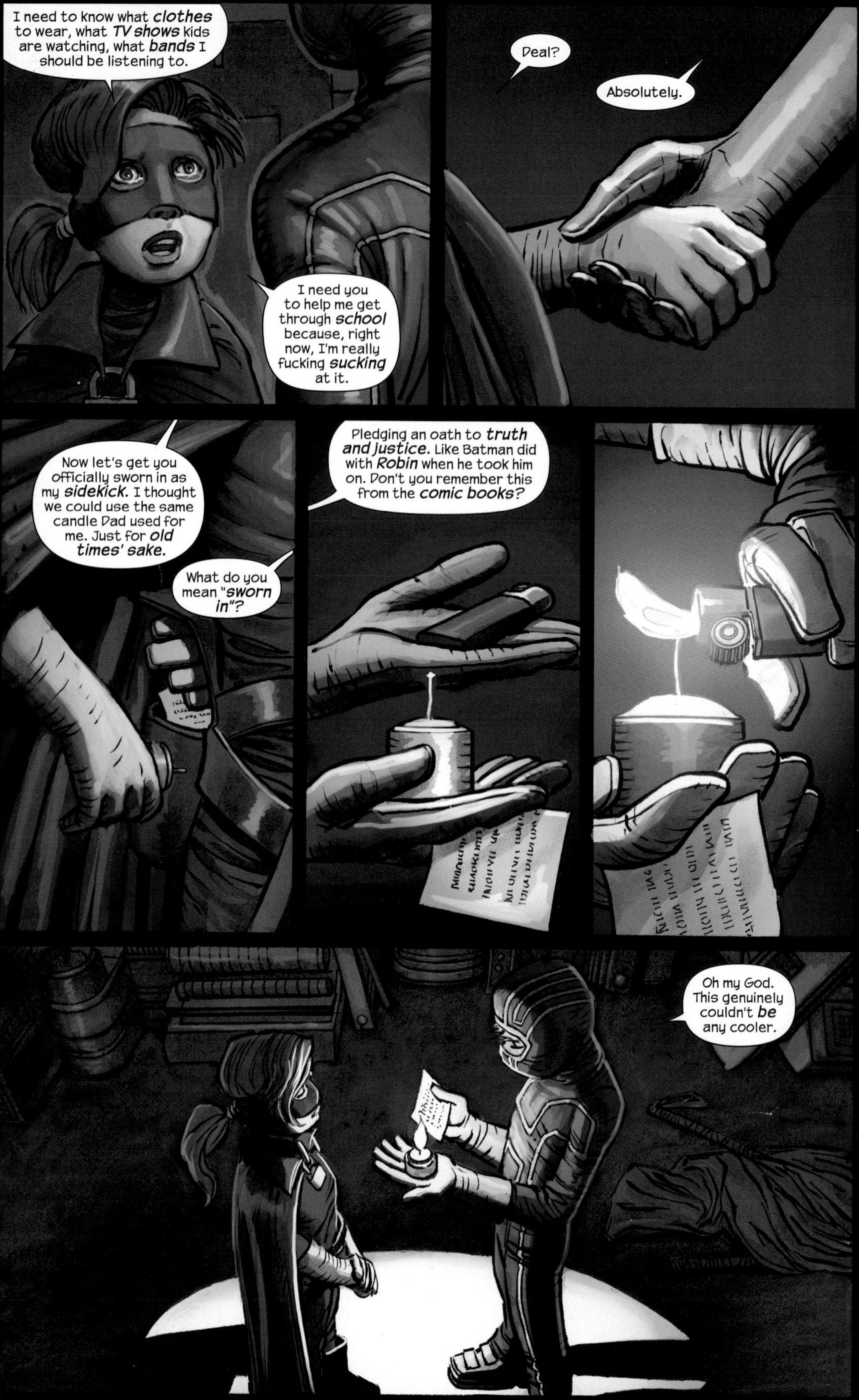
I need to know what clothes to wear, what TV shows kids are watching, what bands I should be listening to.
I need you to help me get through school because, right now, I'm really fucking sucking at it.
Deal?
Absolutely.
Now let's get you officially sworn in as my sidekick. I thought we could use the same candle Dad used for me. Just for old times' sake.
What do you mean "sworn in"?
Pledging an oath to truth and justice. Like Batman did with Robin when he took him on. Don't you remember this from the comic books?
Oh my God. This genuinely couldn't be any cooler.

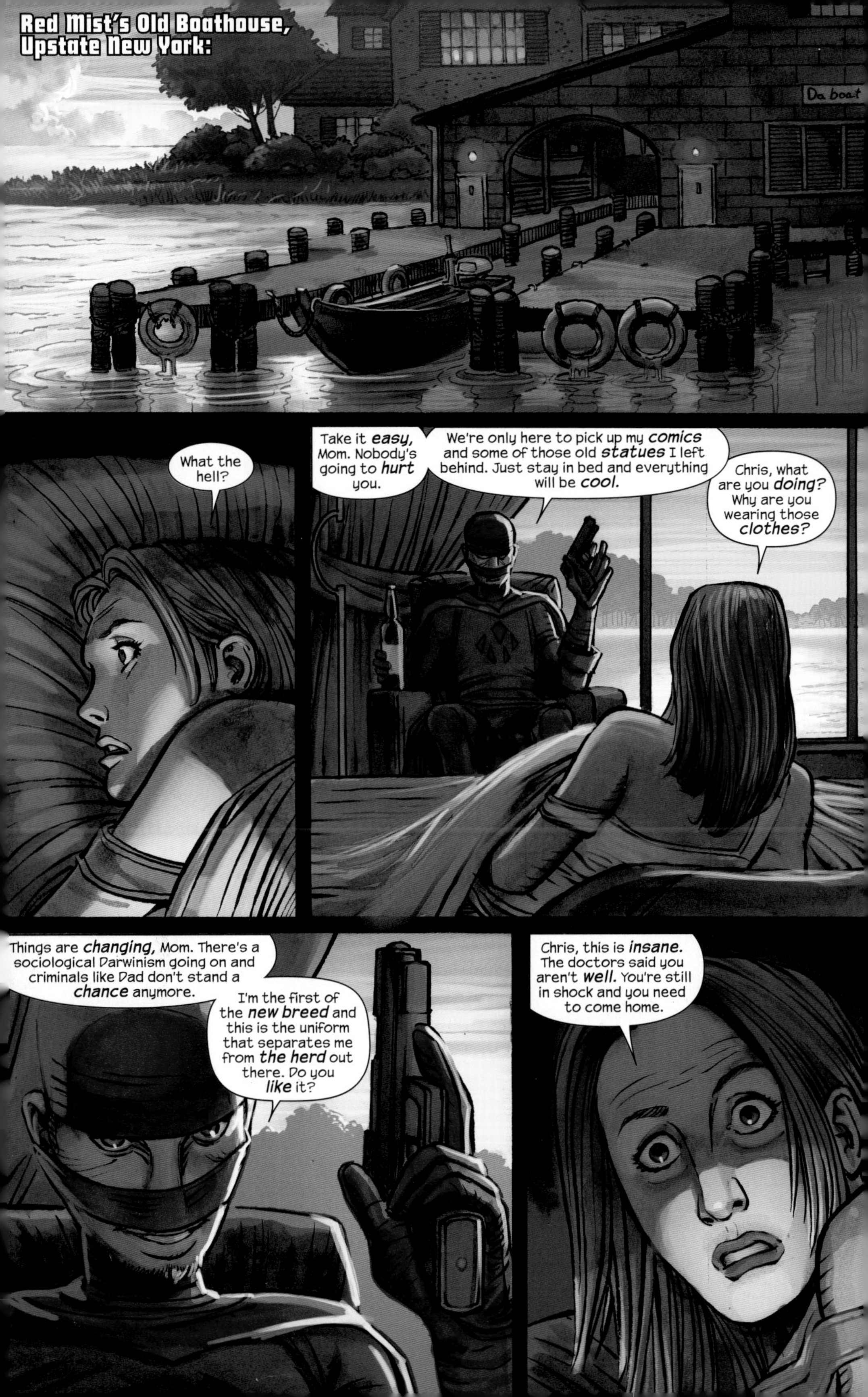
Red Mist's Old Boathouse, Upstate New York:
Da boat
What the hell?
Take it easy, Mom. Nobody's going to hurt you.
We're only here to pick up my comics and some of those old statues I left behind. Just stay in bed and everything will be cool.
Chris, what are you doing? Why are you wearing those clothes?
Things are changing, Mom. There's a sociological Darwinism going on and criminals like Dad don't stand a chance anymore.
I'm the first of the new breed and this is the uniform that separates me from the herd out there. Do you like it?
Chris, this is insane. The doctors said you aren't well. You're still in shock and you need to come home.

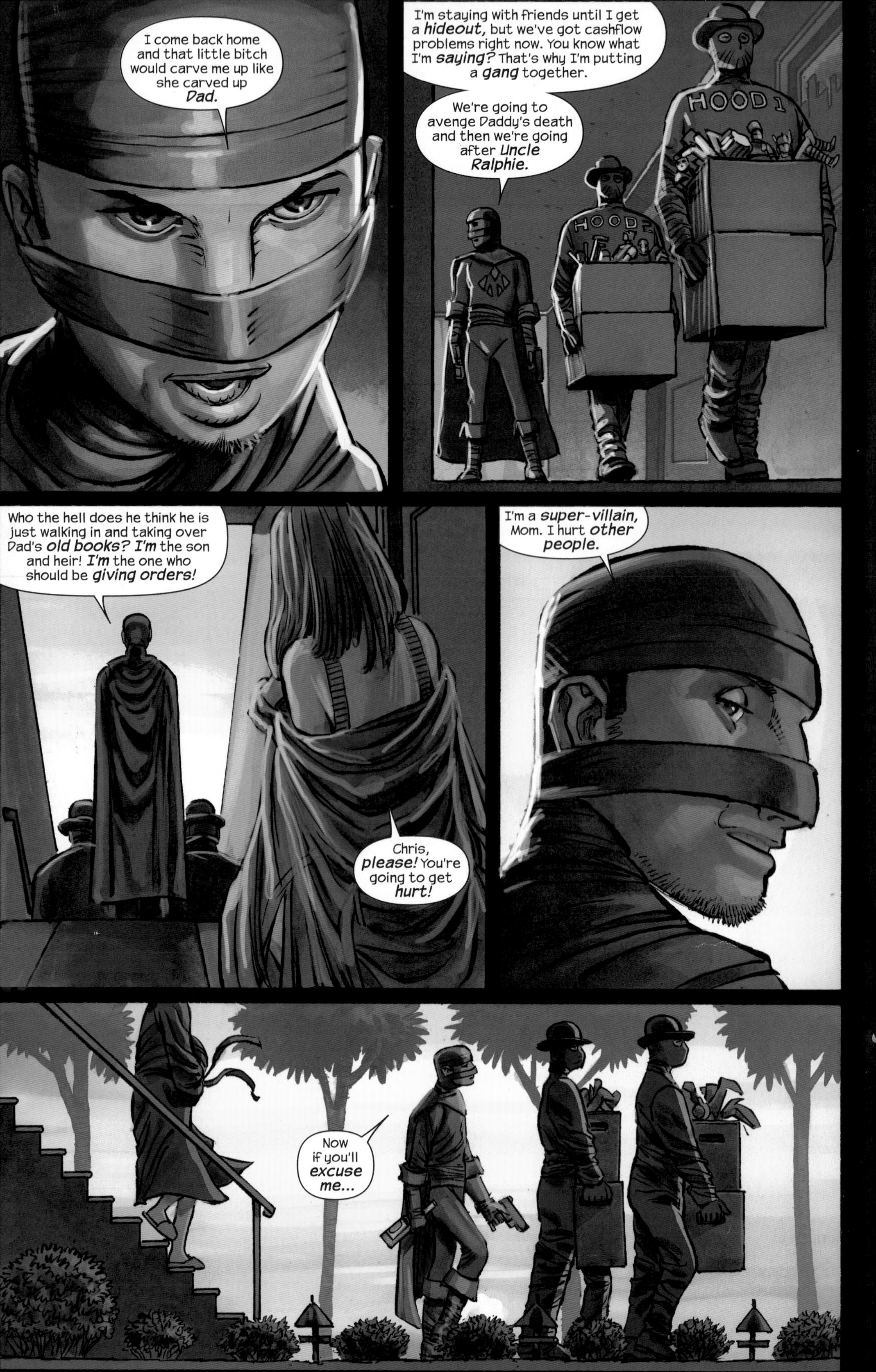
I come back home and that little bitch would carve me up like she carved up Dad.
I'm staying with friends until I get a hideout, but we've got cashflow problems right now. You know what I'm saying? That's why I'm putting a gang together.
We're going to avenge Daddy's death and then we're going after Uncle Ralphie.
HOOD 1
HOOD 2
Who the hell does he think he is just walking in and taking over Dad's old books? I'm the son and heir! I'm the one who should be giving orders!
Chris, please! You're going to get hurt!
I'm a super-villain, Mom. I hurt other people.
Now if you'll excuse me...

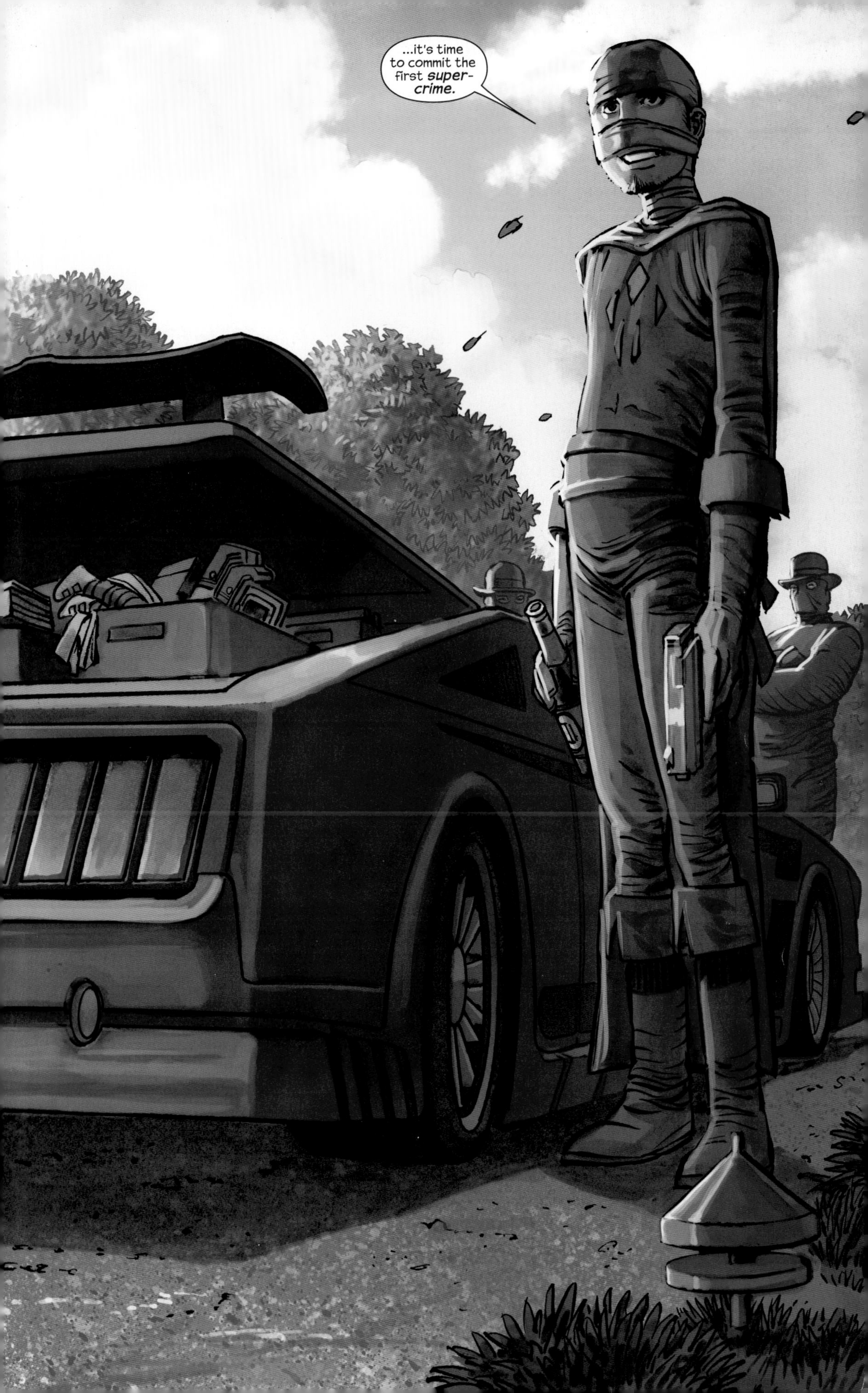
...it's time to commit the first *super-crime.*

TWO

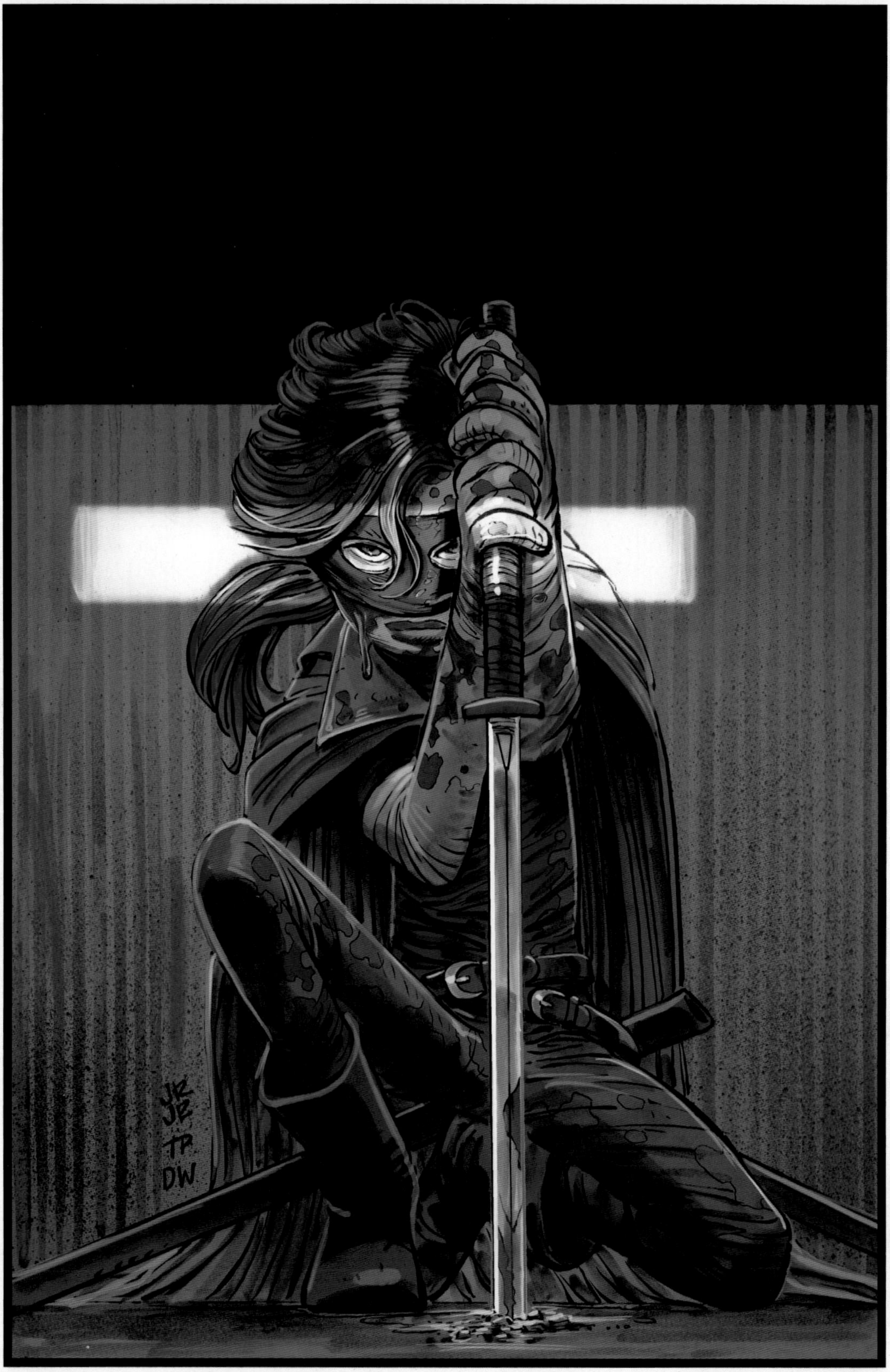

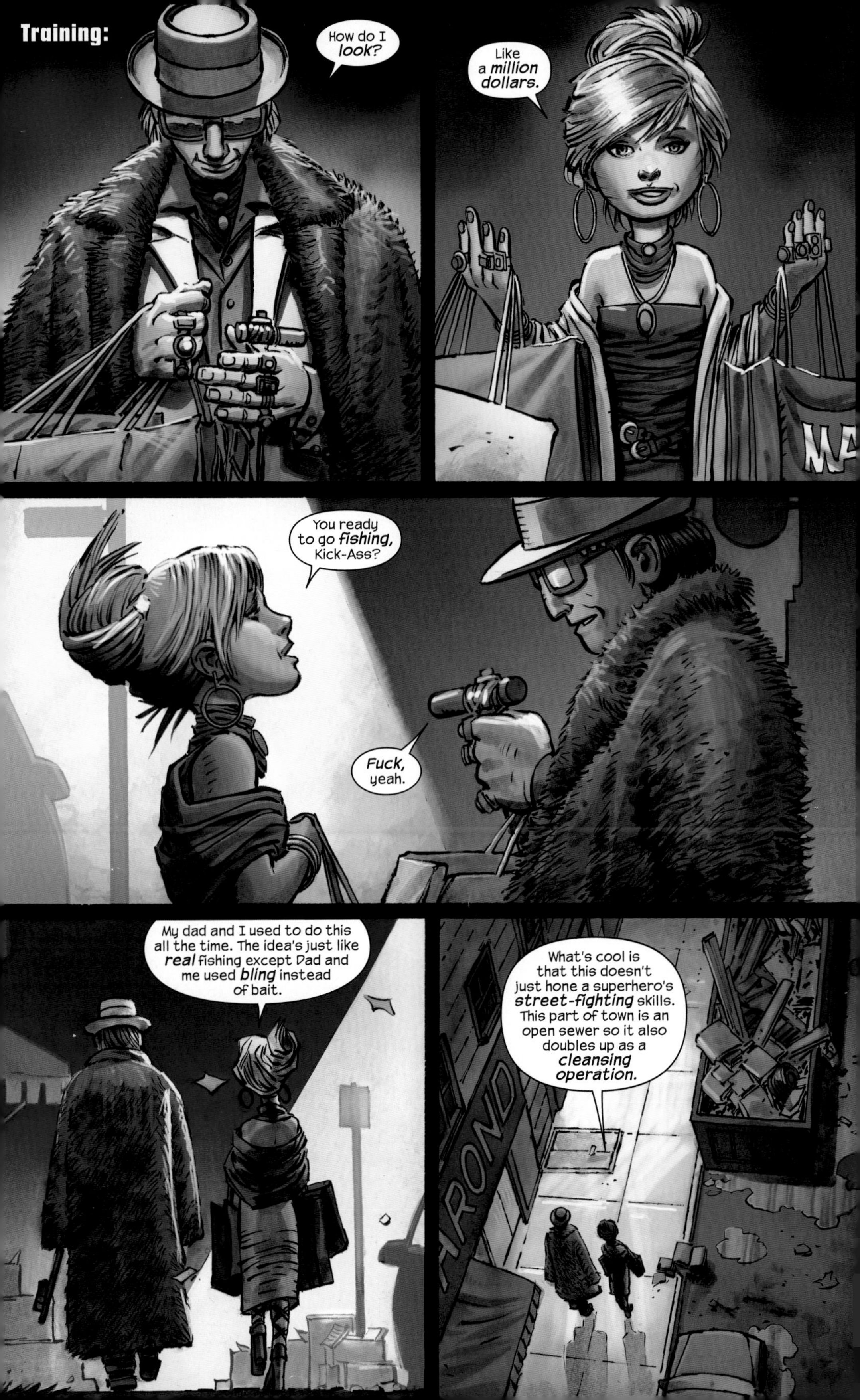

Training:
How do I look?
Like a million dollars.
You ready to go fishing, Kick-Ass?
Fuck, yeah.
My dad and I used to do this all the time. The idea's just like real fishing except Dad and me used bling instead of bait.
What's cool is that this doesn't just hone a superhero's street-fighting skills. This part of town is an open sewer so it also doubles up as a cleansing operation.

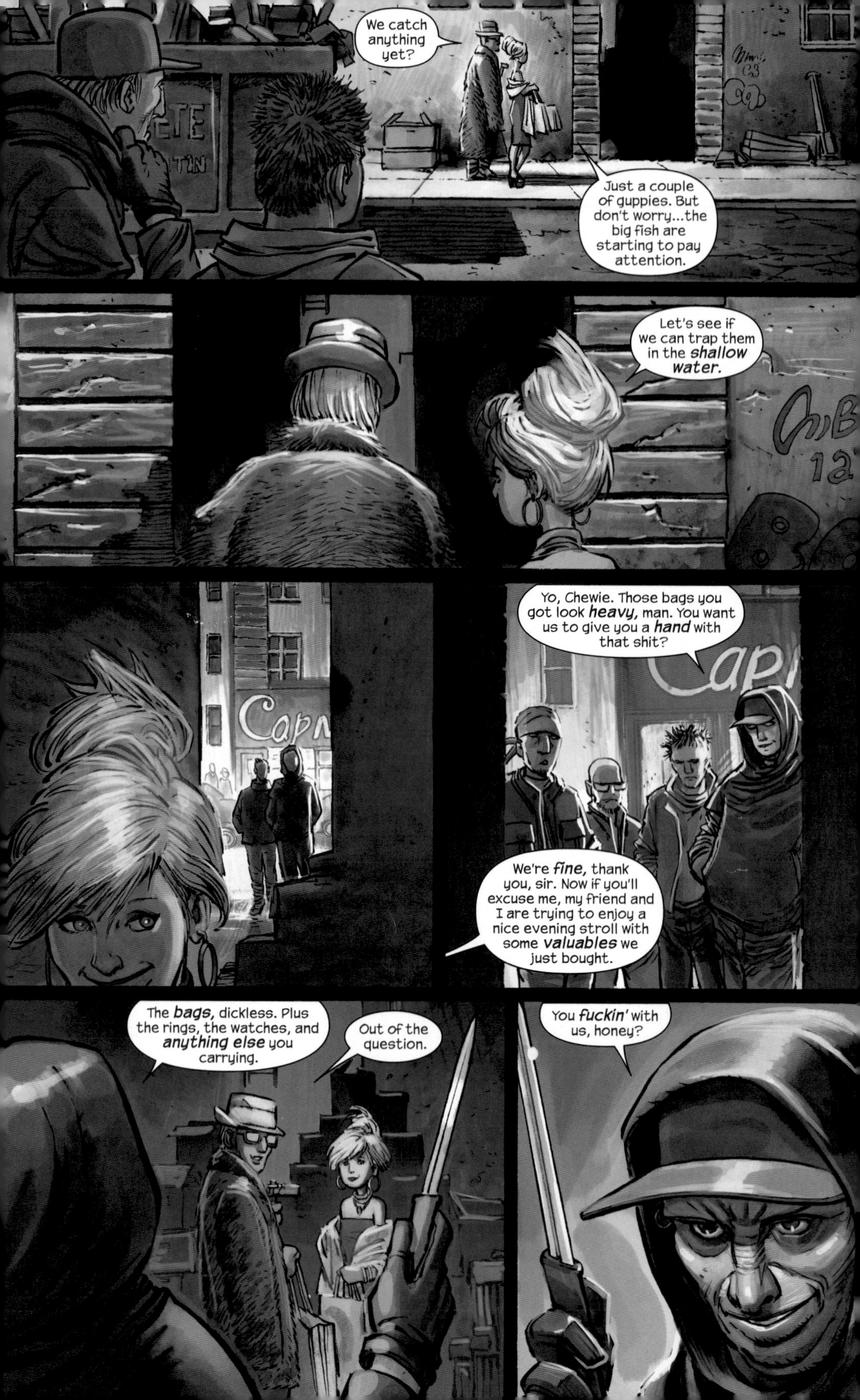

We catch anything yet?
Just a couple of guppies. But don't worry...the big fish are starting to pay attention.
Let's see if we can trap them in the shallow water.
Yo, Chewie. Those bags you got look heavy, man. You want us to give you a hand with that shit?
We're fine, thank you, sir. Now if you'll excuse me, my friend and I are trying to enjoy a nice evening stroll with some valuables we just bought.
The bags, dickless. Plus the rings, the watches, and anything else you carrying.
Out of the question.
You fuckin' with us, honey?

Training:

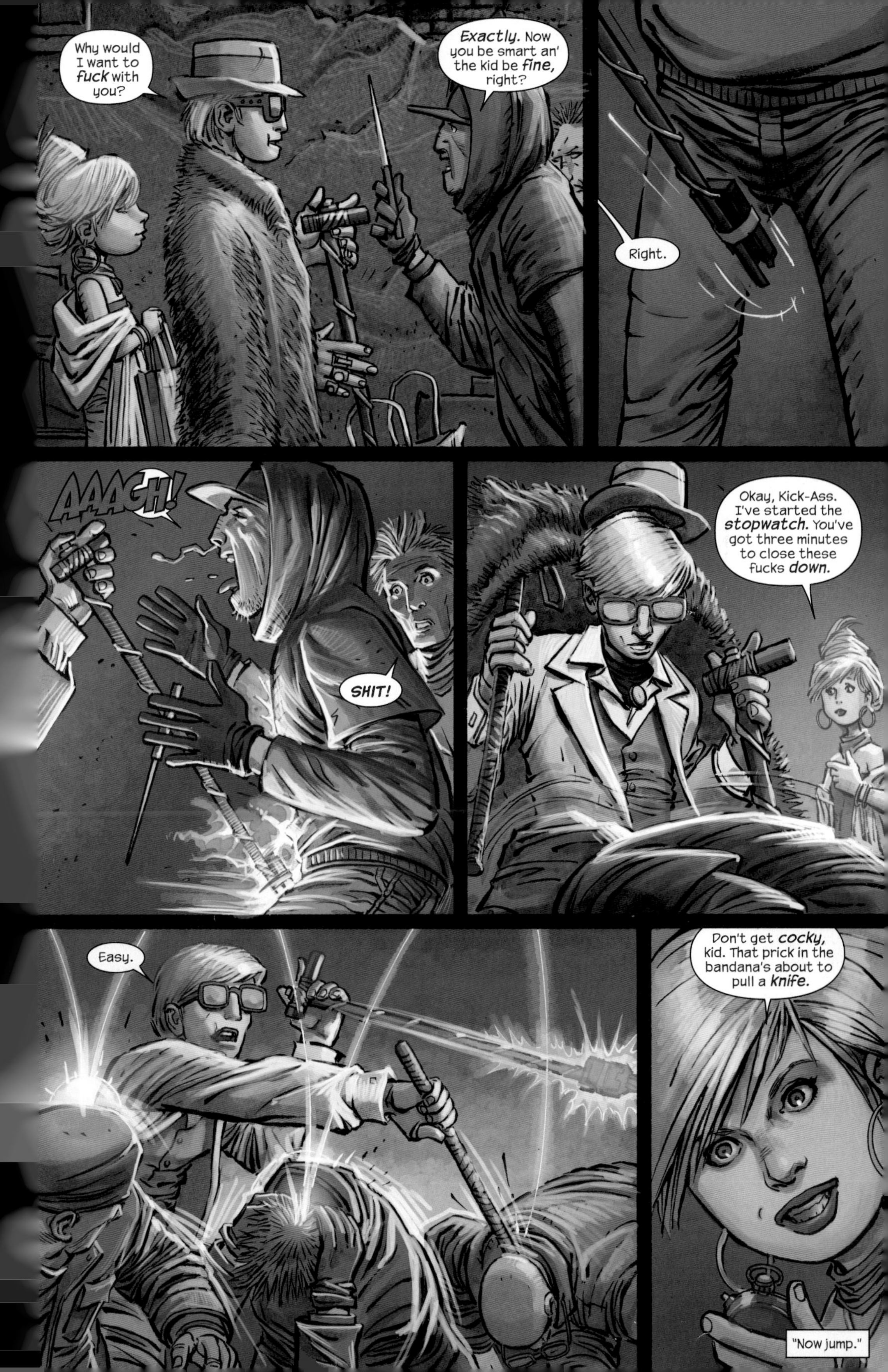
Why would I want to fuck with you?
Exactly. Now you be smart an' the kid be fine, right?
Right.
AAAGH!
SHIT!
Okay, Kick-Ass. I've started the stopwatch. You've got three minutes to close these fucks down.
Easy.
Don't get cocky, kid. That prick in the bandana's about to pull a knife.
"Now jump."

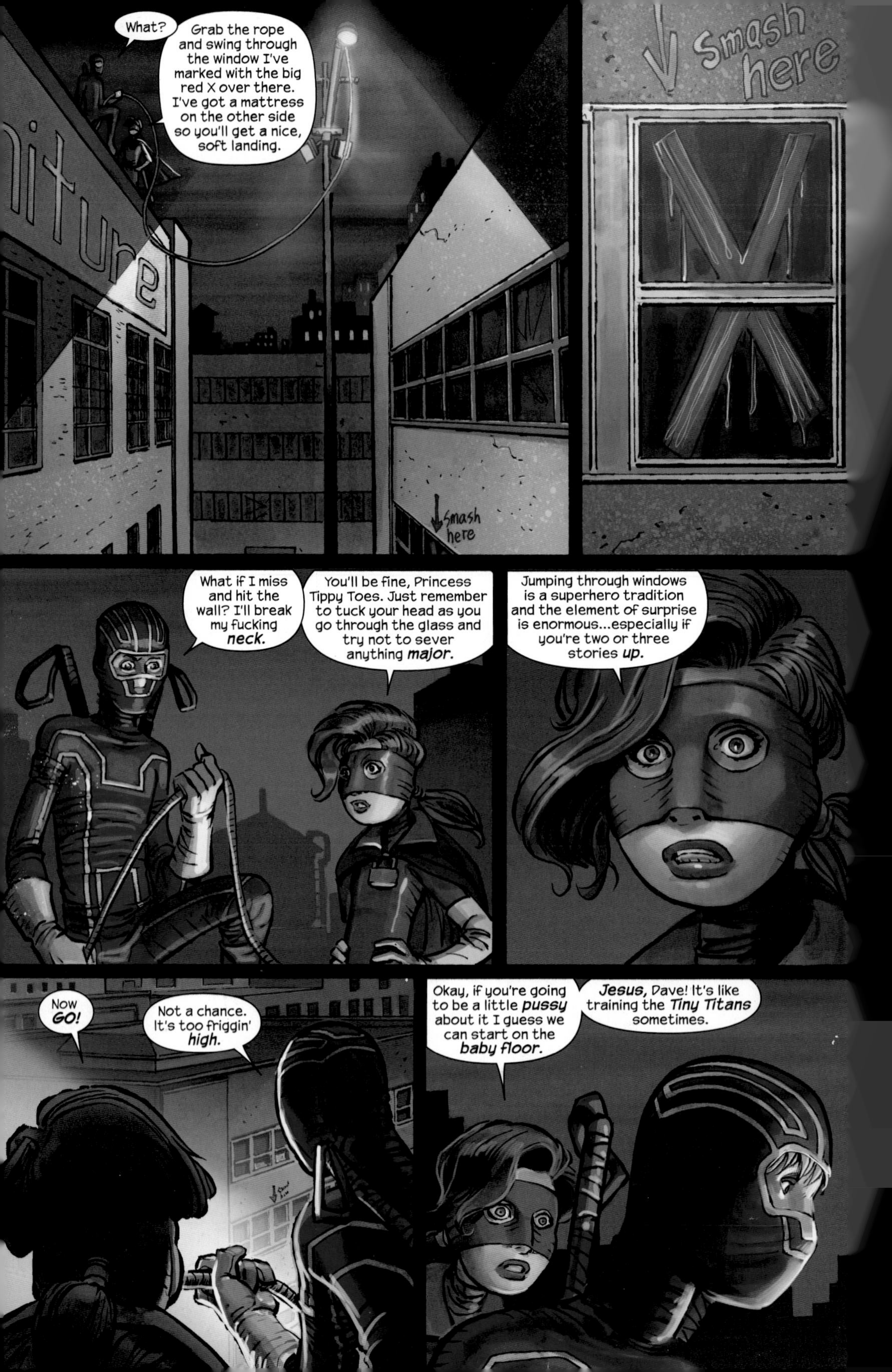
What?
Grab the rope and swing through the window I've marked with the big red X over there. I've got a mattress on the other side so you'll get a nice, soft landing.
Smash here
Smash here
What if I miss and hit the wall? I'll break my fucking neck.
You'll be fine, Princess Tippy Toes. Just remember to tuck your head as you go through the glass and try not to sever anything major.
Jumping through windows is a superhero tradition and the element of surprise is enormous...especially if you're two or three stories up.
Now GO!
Not a chance. It's too friggin' high.
Okay, if you're going to be a little pussy about it I guess we can start on the baby floor.
Jesus, Dave! It's like training the Tiny Titans sometimes.

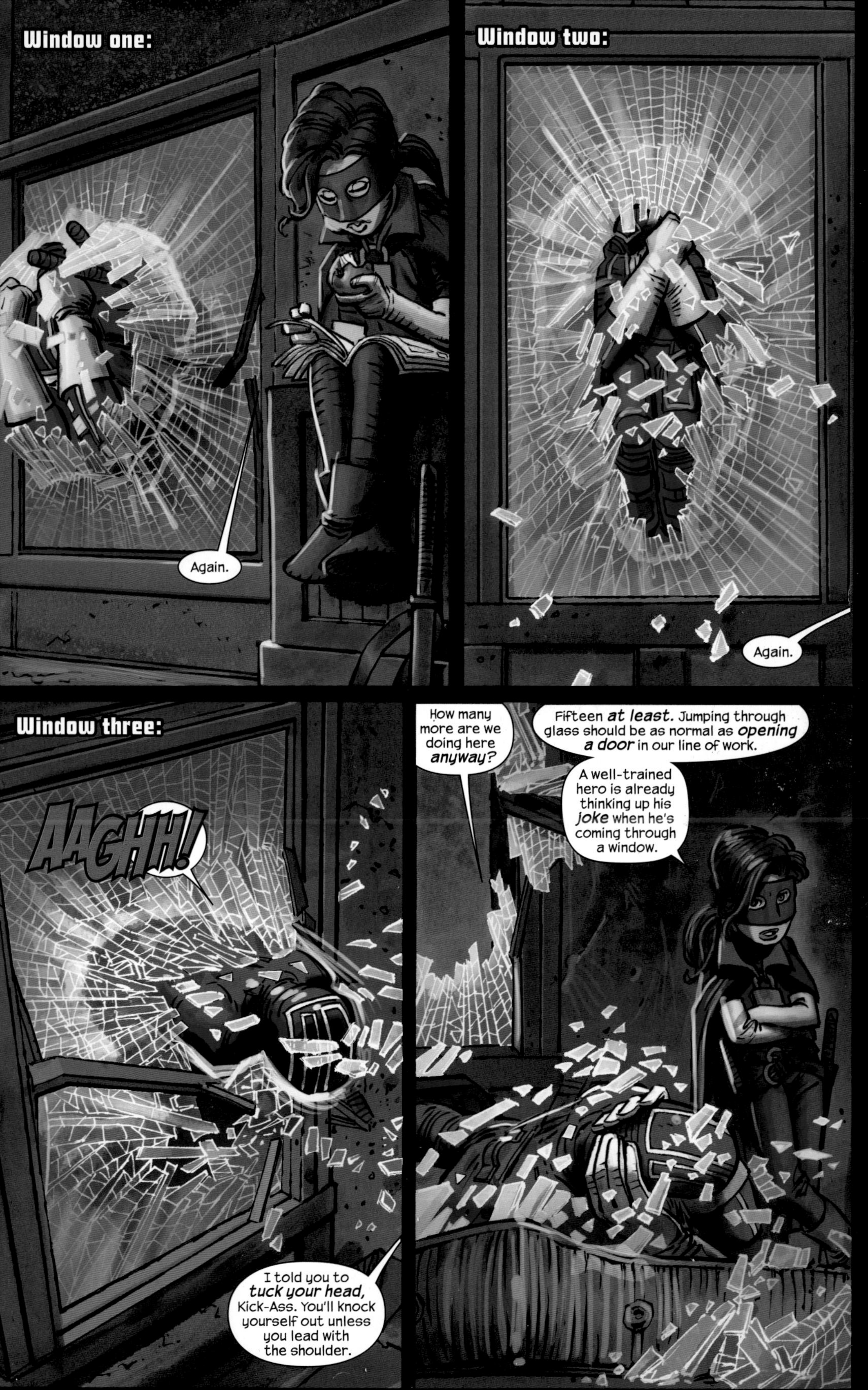

Window one:
Again.
Window two:
Again.
Window three:
AAGHH!
I told you to tuck your head, Kick-Ass. You'll knock yourself out unless you lead with the shoulder.
How many more are we doing here anyway?
Fifteen at least. Jumping through glass should be as normal as opening a door in our line of work.
A well-trained hero is already thinking up his joke when he's coming through a window.

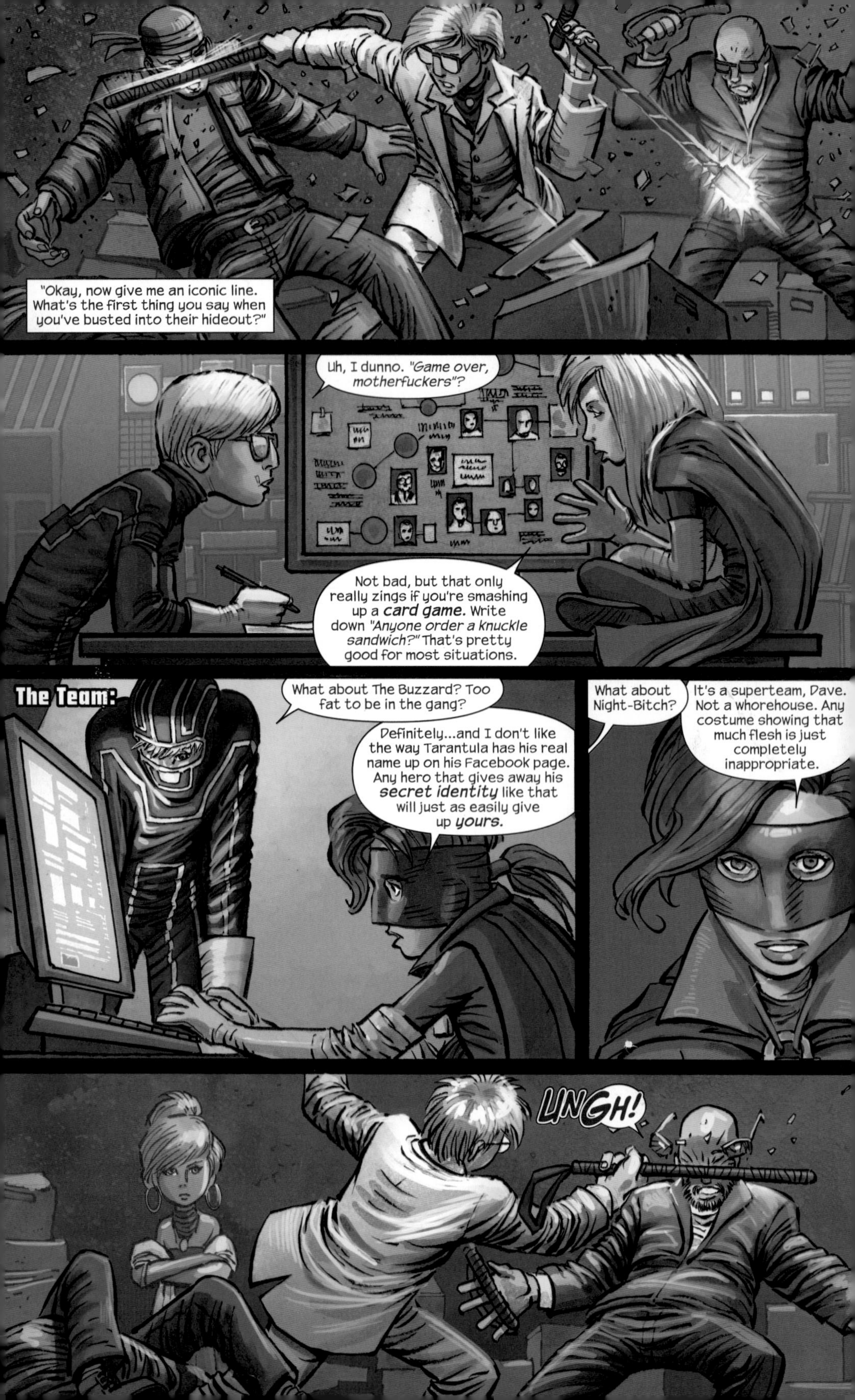
"Okay, now give me an iconic line. What's the first thing you say when you've busted into their hideout?"
Uh, I dunno. "Game over, motherfuckers"?
Not bad, but that only really zings if you're smashing up a card game. Write down "Anyone order a knuckle sandwich?" That's pretty good for most situations.
The Team:
What about The Buzzard? Too fat to be in the gang?
Definitely...and I don't like the way Tarantula has his real name up on his Facebook page. Any hero that gives away his secret identity like that will just as easily give up yours.
What about Night-Bitch?
It's a superteam, Dave. Not a whorehouse. Any costume showing that much flesh is just completely inappropriate.
UNGH!

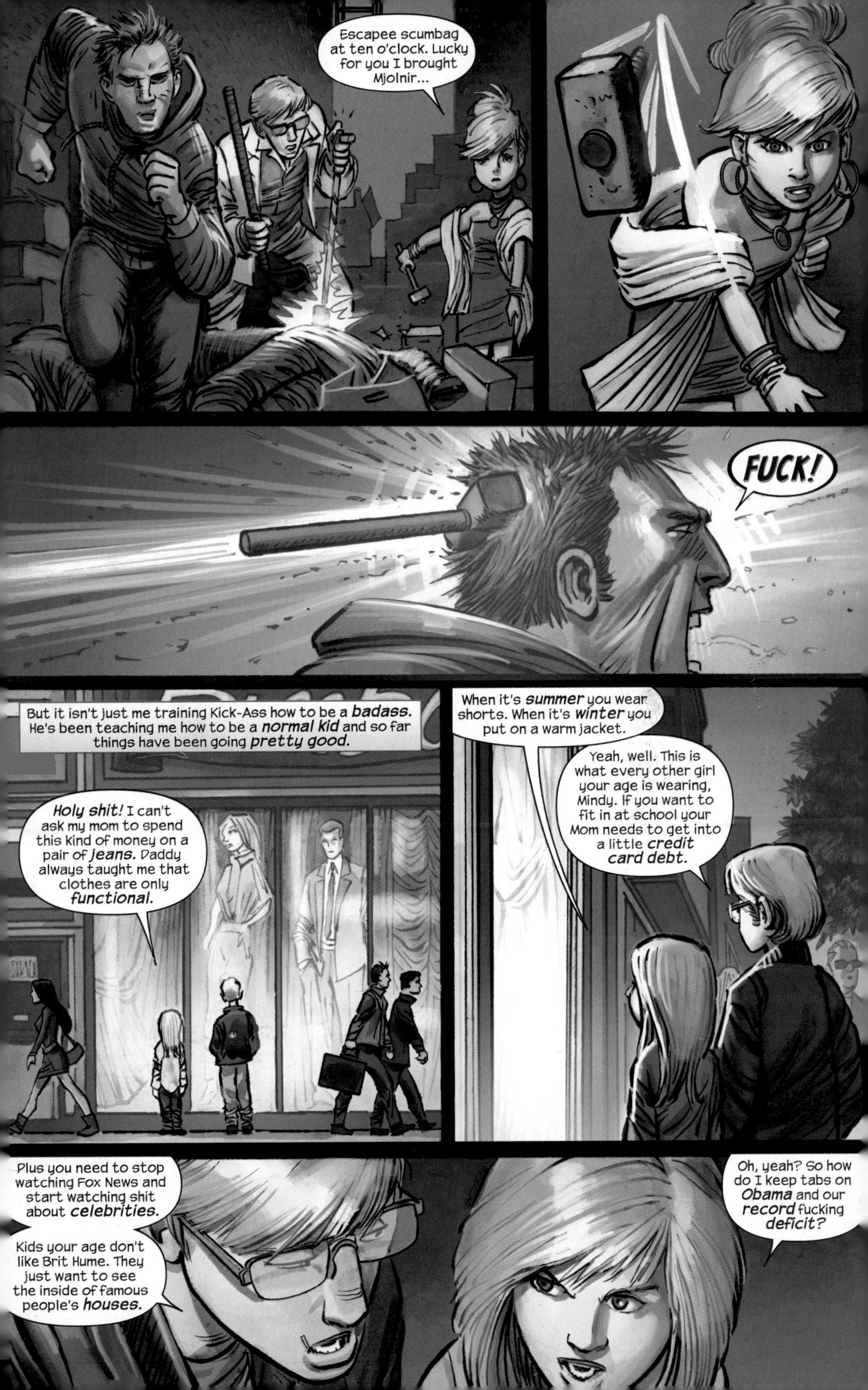

Escapee scumbag at ten o'clock. Lucky for you I brought Mjolnir...
FUCK!
But it isn't just me training Kick-Ass how to be a badass. He's been teaching me how to be a normal kid and so far things have been going pretty good.
Holy shit! I can't ask my mom to spend this kind of money on a pair of jeans. Daddy always taught me that clothes are only functional.
When it's summer you wear shorts. When it's winter you put on a warm jacket.
Yeah, well. This is what every other girl your age is wearing, Mindy. If you want to fit in at school your Mom needs to get into a little credit card debt.
Plus you need to stop watching Fox News and start watching shit about celebrities.
Kids your age don't like Brit Hume. They just want to see the inside of famous people's houses.
Oh, yeah? So how do I keep tabs on Obama and our record fucking deficit?

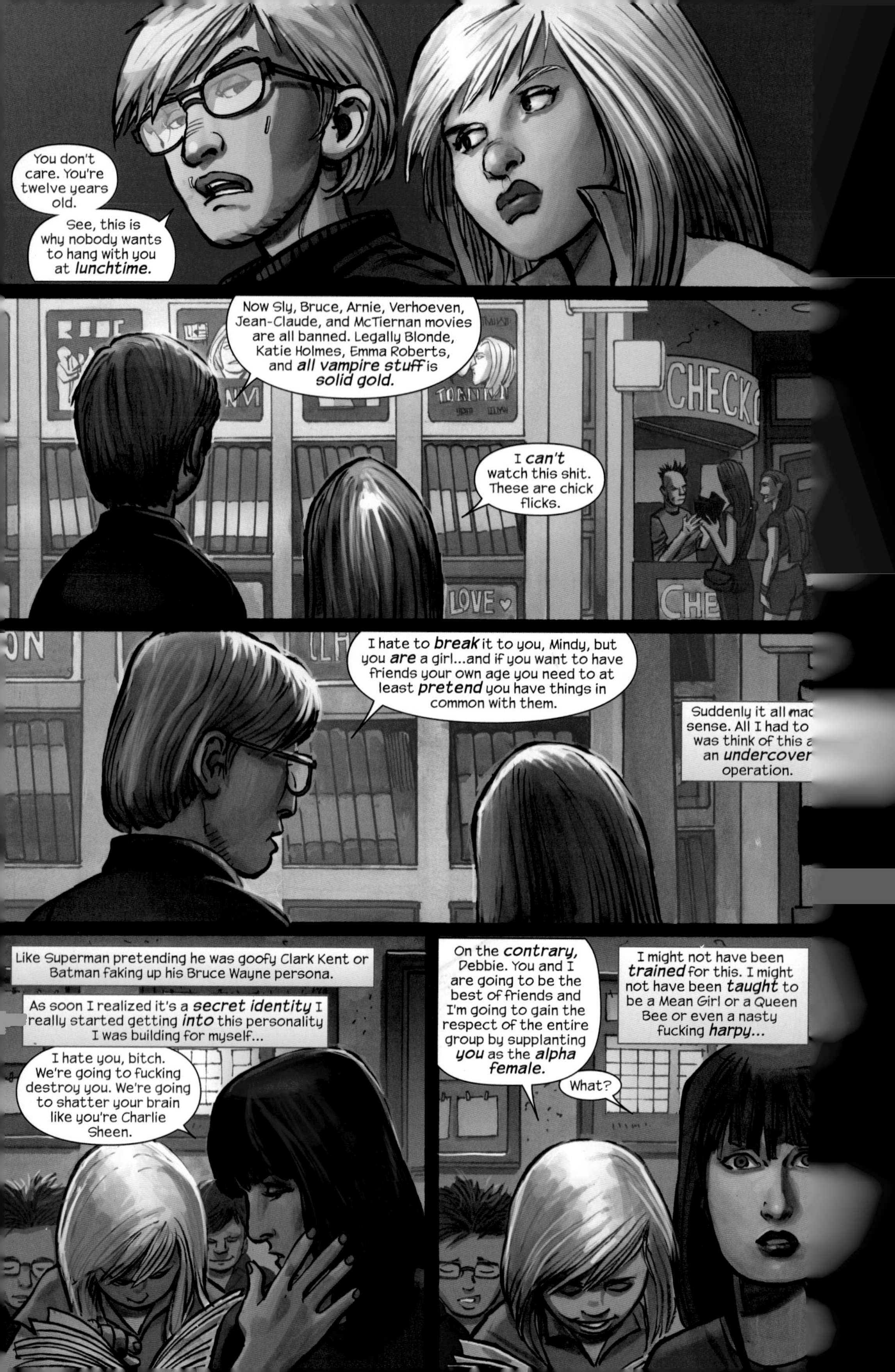

You don't care. You're twelve years old.
See, this is why nobody wants to hang with you at *lunchtime.*
Now Sly, Bruce, Arnie, Verhoeven, Jean-Claude, and McTiernan movies are all banned. Legally Blonde, Katie Holmes, Emma Roberts, and *all vampire stuff* is *solid gold.*
CHECK
I *can't* watch this shit. These are chick flicks.
LOVE
CHE
I hate to *break* it to you, Mindy, but you *are* a girl...and if you want to have friends your own age you need to at least *pretend* you have things in common with them.
Suddenly it all mad sense. All I had to was think of this a an *undercover* operation.
Like Superman pretending he was goofy Clark Kent or Batman faking up his Bruce Wayne persona.
As soon I realized it's a *secret identity* I really started getting *into* this personality I was building for myself...
I hate you, bitch. We're going to fucking destroy you. We're going to shatter your brain like you're Charlie Sheen.
On the *contrary,* Debbie. You and I are going to be the best of friends and I'm going to gain the respect of the entire group by supplanting *you* as the *alpha female.*
What?
I might not have been *trained* for this. I might not have been *taught* to be a Mean Girl or a Queen Bee or even a nasty fucking *harpy...*

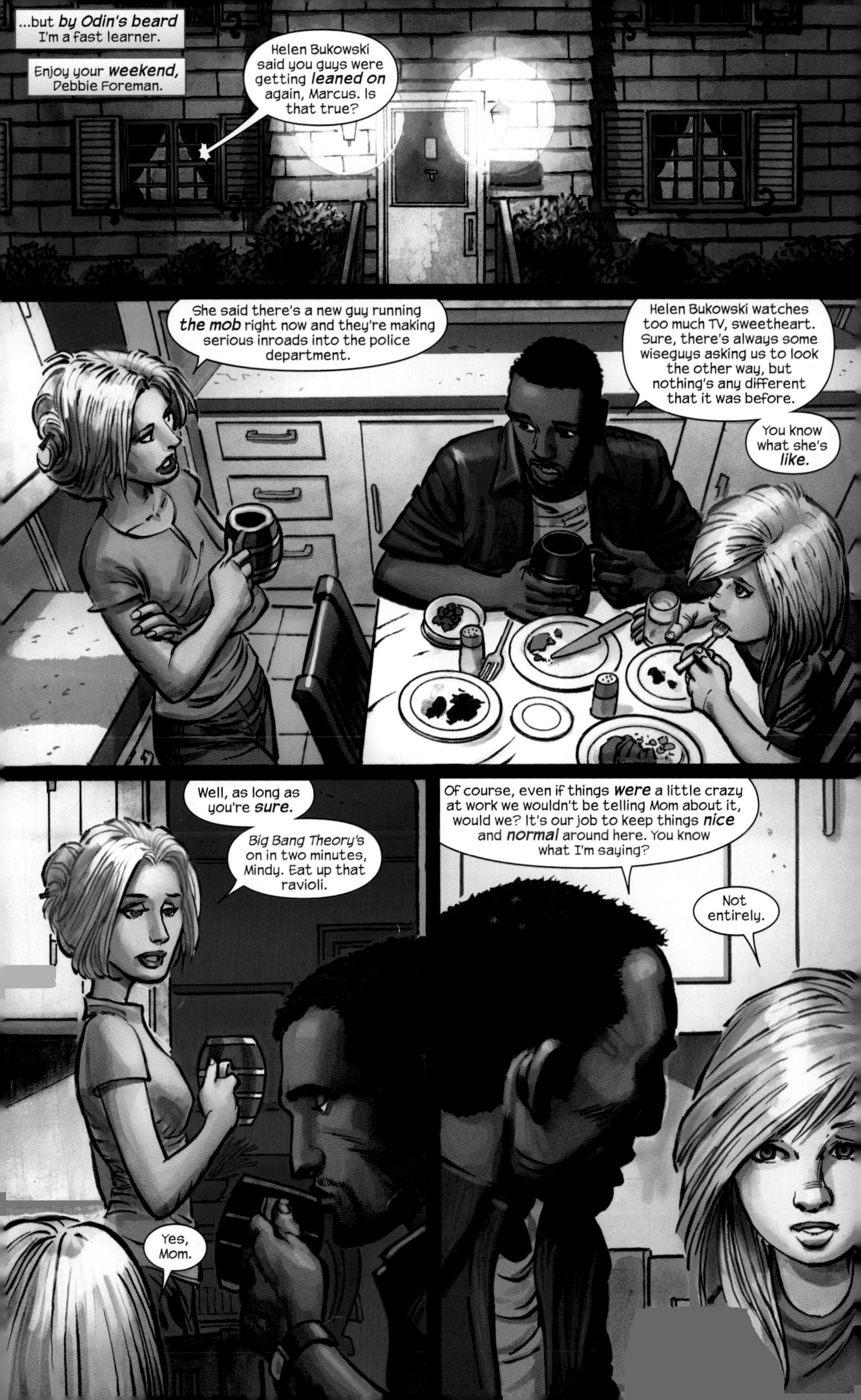
...but by Odin's beard I'm a fast learner.
Enjoy your weekend, Debbie Foreman.
Helen Bukowski said you guys were getting leaned on again, Marcus. Is that true?
She said there's a new guy running the mob right now and they're making serious inroads into the police department.
Helen Bukowski watches too much TV, sweetheart. Sure, there's always some wiseguys asking us to look the other way, but nothing's any different that it was before.
You know what she's like.
Well, as long as you're sure.
Big Bang Theory's on in two minutes, Mindy. Eat up that ravioli.
Yes, Mom.
Of course, even if things were a little crazy at work we wouldn't be telling Mom about it, would we? It's our job to keep things nice and normal around here. You know what I'm saying?
Not entirely.

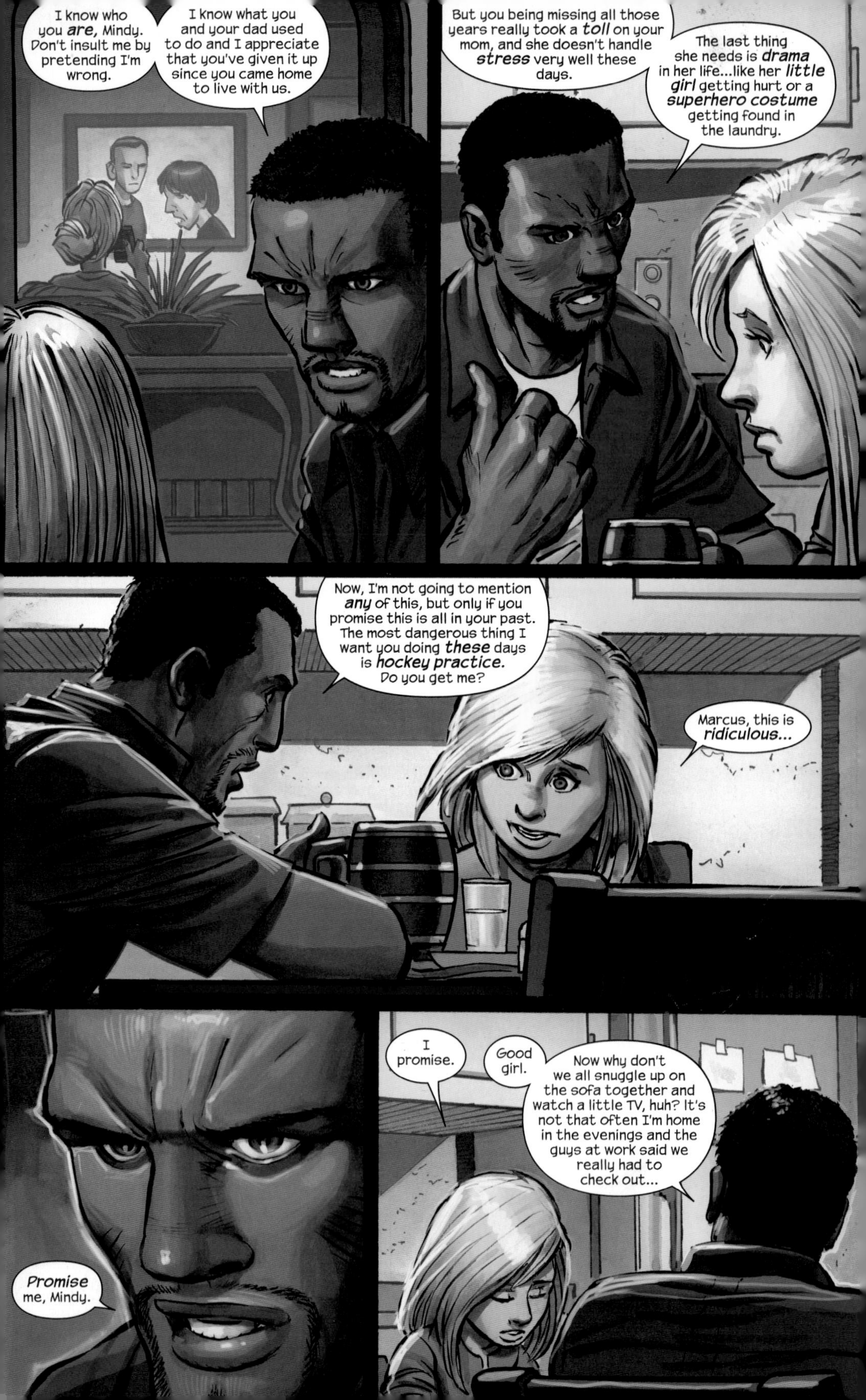

I know who you are, Mindy. Don't insult me by pretending I'm wrong.
I know what you and your dad used to do and I appreciate that you've given it up since you came home to live with us.
But you being missing all those years really took a toll on your mom, and she doesn't handle stress very well these days.
The last thing she needs is drama in her life...like her little girl getting hurt or a superhero costume getting found in the laundry.
Now, I'm not going to mention any of this, but only if you promise this is all in your past. The most dangerous thing I want you doing these days is hockey practice. Do you get me?
Marcus, this is ridiculous...
Promise me, Mindy.
I promise.
Good girl.
Now why don't we all snuggle up on the sofa together and watch a little TV, huh? It's not that often I'm home in the evenings and the guys at work said we really had to check out...

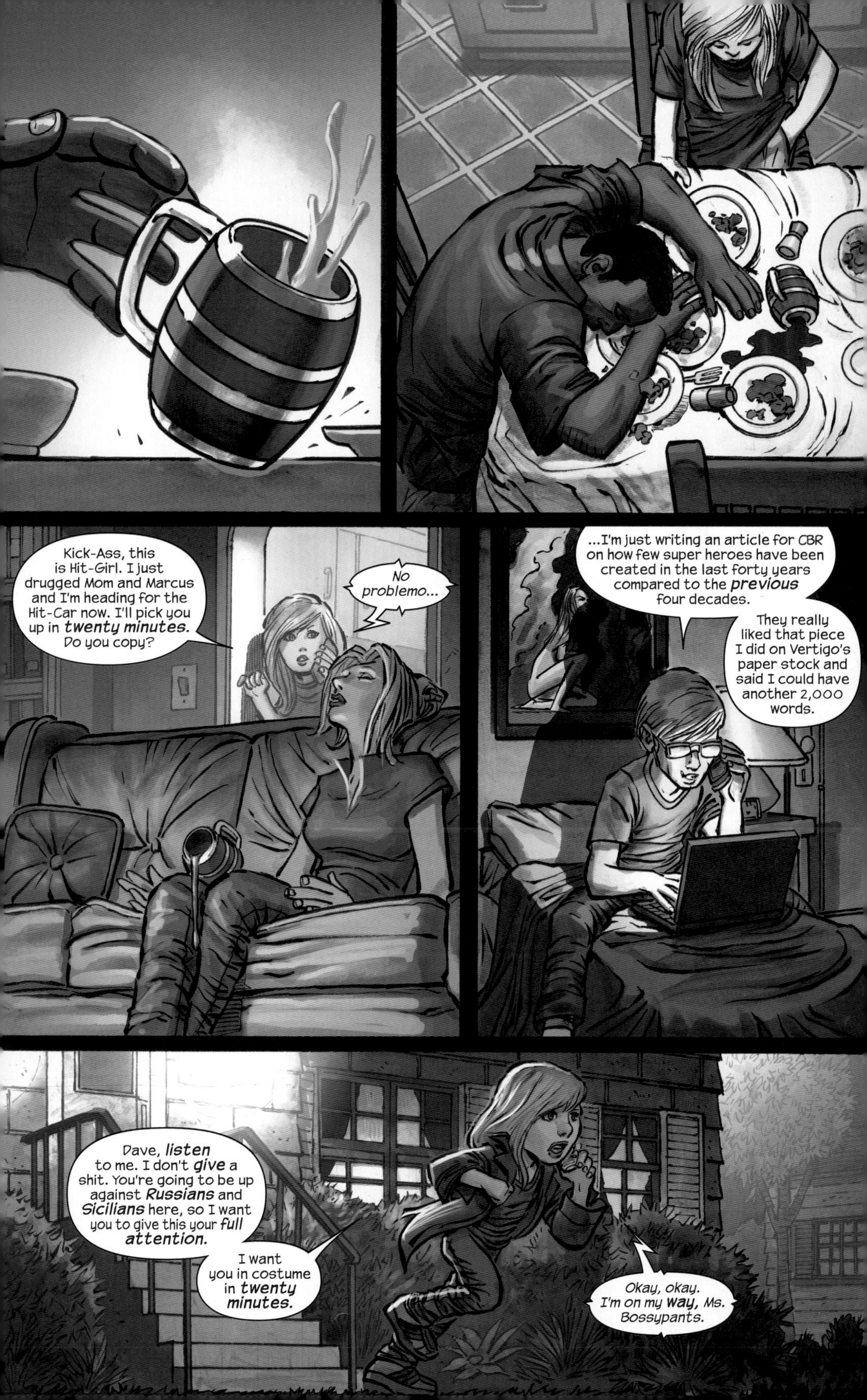

Kick-Ass, this is Hit-Girl. I just drugged Mom and Marcus and I'm heading for the Hit-Car now. I'll pick you up in twenty minutes. Do you copy?
No problemo...
...I'm just writing an article for CBR on how few super heroes have been created in the last forty years compared to the previous four decades.
They really liked that piece I did on Vertigo's paper stock and said I could have another 2,000 words.
Dave, listen to me. I don't give a shit. You're going to be up against Russians and Sicilians here, so I want you to give this your full attention.
I want you in costume in twenty minutes.
Okay, okay. I'm on my way, Ms. Bossypants.

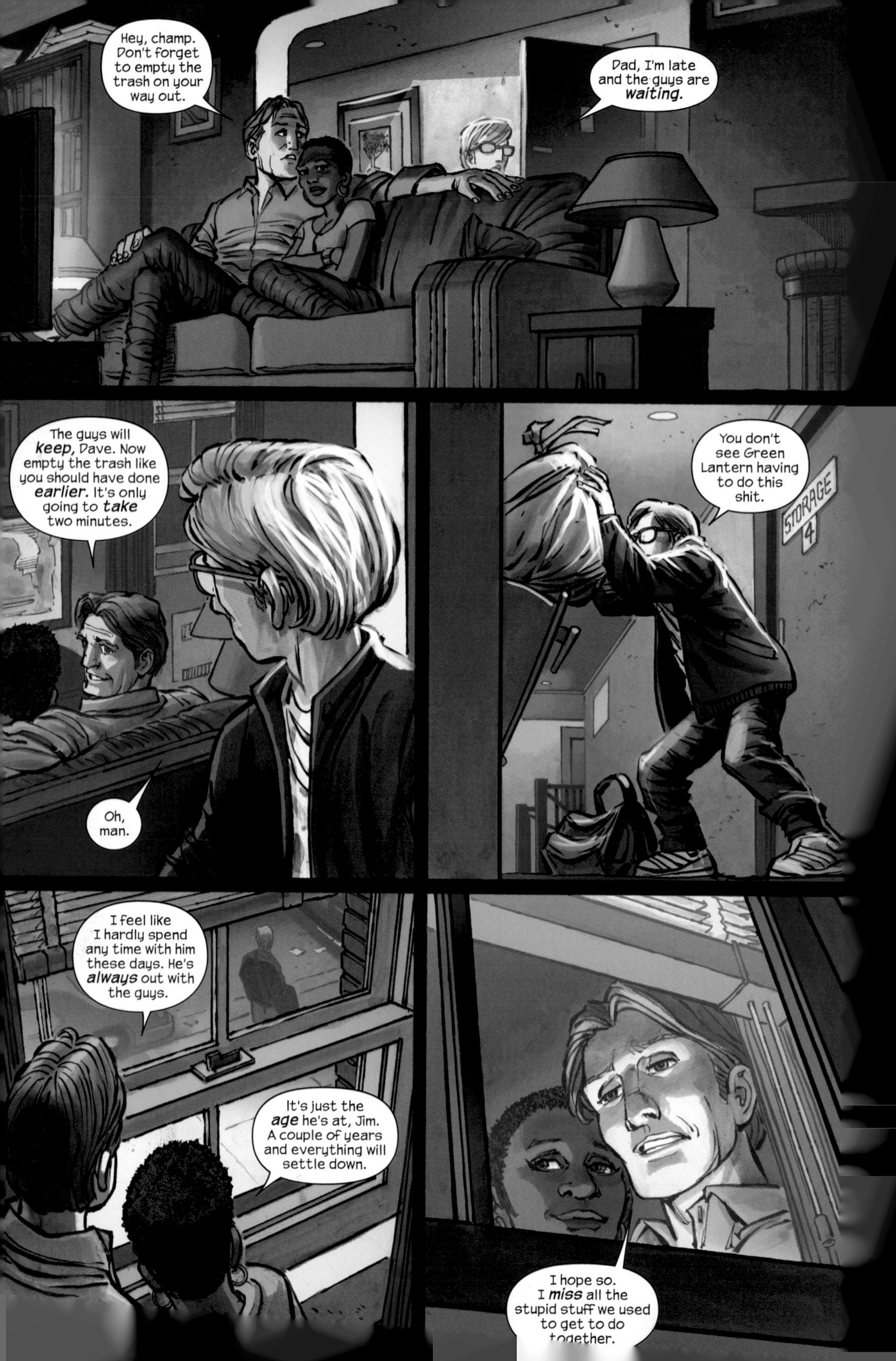
Hey, champ. Don't forget to empty the trash on your way out.
Dad, I'm late and the guys are *waiting.*
The guys will *keep,* Dave. Now empty the trash like you should have done *earlier.* It's only going to *take* two minutes.
Oh, man.
You don't see Green Lantern having to do this shit.
STORAGE 4
I feel like I hardly spend any time with him these days. He's *always* out with the guys.
It's just the *age* he's at, Jim. A couple of years and everything will settle down.
I hope so. I *miss* all the stupid stuff we used to get to do together.

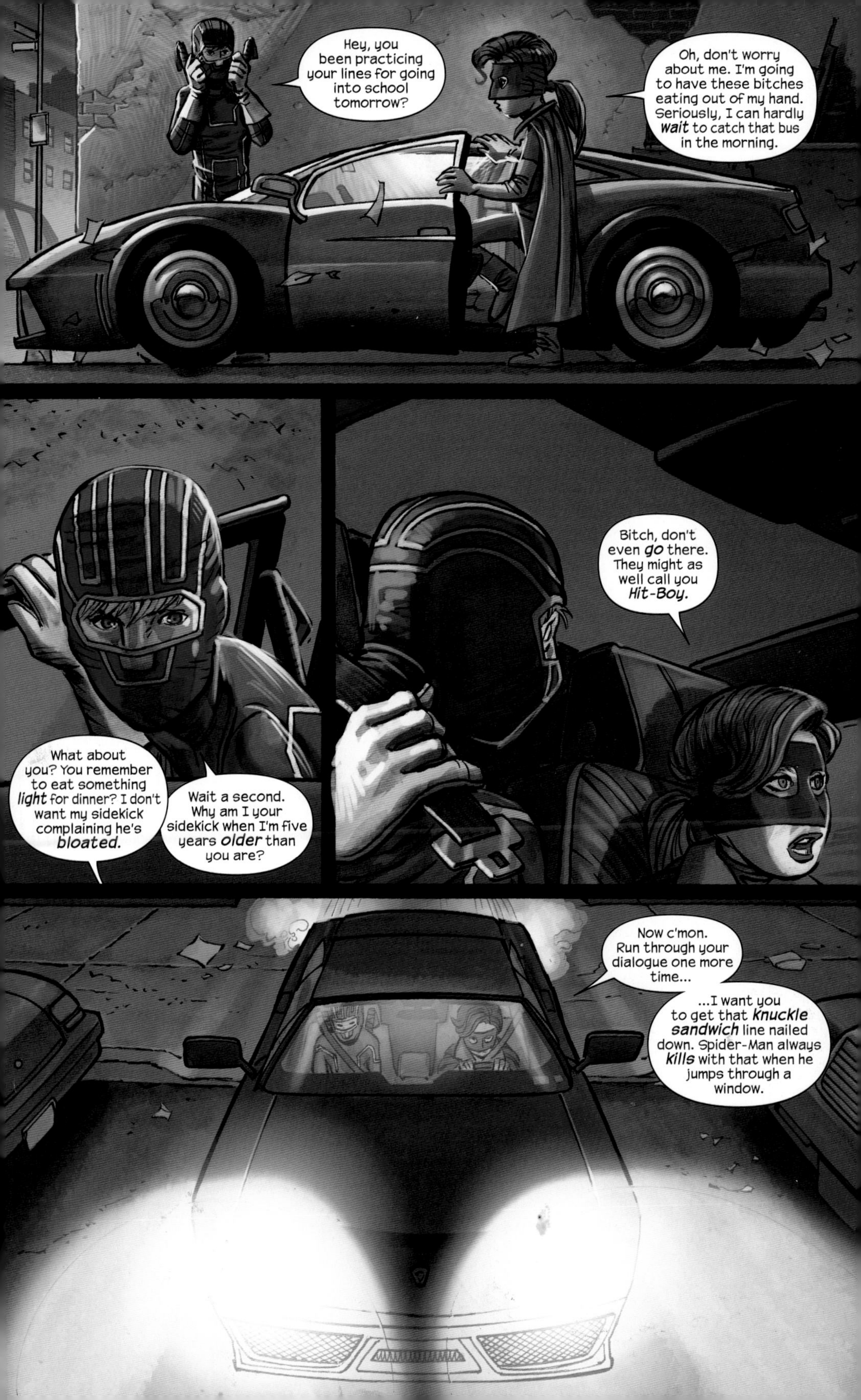
Hey, you been practicing your lines for going into school tomorrow?
Oh, don't worry about me. I'm going to have these bitches eating out of my hand. Seriously, I can hardly wait to catch that bus in the morning.
What about you? You remember to eat something light for dinner? I don't want my sidekick complaining he's bloated.
Wait a second. Why am I your sidekick when I'm five years older than you are?
Bitch, don't even go there. They might as well call you Hit-Boy.
Now c'mon. Run through your dialogue one more time...
...I want you to get that knuckle sandwich line nailed down. Spider-Man always kills with that when he jumps through a window.

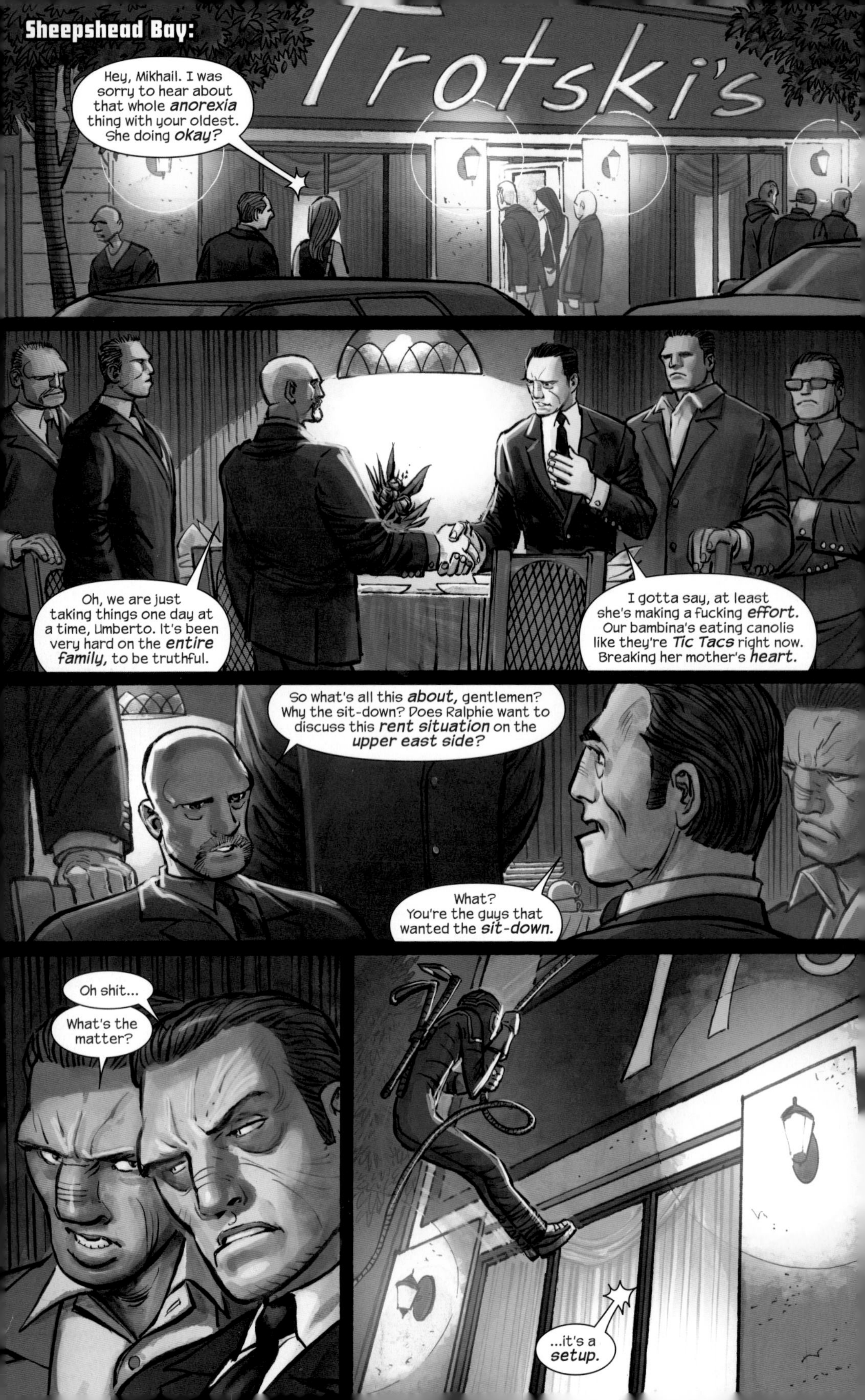
Sheepshead Bay:
Trotski's
Hey, Mikhail. I was sorry to hear about that whole *anorexia* thing with your oldest. She doing *okay?*
Oh, we are just taking things one day at a time, Umberto. It's been very hard on the *entire family,* to be truthful.
I gotta say, at least she's making a fucking *effort.* Our bambina's eating canolis like they're *Tic Tacs* right now. Breaking her mother's *heart.*
So what's all this *about,* gentlemen? Why the sit-down? Does Ralphie want to discuss this *rent situation* on the *upper east side?*
What? You're the guys that wanted the *sit-down.*
Oh shit...
What's the matter?
...it's a *setup.*

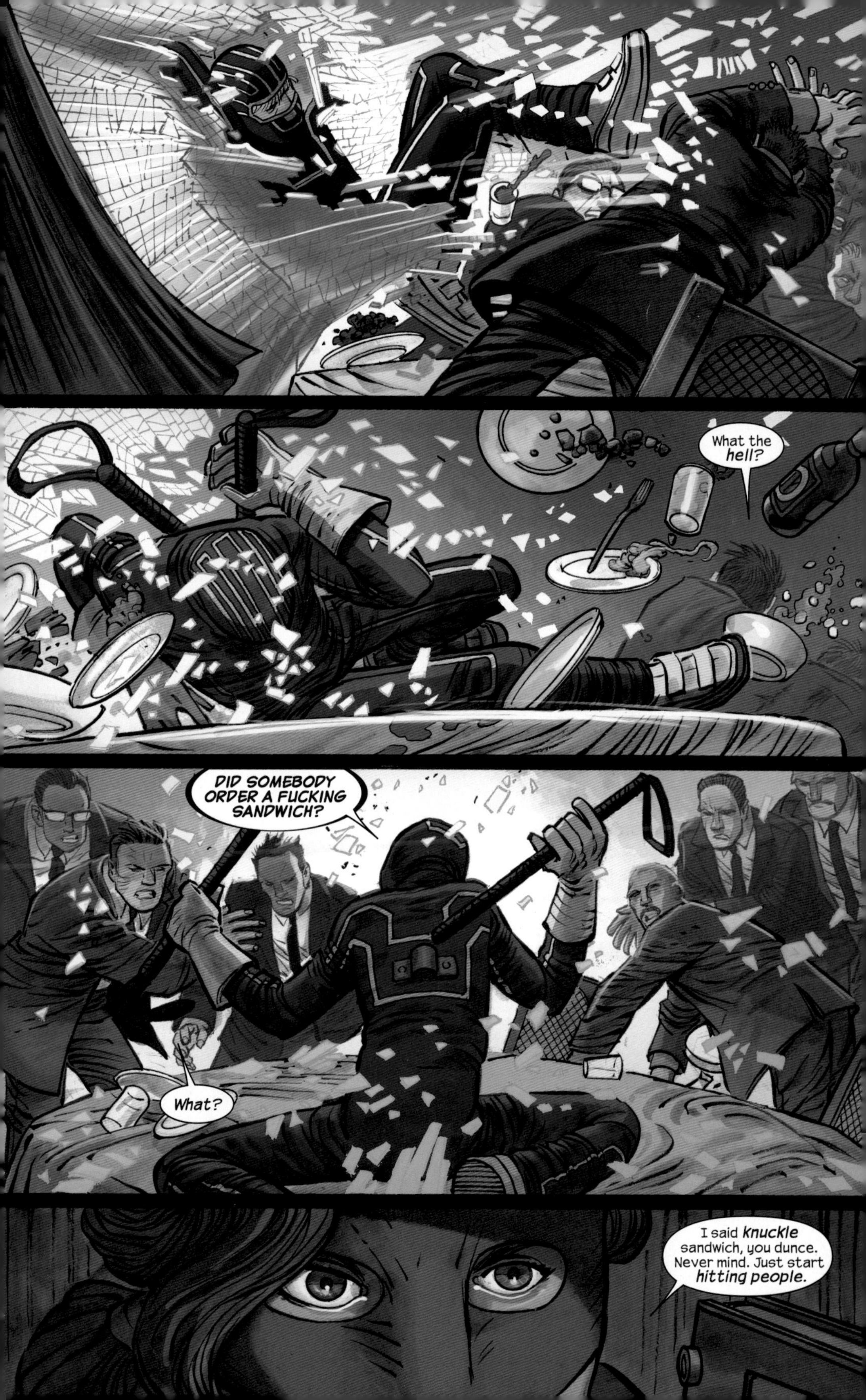
What the hell?
DID SOMEBODY ORDER A FUCKING SANDWICH?
What?
I said knuckle sandwich, you dunce. Never mind. Just start hitting people.

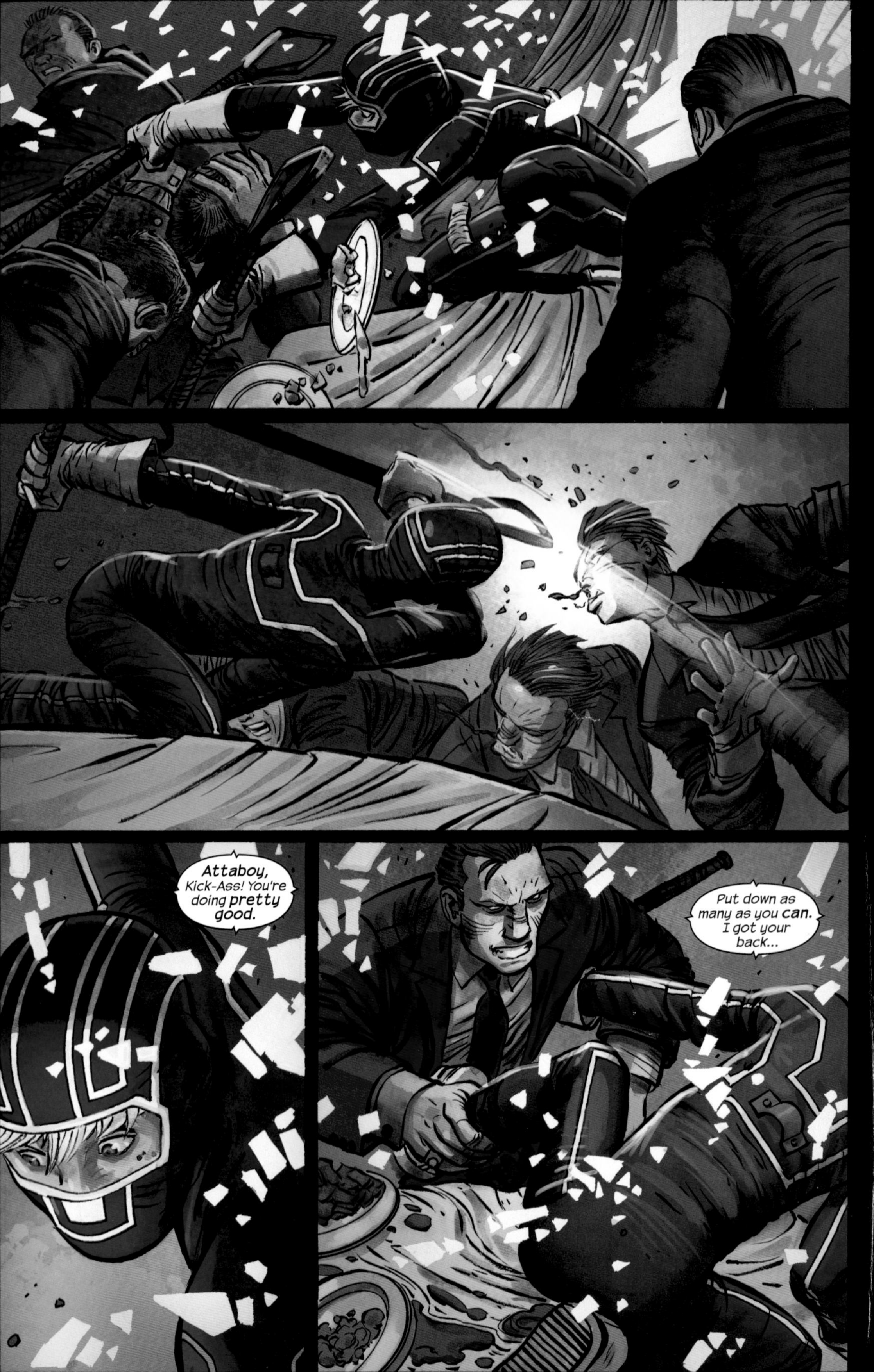
Attaboy, Kick-Ass! You're doing pretty good.
Put down as many as you can. I got your back...

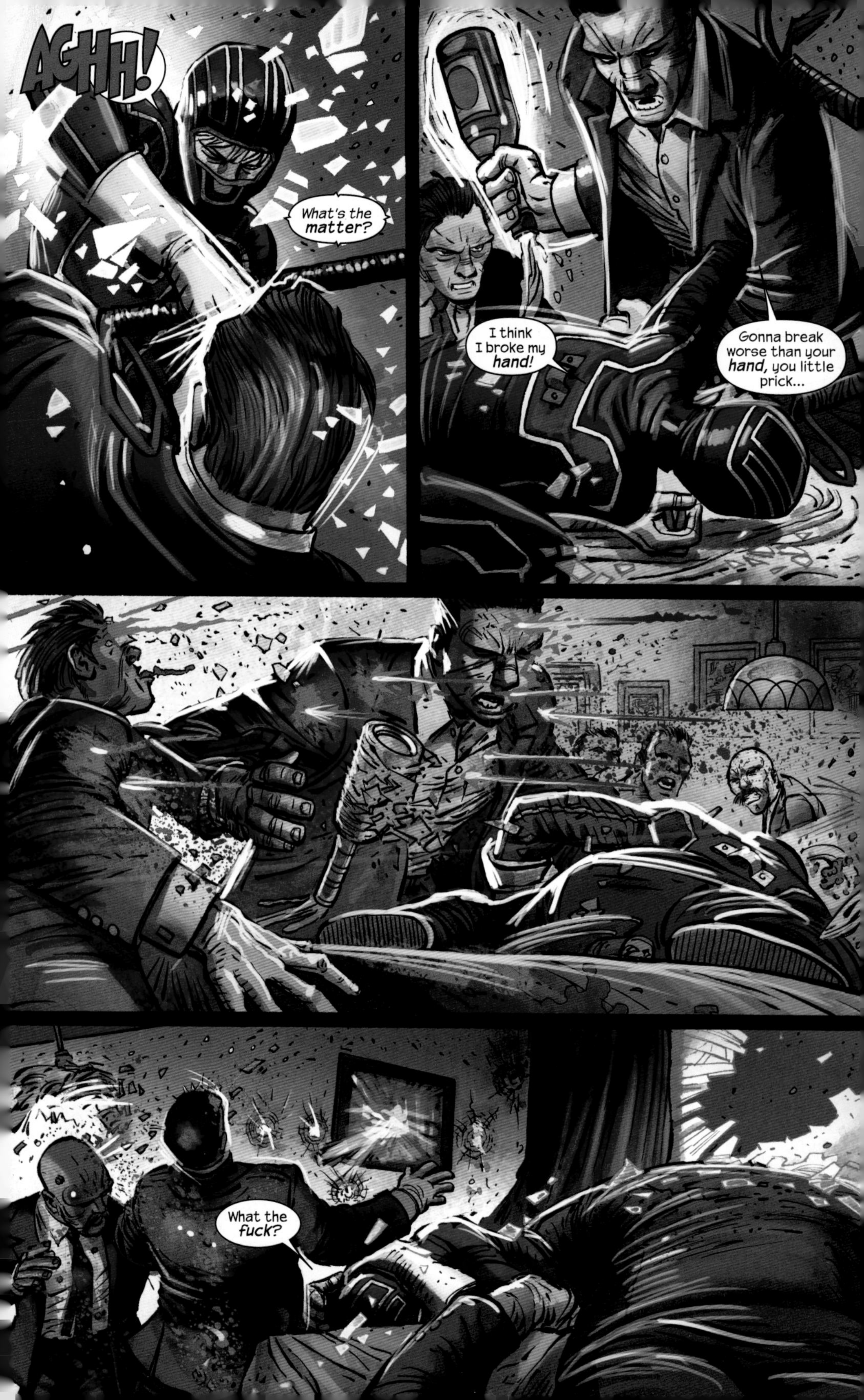
AGHH!
What's the matter?
I think I broke my hand!
Gonna break worse than your hand, you little prick...
What the fuck?

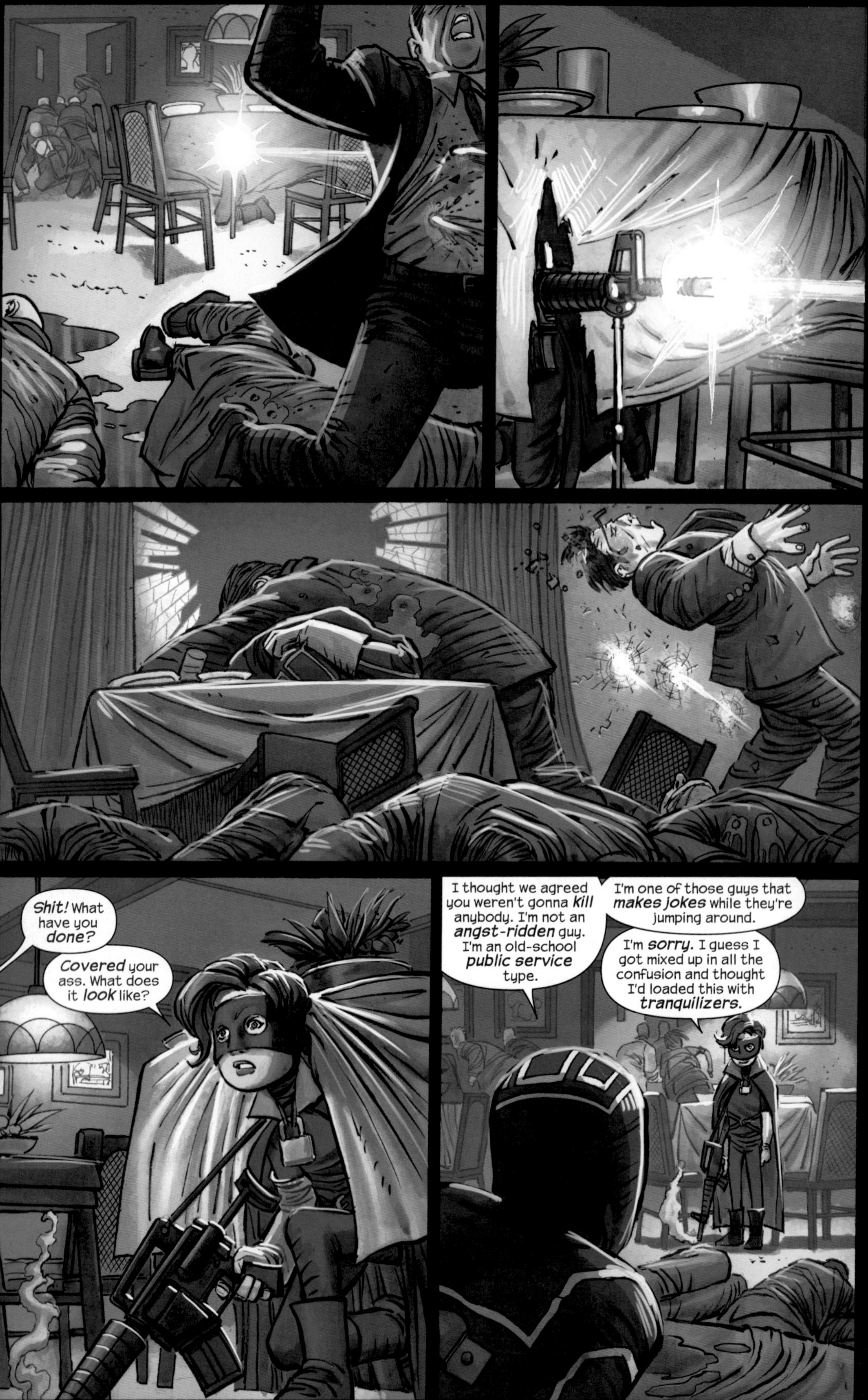
Shit! What have you done?
Covered your ass. What does it look like?
I thought we agreed you weren't gonna kill anybody. I'm not an angst-ridden guy. I'm an old-school public service type.
I'm one of those guys that makes jokes while they're jumping around.
I'm sorry. I guess I got mixed up in all the confusion and thought I'd loaded this with tranquilizers.

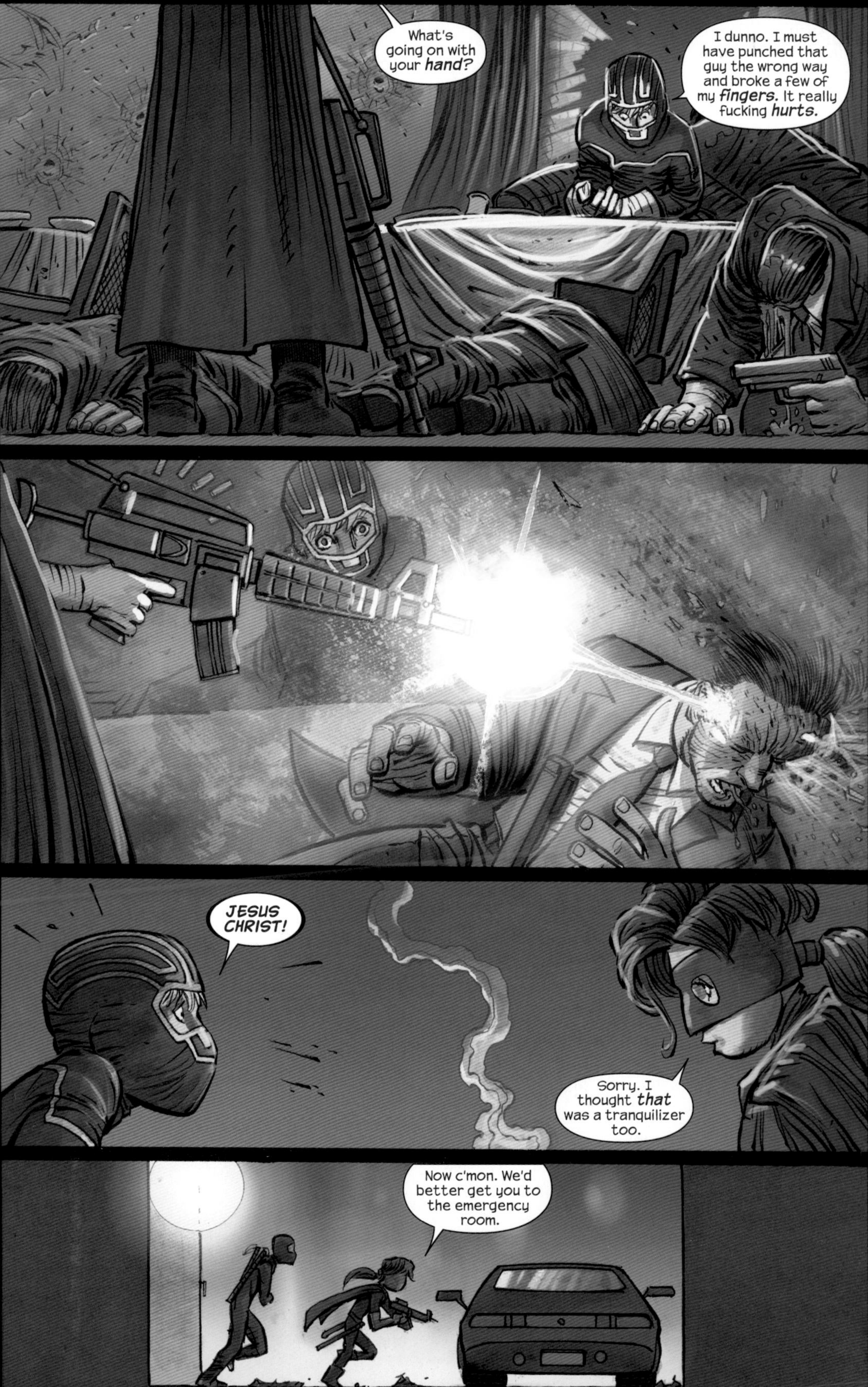
What's going on with your *hand?*
I dunno. I must have punched that guy the wrong way and broke a few of my *fingers.* It really fucking *hurts.*
JESUS CHRIST!
Sorry. I thought *that* was a tranquilizer too.
Now c'mon. We'd better get you to the emergency room.

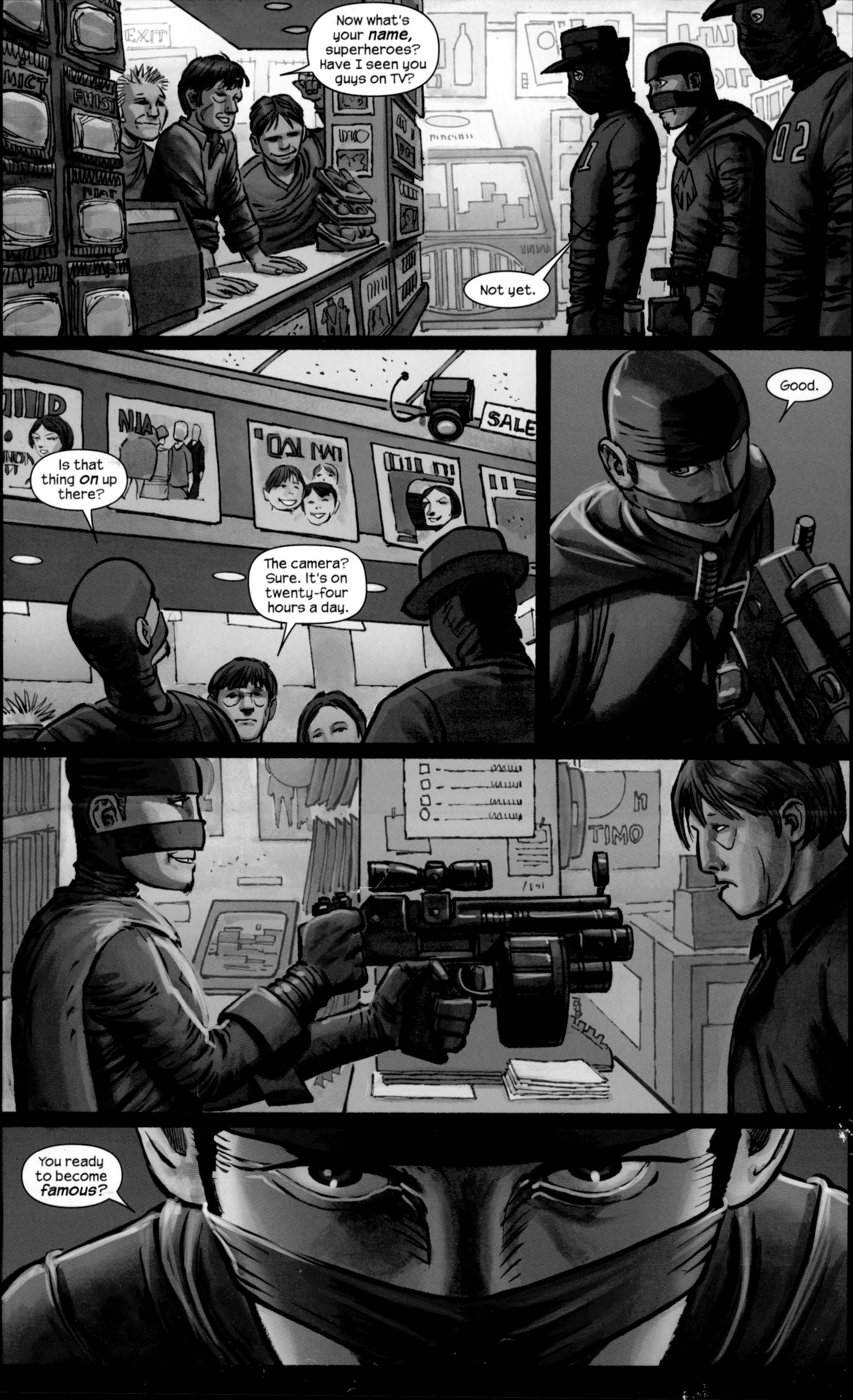

Now what's your **name,** superheroes? Have I seen you guys on TV?
Not yet.
Is that thing ***on*** up there?
The camera? Sure. It's on twenty-four hours a day.
Good.
You ready to become ***famous?***

THREE

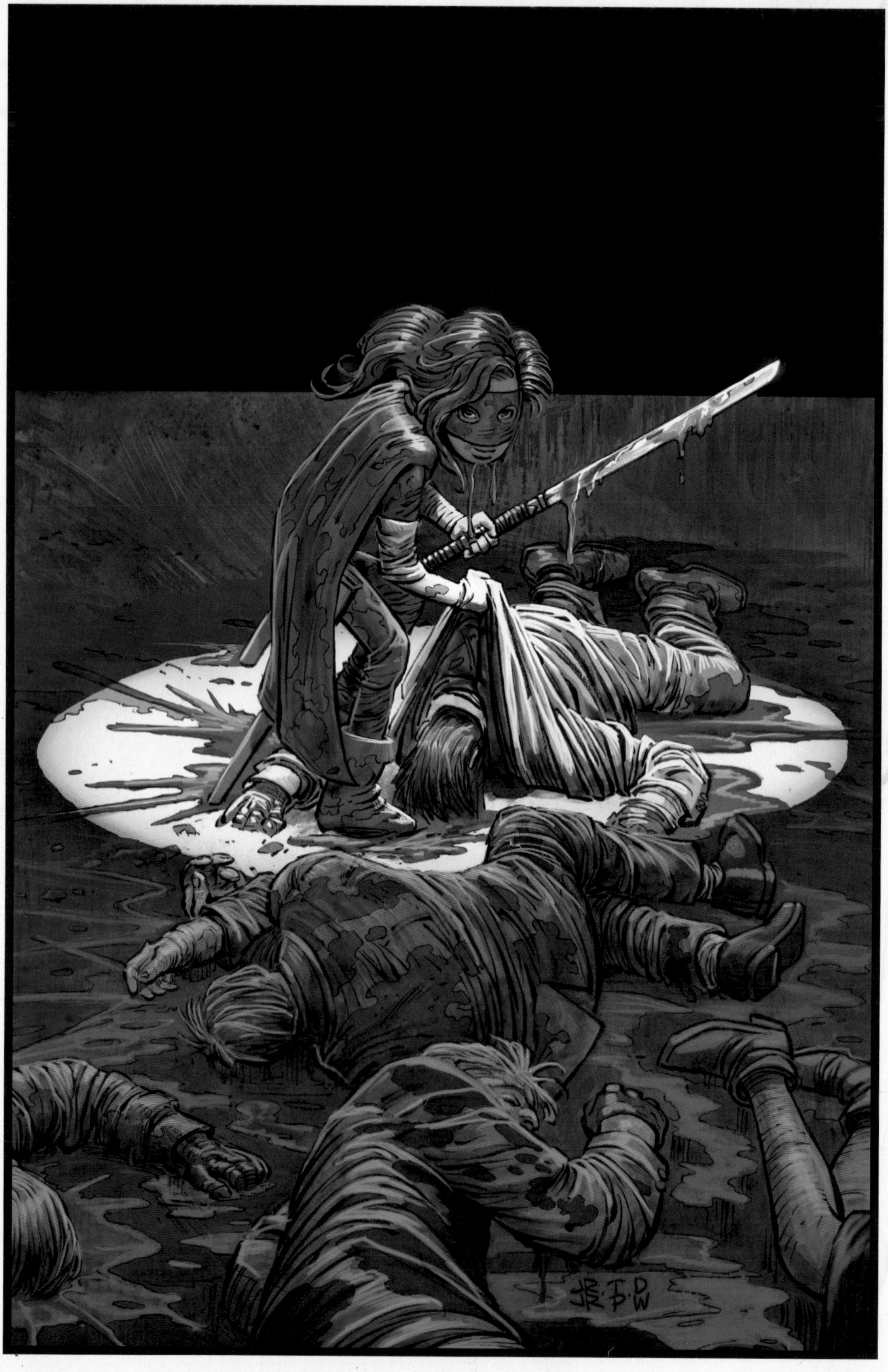

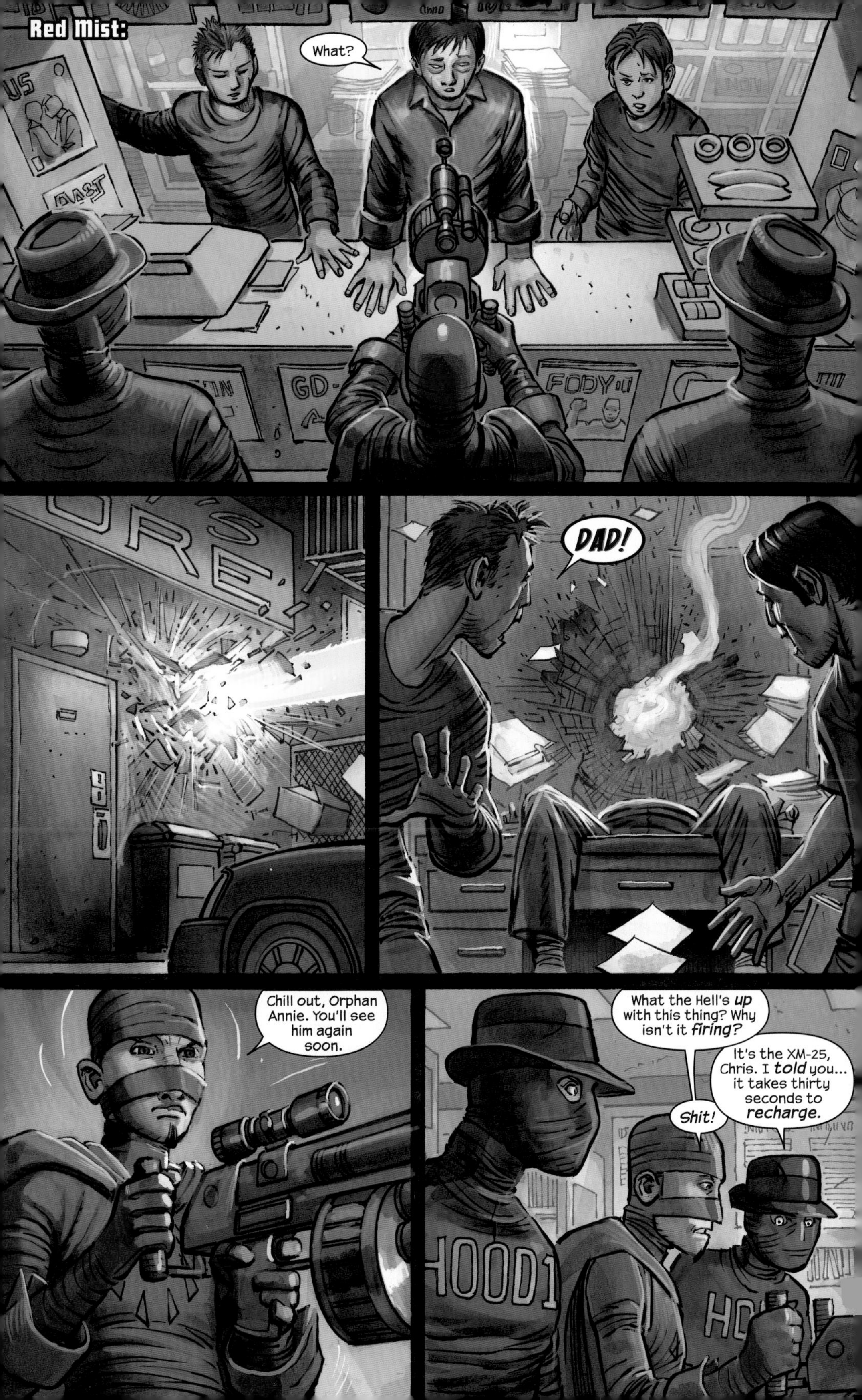
Red Mist:
What?
DAD!
Chill out, Orphan Annie. You'll see him again soon.
What the Hell's up with this thing? Why isn't it firing?
Shit!
It's the XM-25, Chris. I told you... it takes thirty seconds to recharge.
HOOD1

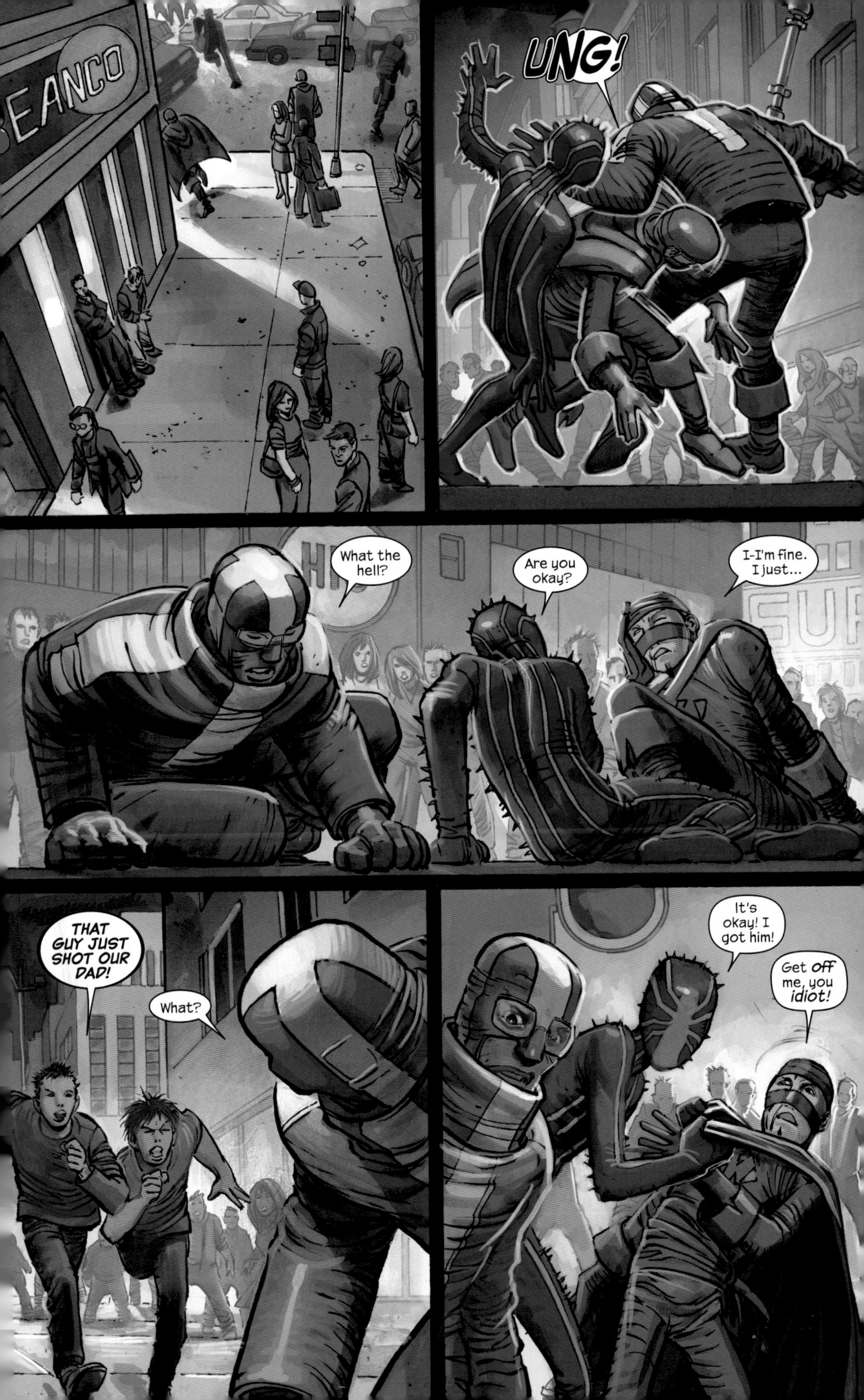
EANCO
UNG!
What the hell?
Are you okay?
I-I'm fine. I just...
THAT GUY JUST SHOT OUR DAD!
What?
It's okay! I got him!
Get off me, you idiot!

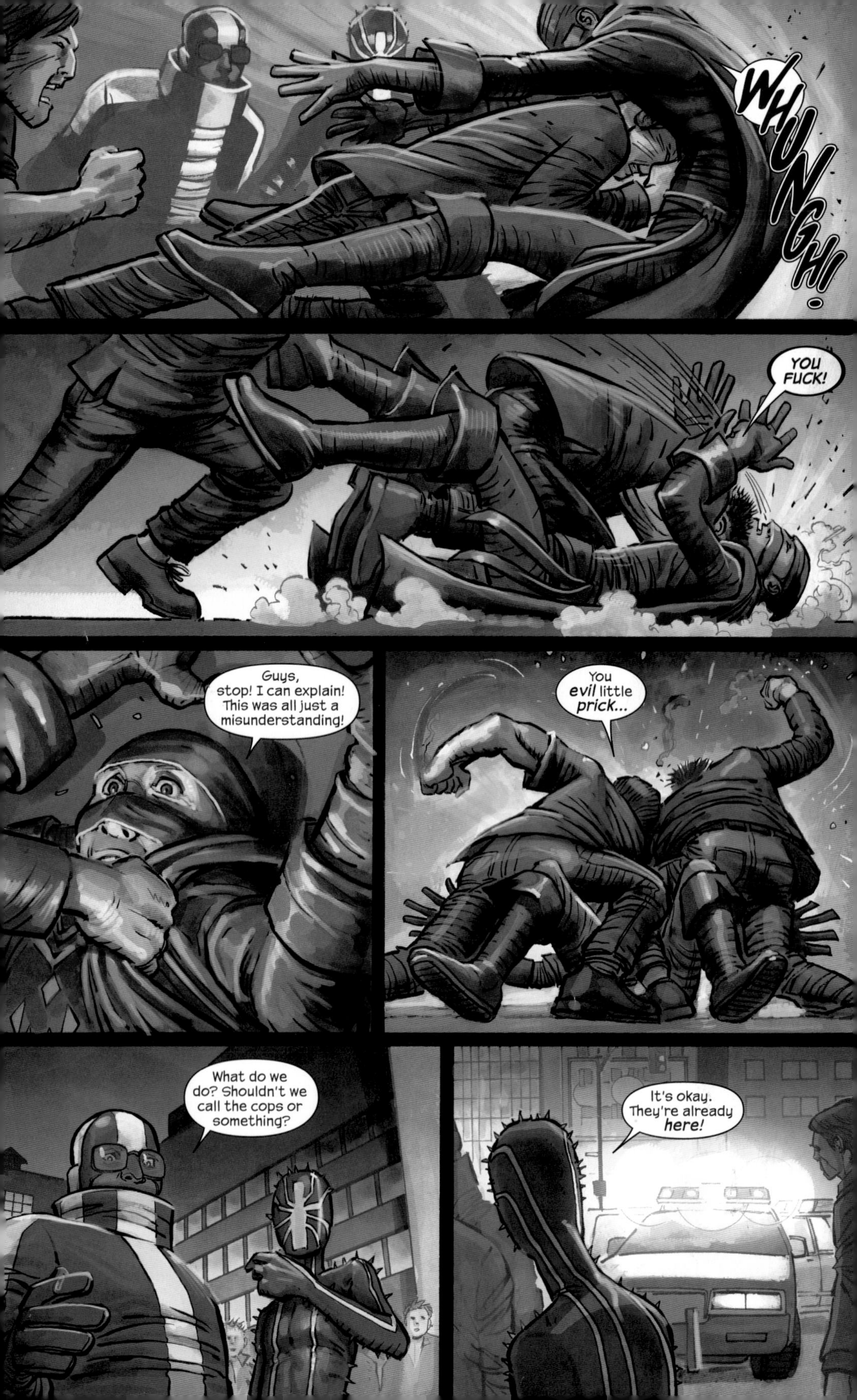
WHUNGH!
YOU FUCK!
Guys, stop! I can explain! This was all just a misunderstanding!
You evil little prick...
What do we do? Shouldn't we call the cops or something?
It's okay. They're already here!

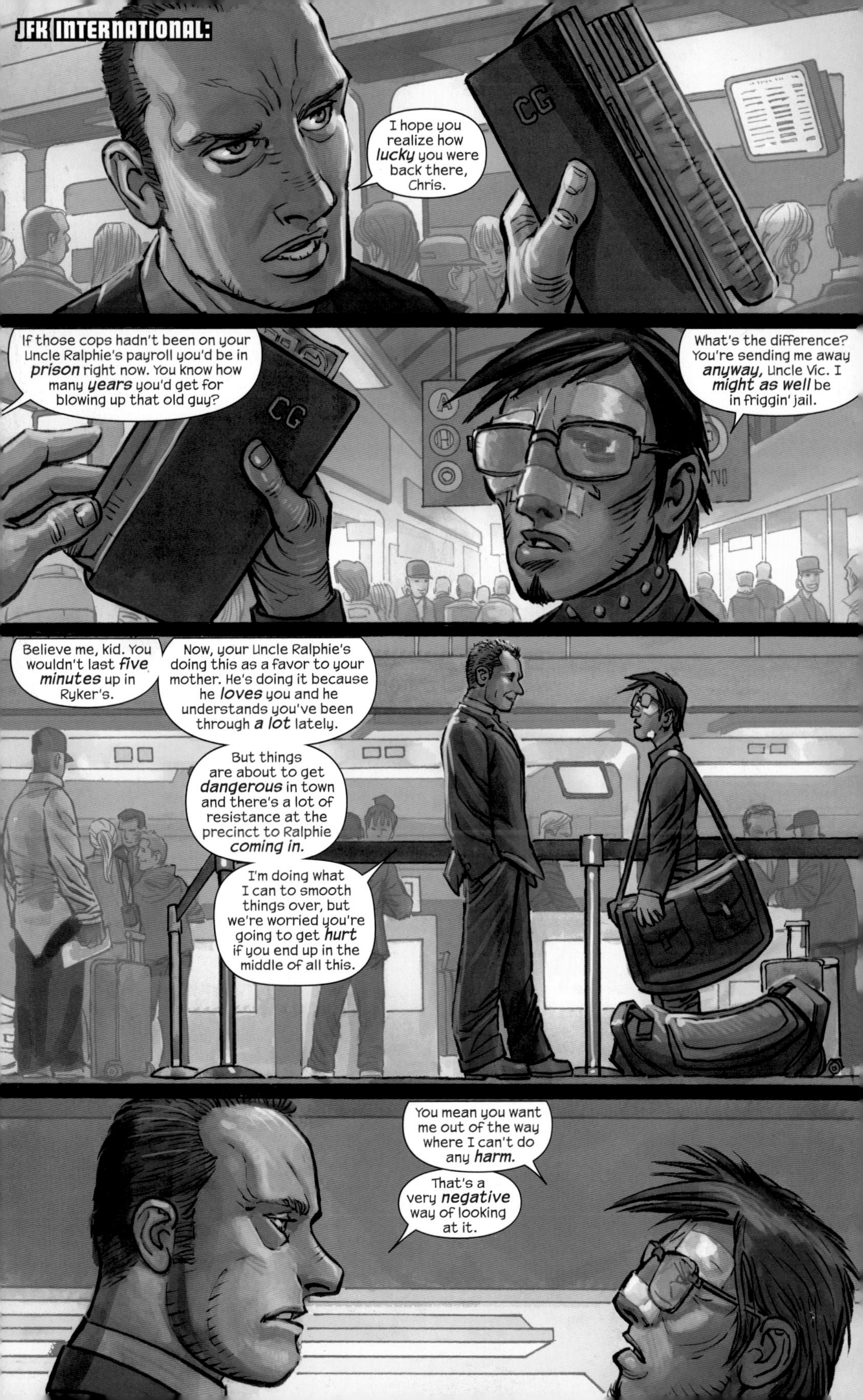
JFK INTERNATIONAL:
I hope you realize how *lucky* you were back there, Chris.
If those cops hadn't been on your Uncle Ralphie's payroll you'd be in *prison* right now. You know how many *years* you'd get for blowing up that old guy?
What's the difference? You're sending me away *anyway,* Uncle Vic. I *might as well* be in friggin' jail.
Believe me, kid. You wouldn't last *five minutes* up in Ryker's.
Now, your Uncle Ralphie's doing this as a favor to your mother. He's doing it because he *loves* you and he understands you've been through *a lot* lately.
But things are about to get *dangerous* in town and there's a lot of resistance at the precinct to Ralphie *coming in.*
I'm doing what I can to smooth things over, but we're worried you're going to get *hurt* if you end up in the middle of all this.
You mean you want me out of the way where I can't do any *harm.*
That's a very *negative* way of looking at it.

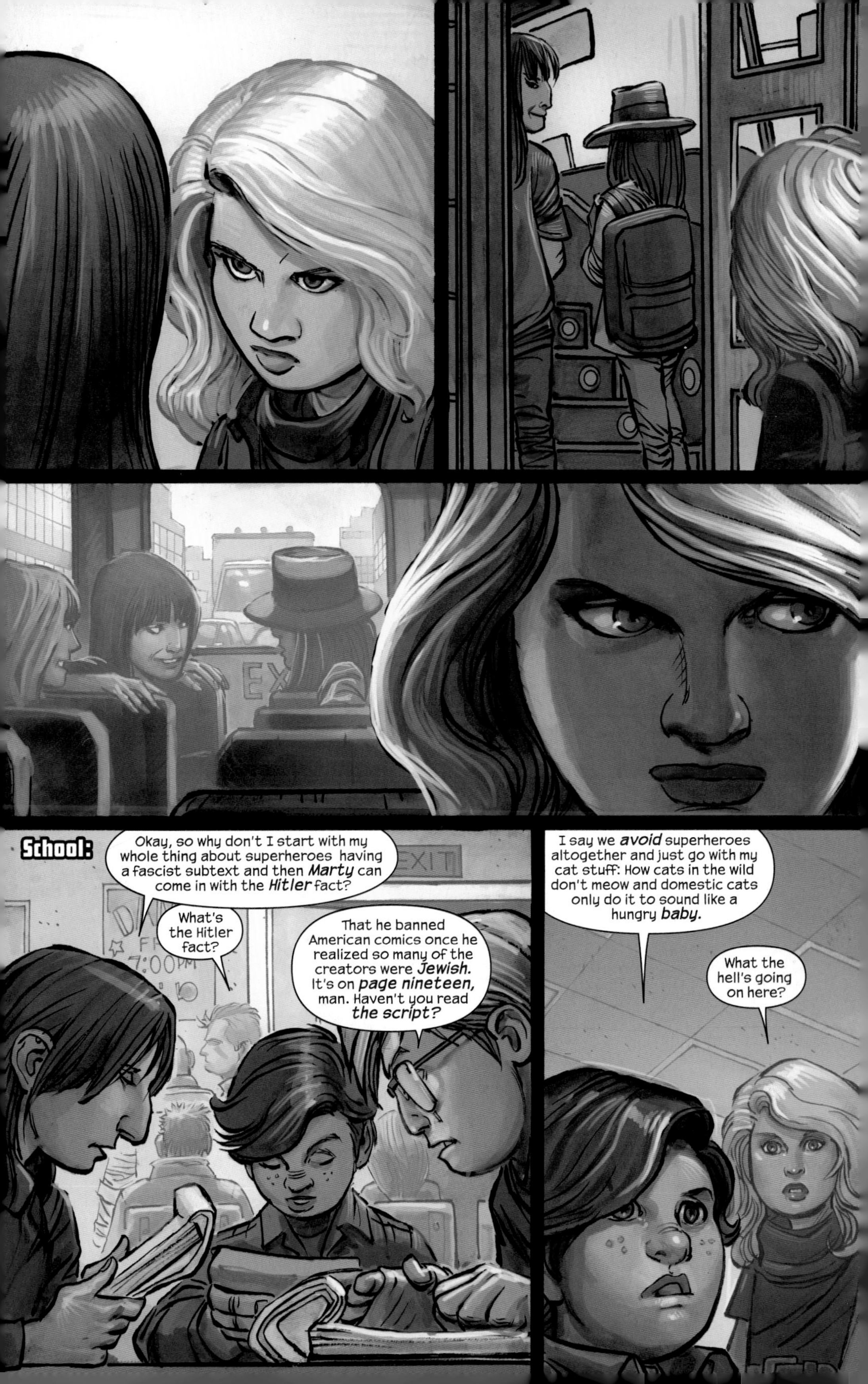
School:
Okay, so why don't I start with my whole thing about superheroes having a fascist subtext and then Marty can come in with the Hitler fact?
What's the Hitler fact?
That he banned American comics once he realized so many of the creators were Jewish. It's on page nineteen, man. Haven't you read the script?
EXIT
I say we avoid superheroes altogether and just go with my cat stuff: How cats in the wild don't meow and domestic cats only do it to sound like a hungry baby.
What the hell's going on here?

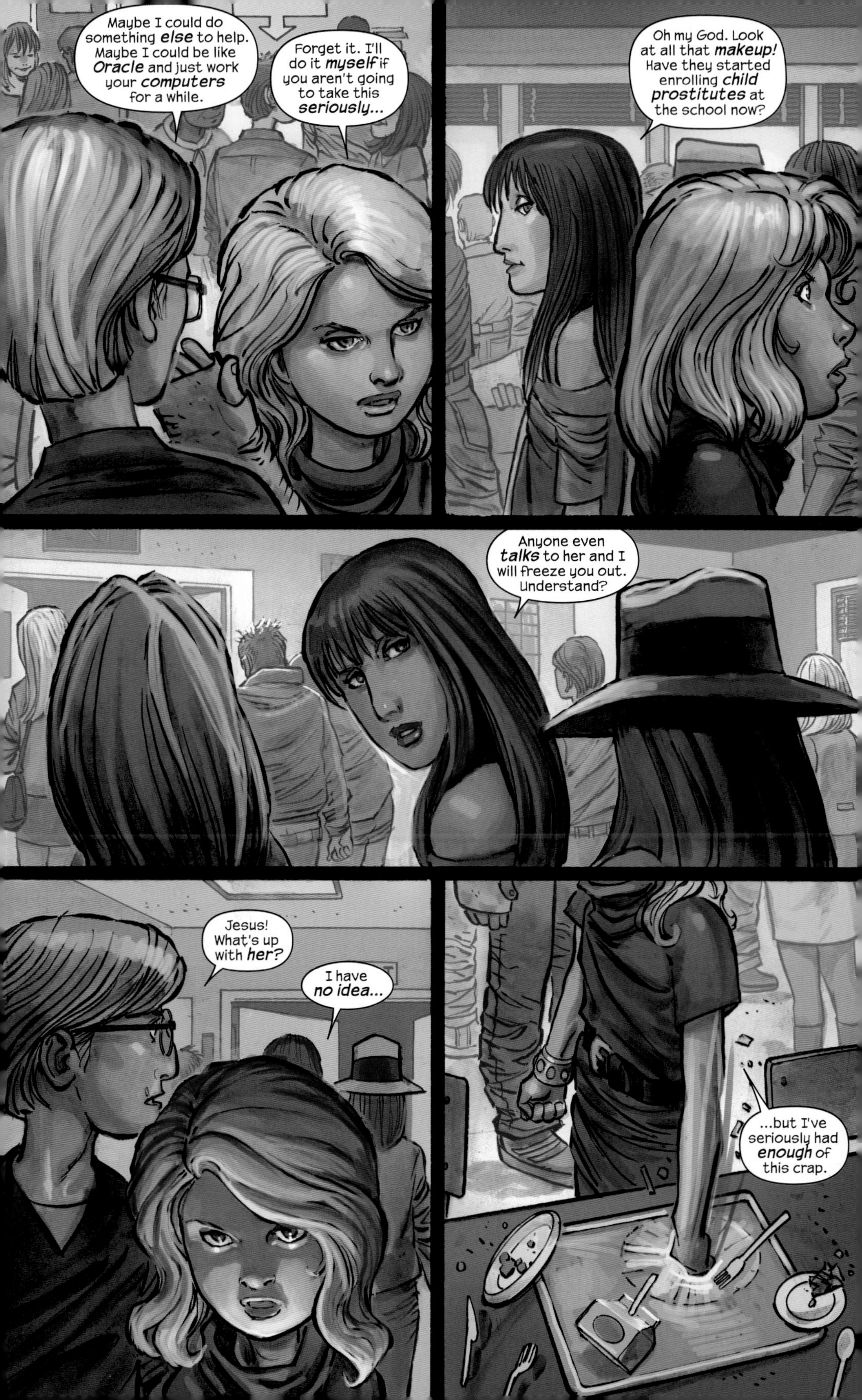

Maybe I could do something *else* to help. Maybe I could be like *Oracle* and just work your *computers* for a while.
Forget it. I'll do it *myself* if you aren't going to take this *seriously...*
Oh my God. Look at all that *makeup!* Have they started enrolling *child prostitutes* at the school now?
Anyone even *talks* to her and I will freeze you out. Understand?
Jesus! What's up with *her*?
I have *no idea...*
...but I've seriously had *enough* of this crap.

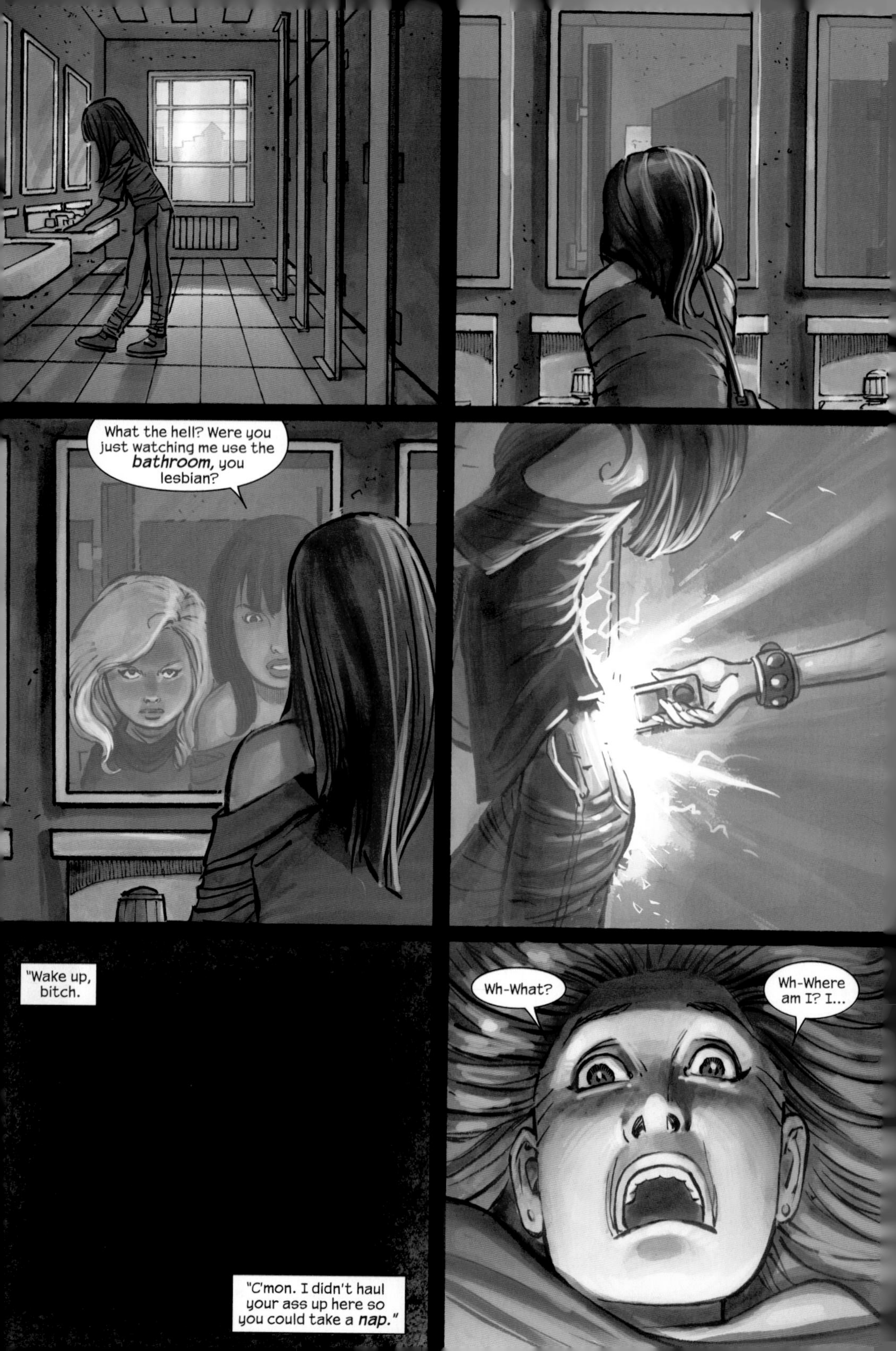
What the hell? Were you just watching me use the *bathroom*, you lesbian?
"Wake up, bitch.
"C'mon. I didn't haul your ass up here so you could take a *nap*."
Wh-What?
Wh-Where am I? I...

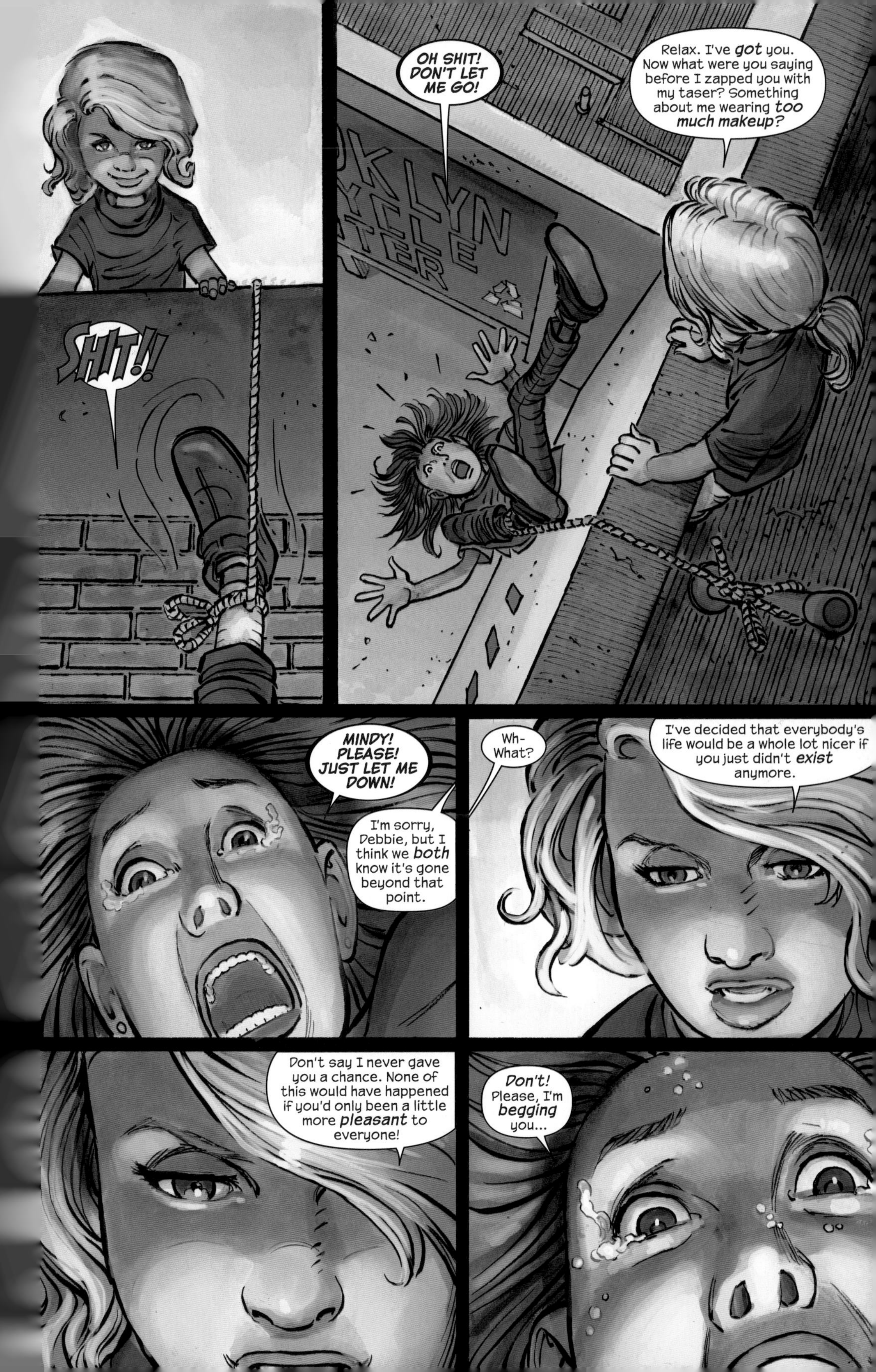
SHIT!!
OH SHIT! DON'T LET ME GO!
Relax. I've *got* you. Now what were you saying before I zapped you with my taser? Something about me wearing *too much makeup?*
MINDY! PLEASE! JUST LET ME DOWN!
I'm sorry, Debbie, but I think we *both* know it's gone beyond that point.
Wh- What?
I've decided that everybody's life would be a whole lot nicer if you just didn't *exist* anymore.
Don't say I never gave you a chance. None of this would have happened if you'd only been a little more *pleasant* to everyone!
Don't! Please, I'm *begging* you...

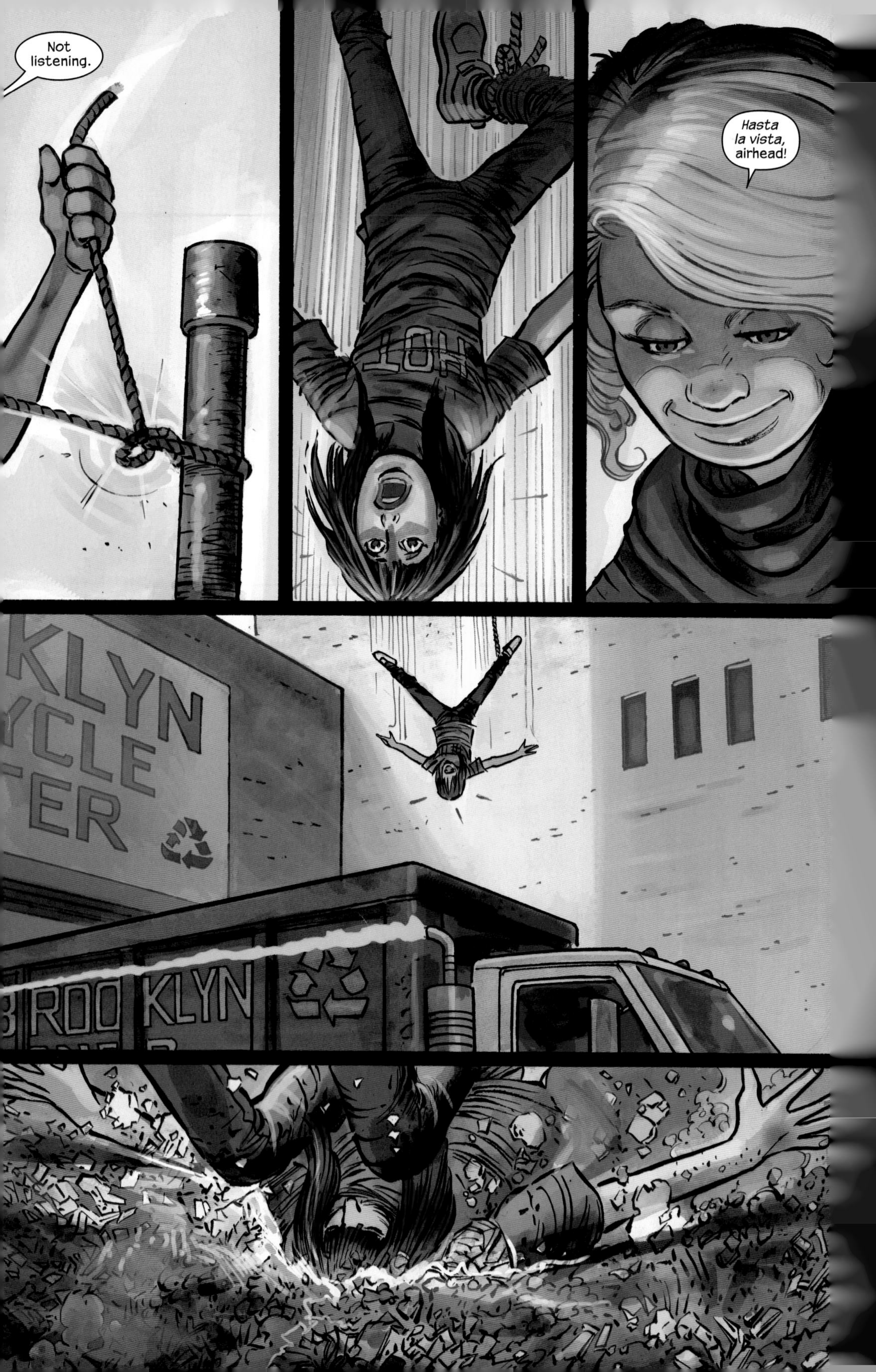
Not listening.
HOT
Hasta la vista, airhead!
KLYN
YCLE
TER
BROOKLYN

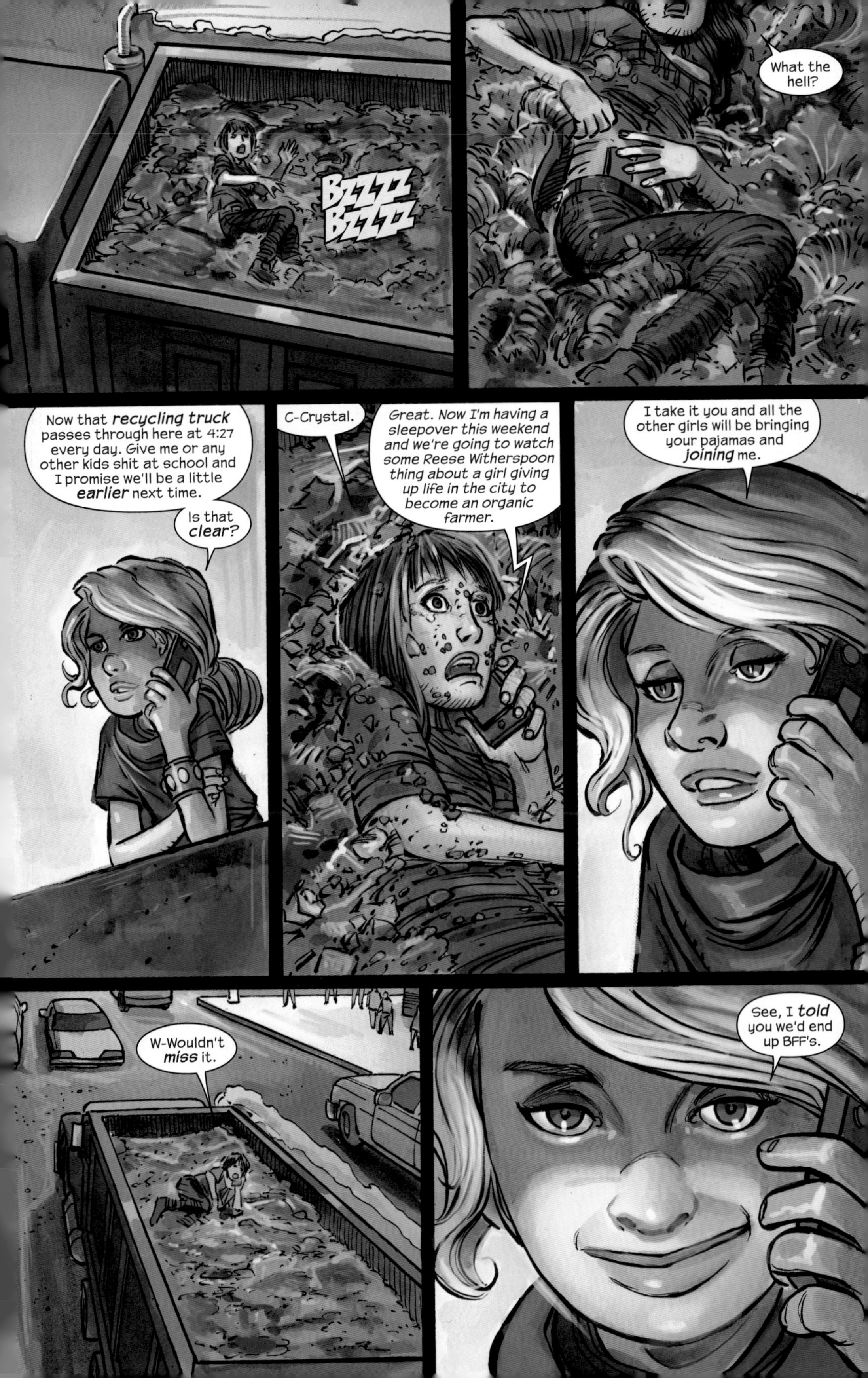
BZZZZ BZZZZ
What the hell?
Now that recycling truck passes through here at 4:27 every day. Give me or any other kids shit at school and I promise we'll be a little earlier next time.
Is that clear?
C-Crystal.
Great. Now I'm having a sleepover this weekend and we're going to watch some Reese Witherspoon thing about a girl giving up life in the city to become an organic farmer.
I take it you and all the other girls will be bringing your pajamas and joining me.
W-Wouldn't miss it.
See, I told you we'd end up BFF's.

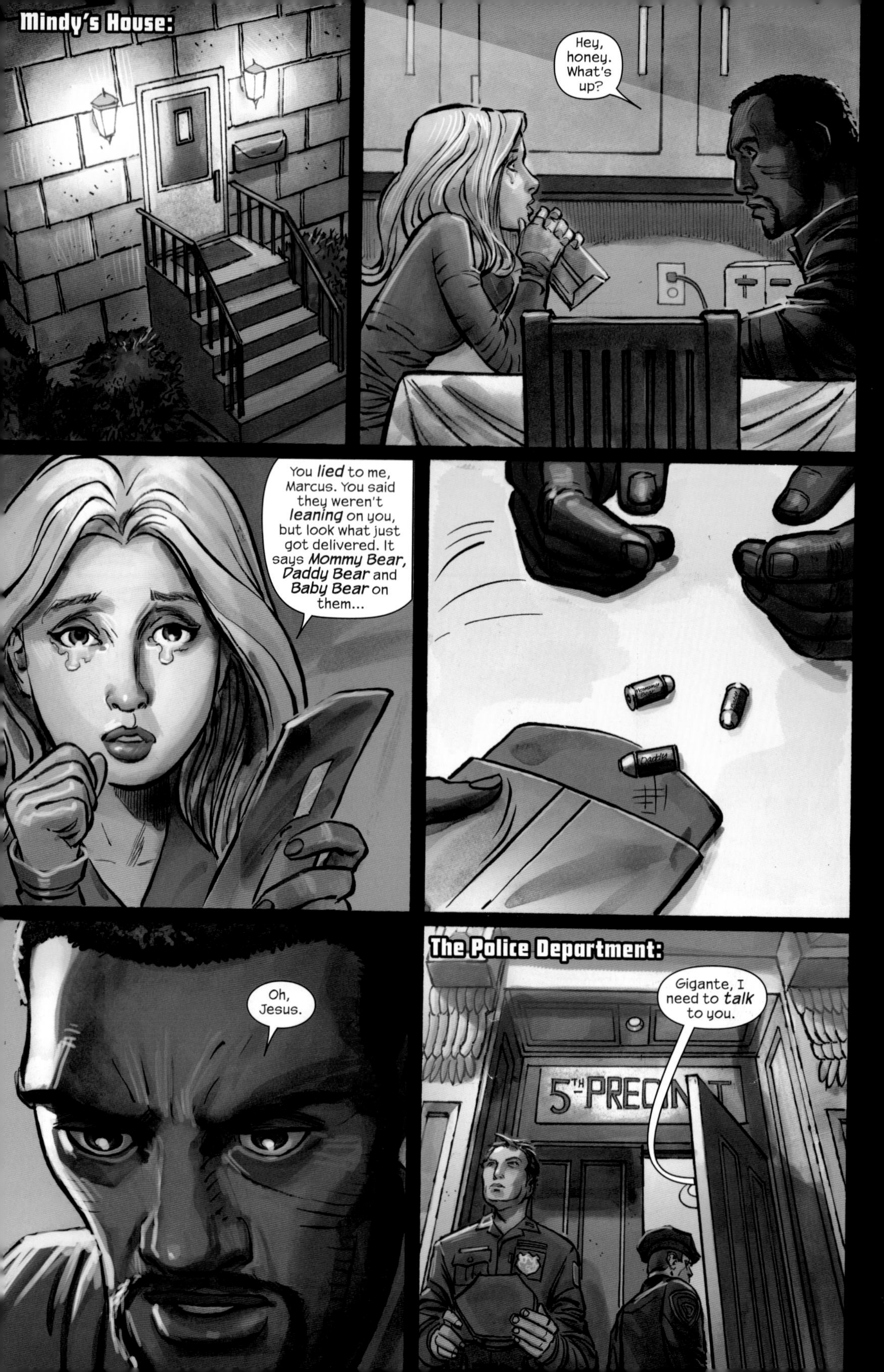
Mindy's House:
Hey, honey. What's up?
You lied to me, Marcus. You said they weren't leaning on you, but look what just got delivered. It says Mommy Bear, Daddy Bear and Baby Bear on them...
Oh, Jesus.
The Police Department:
Gigante, I need to talk to you.

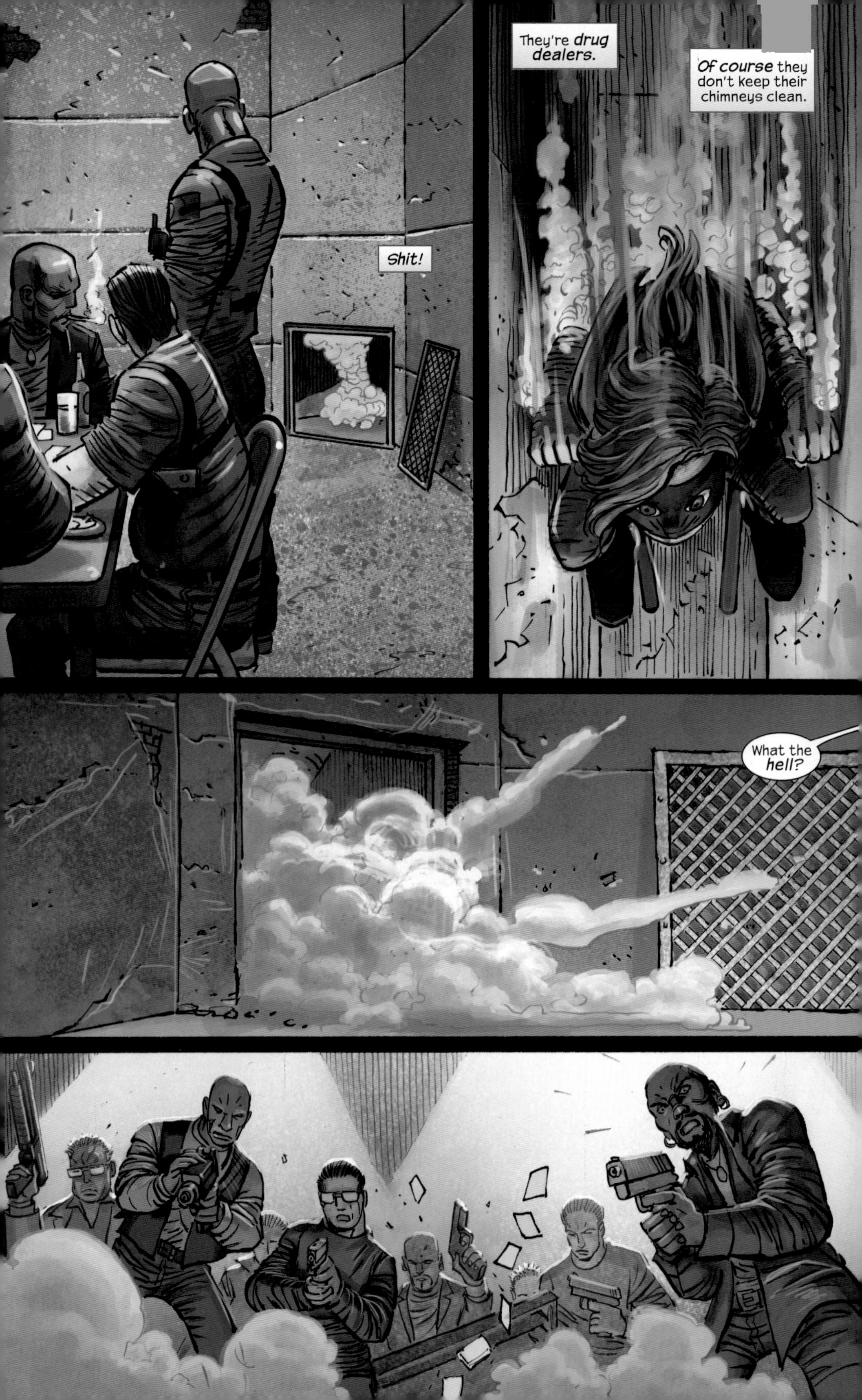
Shit!
They're drug dealers.
Of course they don't keep their chimneys clean.
What the hell?

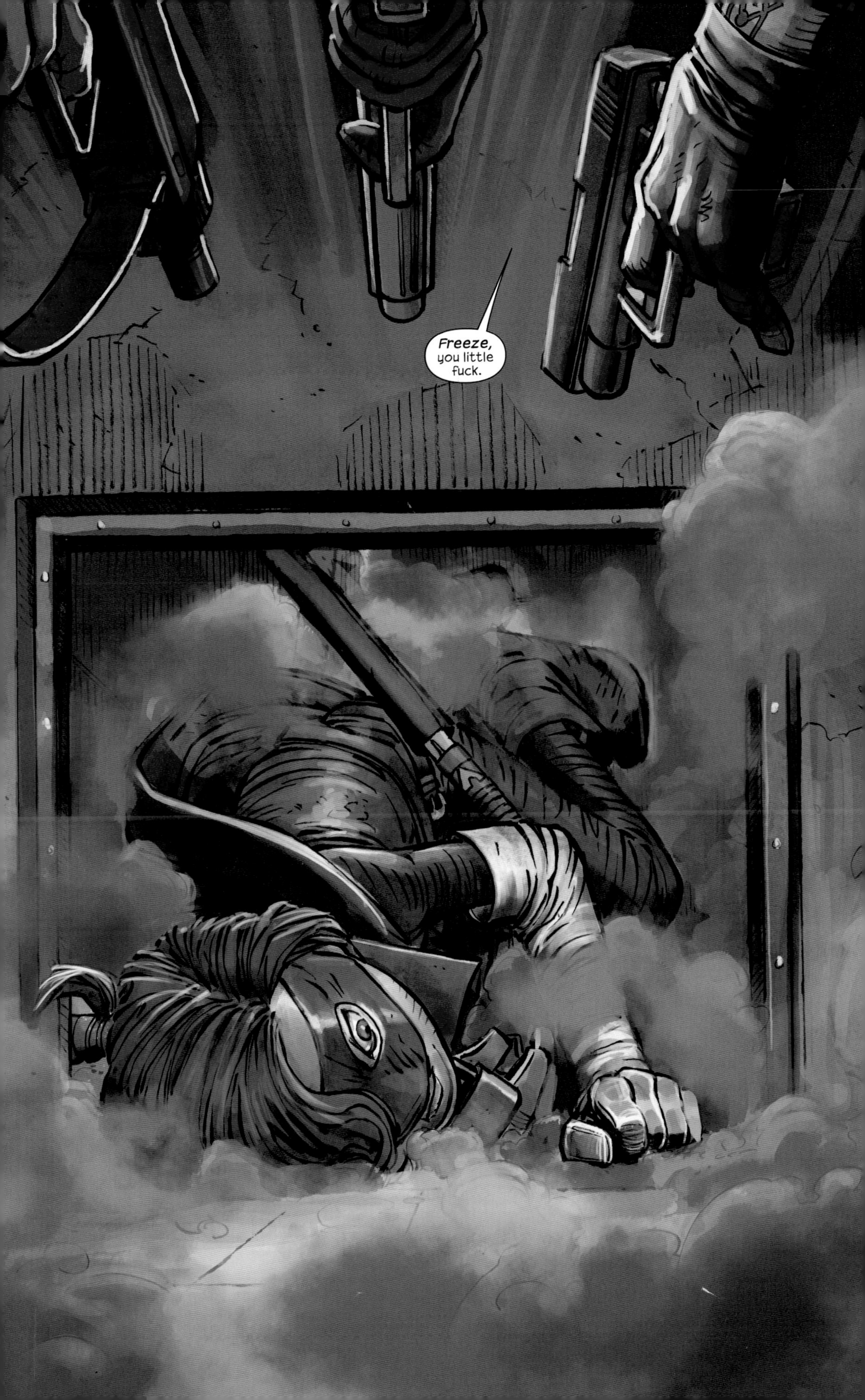
Freeze, you little fuck.

FOUR

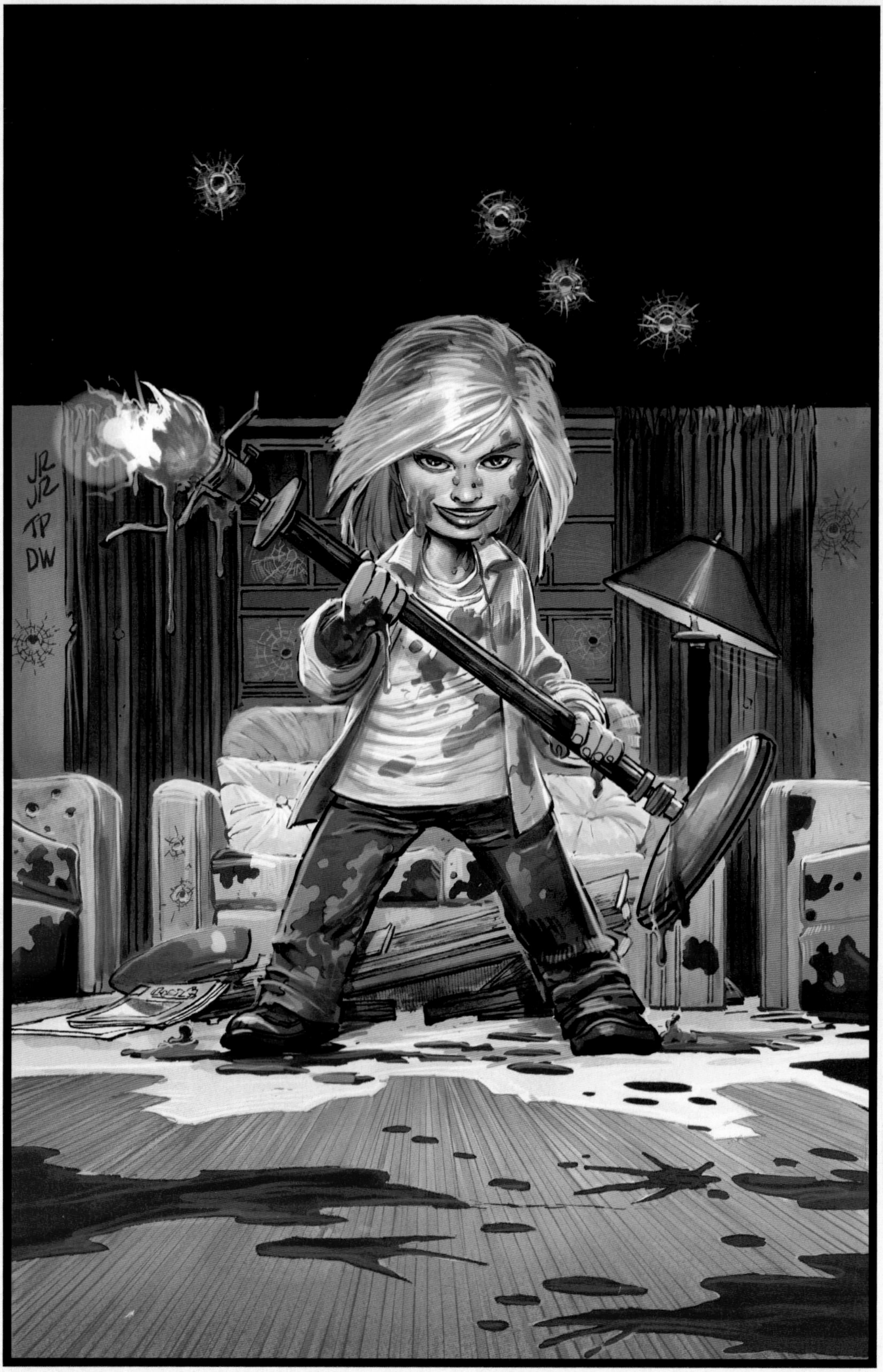
JR
JR
TP
DW

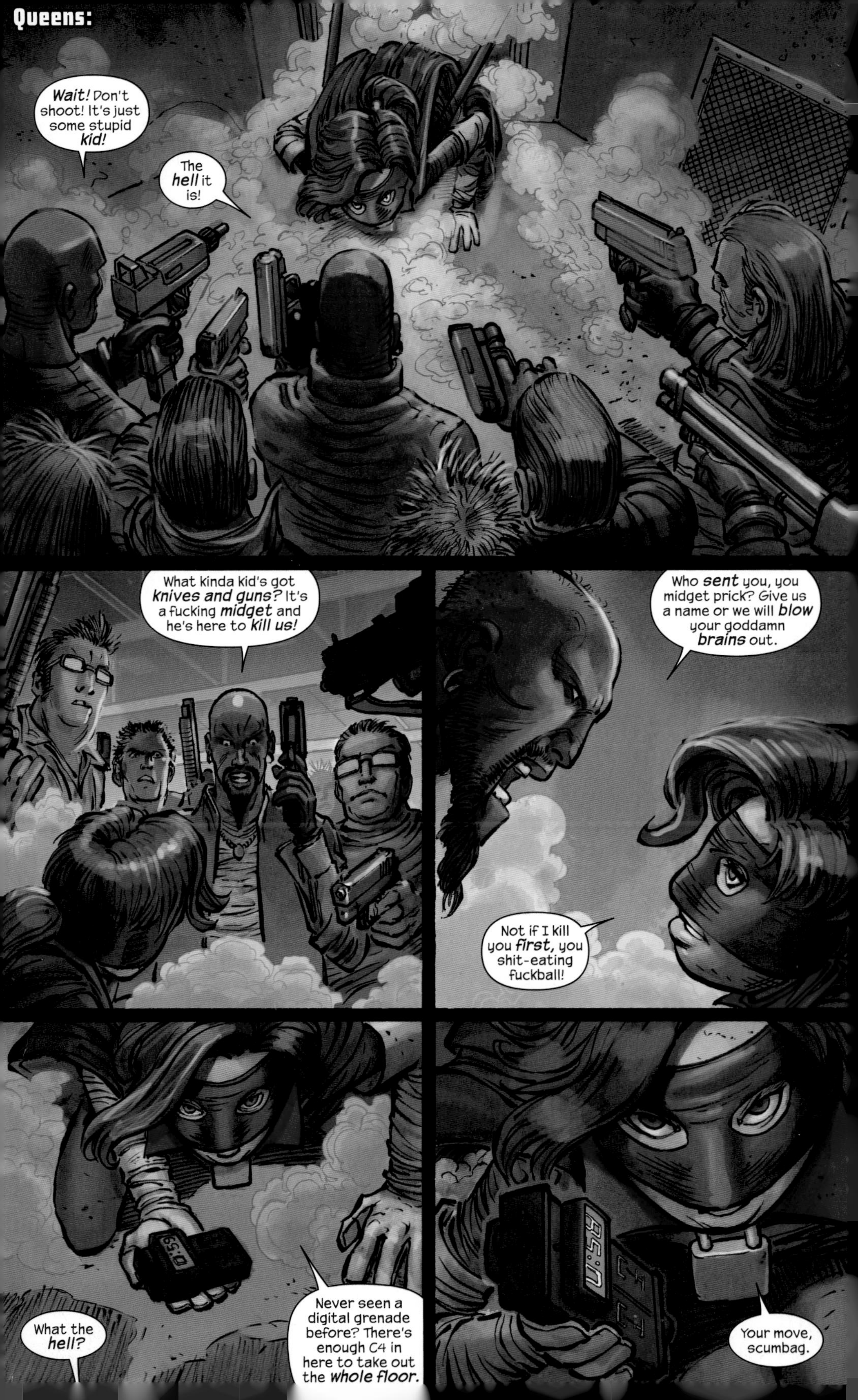
Queens:
Wait! Don't shoot! It's just some stupid kid!
The hell it is!
What kinda kid's got knives and guns? It's a fucking midget and he's here to kill us!
Who sent you, you midget prick? Give us a name or we will blow your goddamn brains out.
Not if I kill you first, you shit-eating fuckball!
What the hell?
Never seen a digital grenade before? There's enough C4 in here to take out the whole floor.
Your move, scumbag.

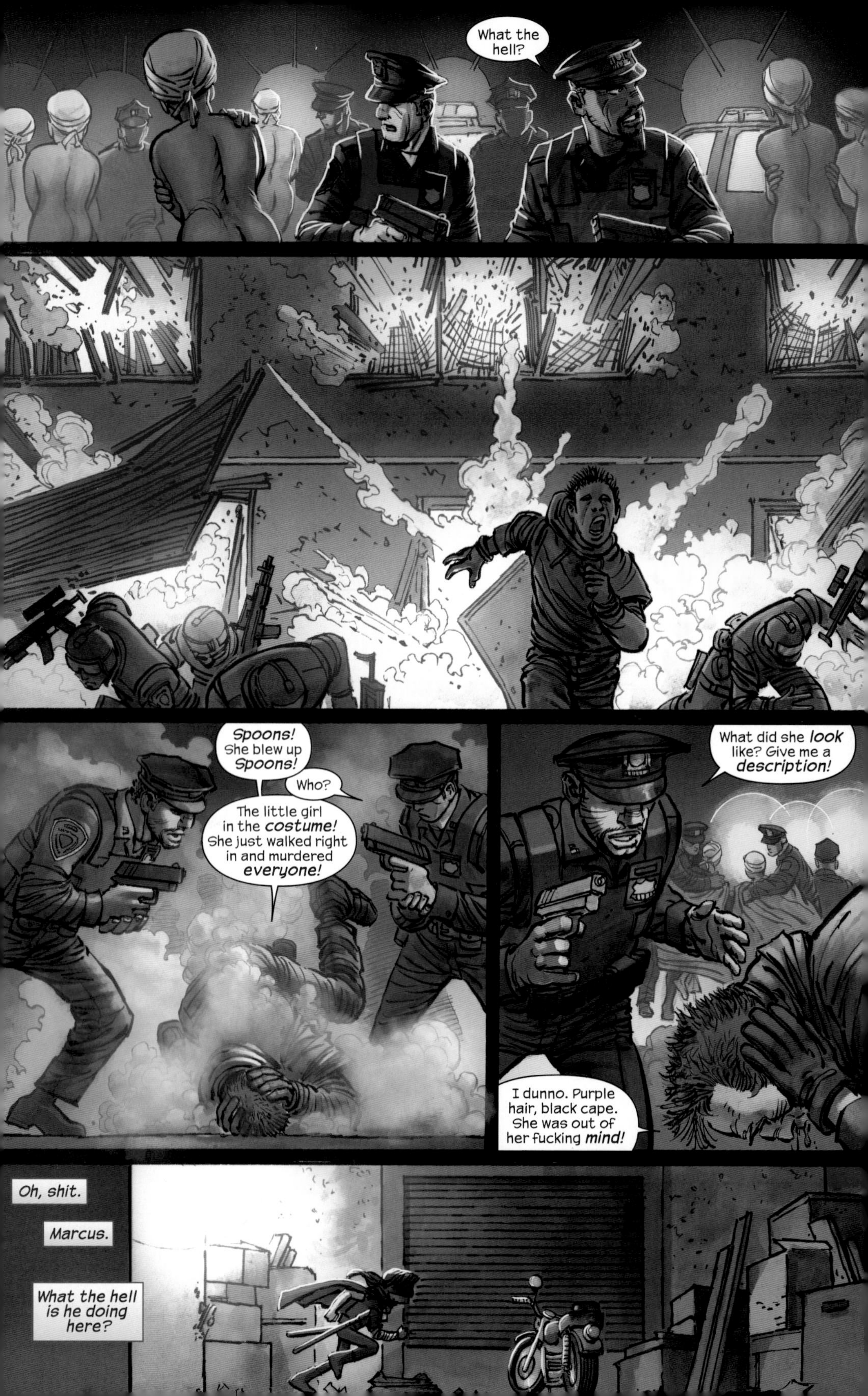

What the hell?
Spoons! She blew up Spoons!
Who?
The little girl in the costume! She just walked right in and murdered everyone!
What did she look like? Give me a description!
I dunno. Purple hair, black cape. She was out of her fucking mind!
Oh, shit.
Marcus.
What the hell is he doing here?

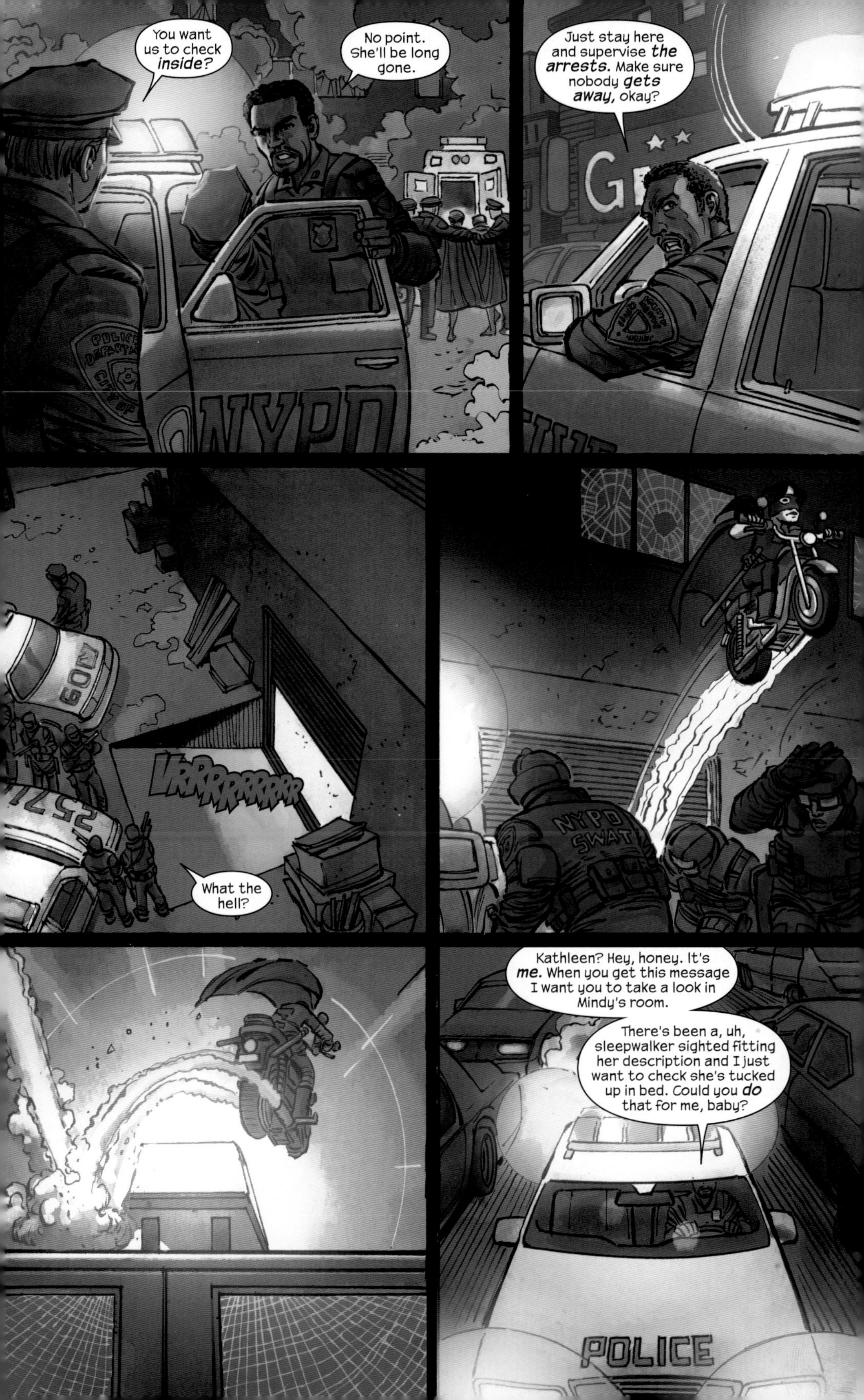
You want us to check *inside*?
No point. She'll be long gone.
Just stay here and supervise ***the arrests.*** Make sure nobody ***gets away,*** okay?
NYPD
VRRRRRRRRRR
What the hell?
NYPD SWAT
Kathleen? Hey, honey. It's ***me.*** When you get this message I want you to take a look in Mindy's room.
There's been a, uh, sleepwalker sighted fitting her description and I just want to check she's tucked up in bed. Could you ***do*** that for me, baby?
POLICE

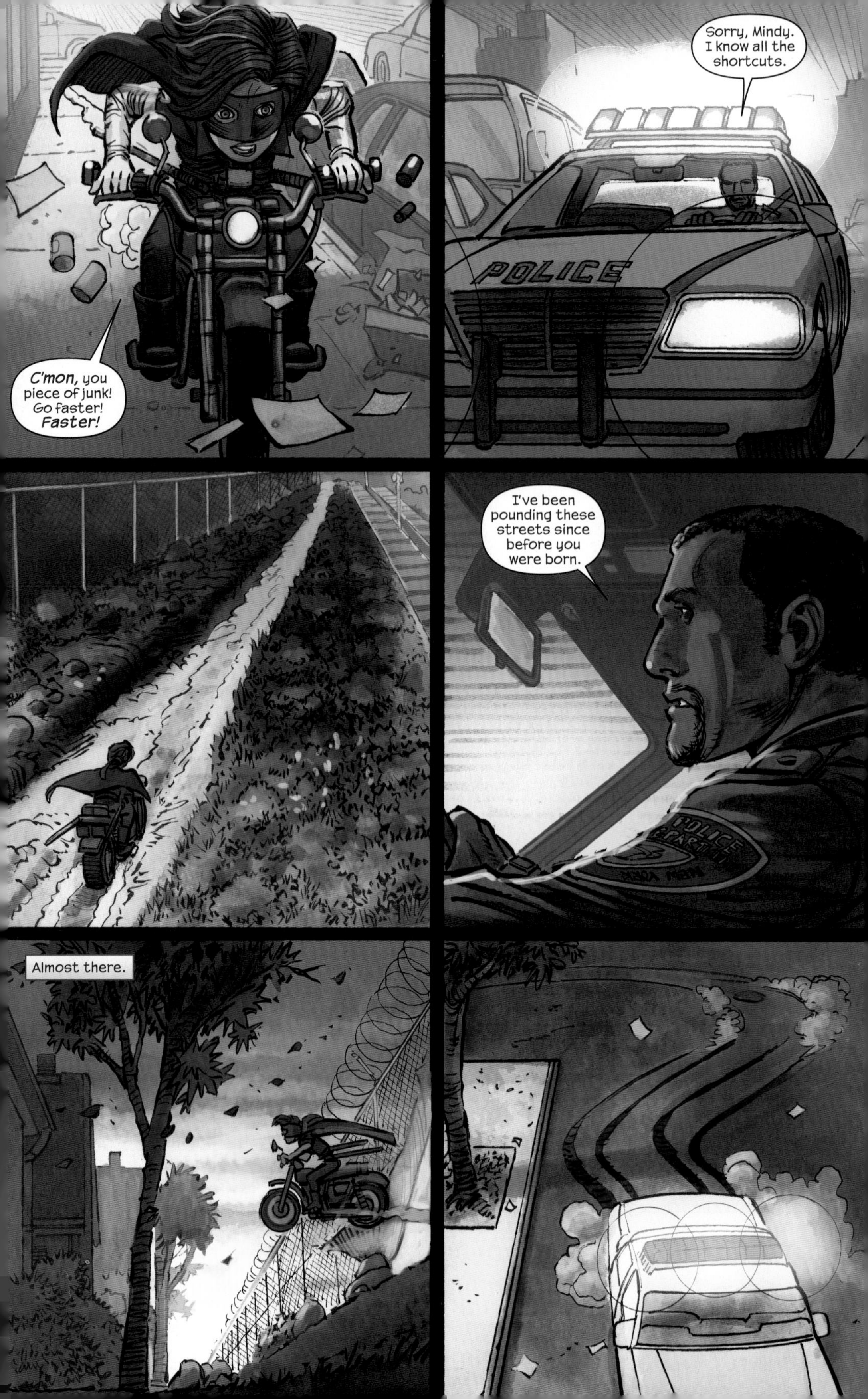
C'mon, you piece of junk! Go faster! Faster!
Sorry, Mindy. I know all the shortcuts.
POLICE
I've been pounding these streets since before you were born.
Almost there.

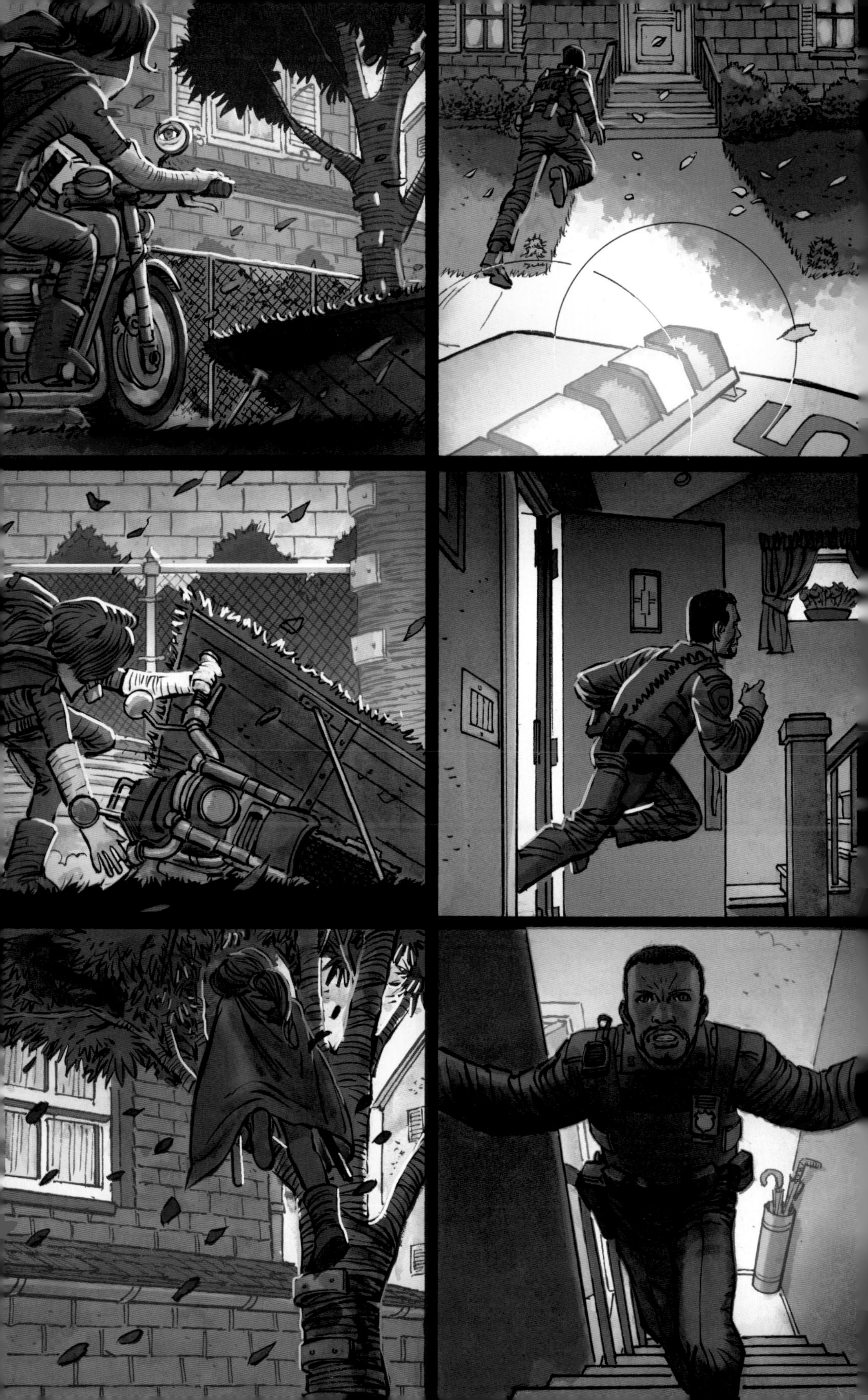

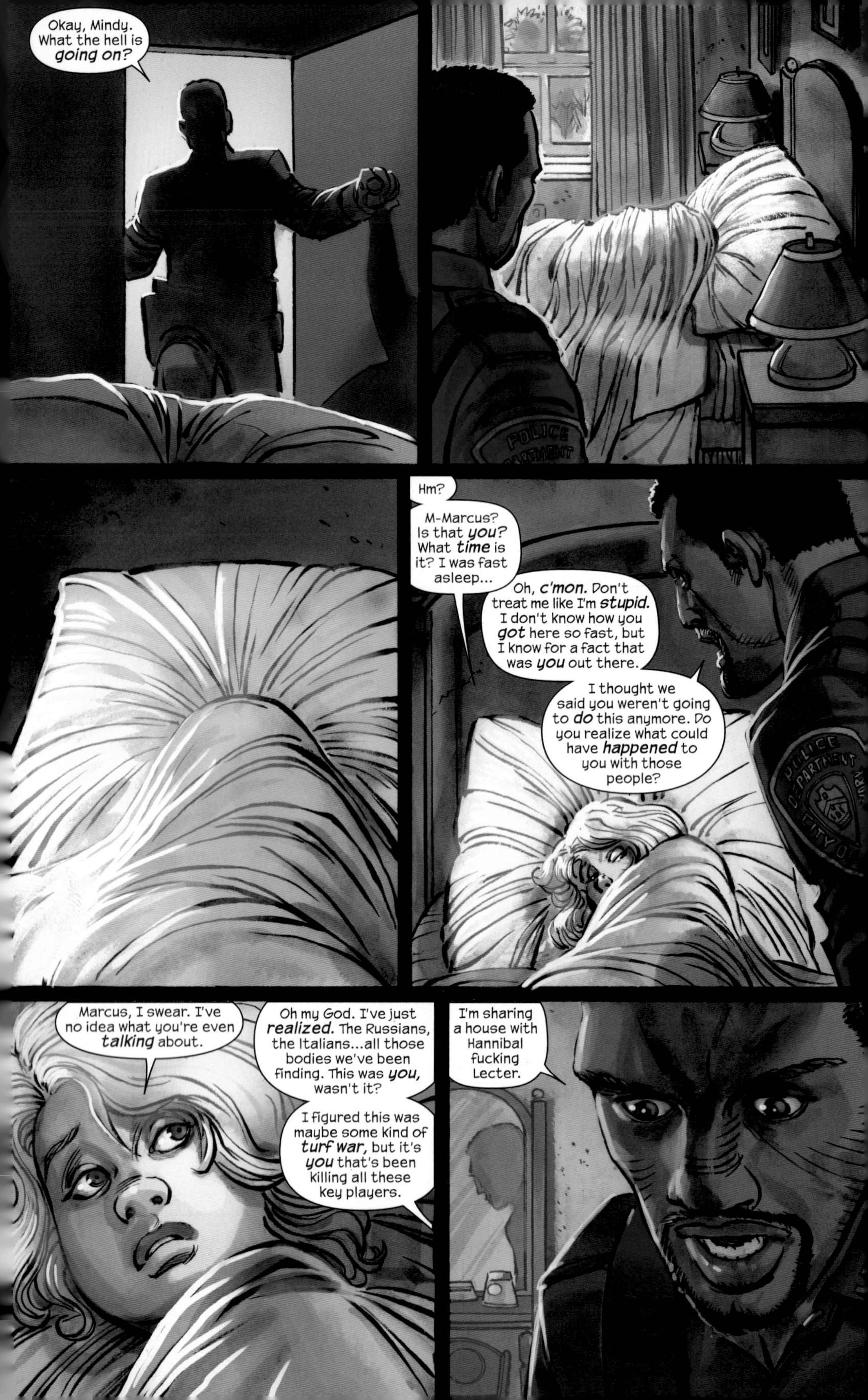
Okay, Mindy. What the hell is *going on?*
POLICE DEPARTMENT
Hm?
M-Marcus? Is that *you?* What *time* is it? I was fast asleep...
Oh, *c'mon.* Don't treat me like I'm *stupid.* I don't know how you *got* here so fast, but I know for a fact that was *you* out there.
I thought we said you weren't going to *do* this anymore. Do you realize what could have *happened* to you with those people?
POLICE DEPARTMENT
Marcus, I swear. I've no idea what you're even *talking* about.
Oh my God. I've just *realized.* The Russians, the Italians...all those bodies we've been finding. This was *you,* wasn't it?
I figured this was maybe some kind of *turf war,* but it's *you* that's been killing all these key players.
I'm sharing a house with Hannibal fucking Lecter.

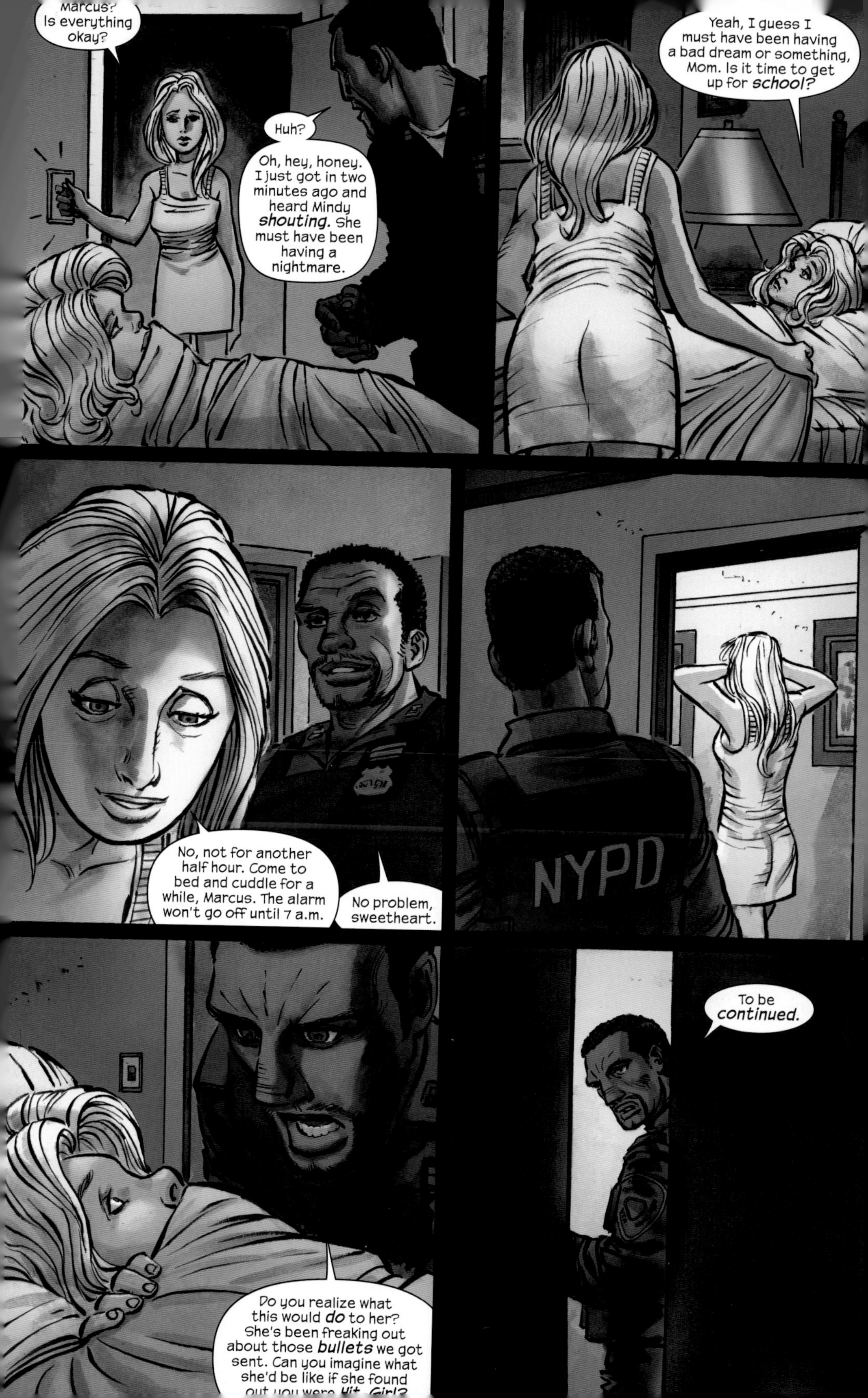
Marcus? Is everything okay?
Huh?
Oh, hey, honey. I just got in two minutes ago and heard Mindy *shouting*. She must have been having a nightmare.
Yeah, I guess I must have been having a bad dream or something, Mom. Is it time to get up for *school?*
No, not for another half hour. Come to bed and cuddle for a while, Marcus. The alarm won't go off until 7 a.m.
No problem, sweetheart.
NYPD
Do you realize what this would *do* to her? She's been freaking out about those *bullets* we got sent. Can you imagine what she'd be like if she found out you were *Hit-Girl?*
To be *continued.*

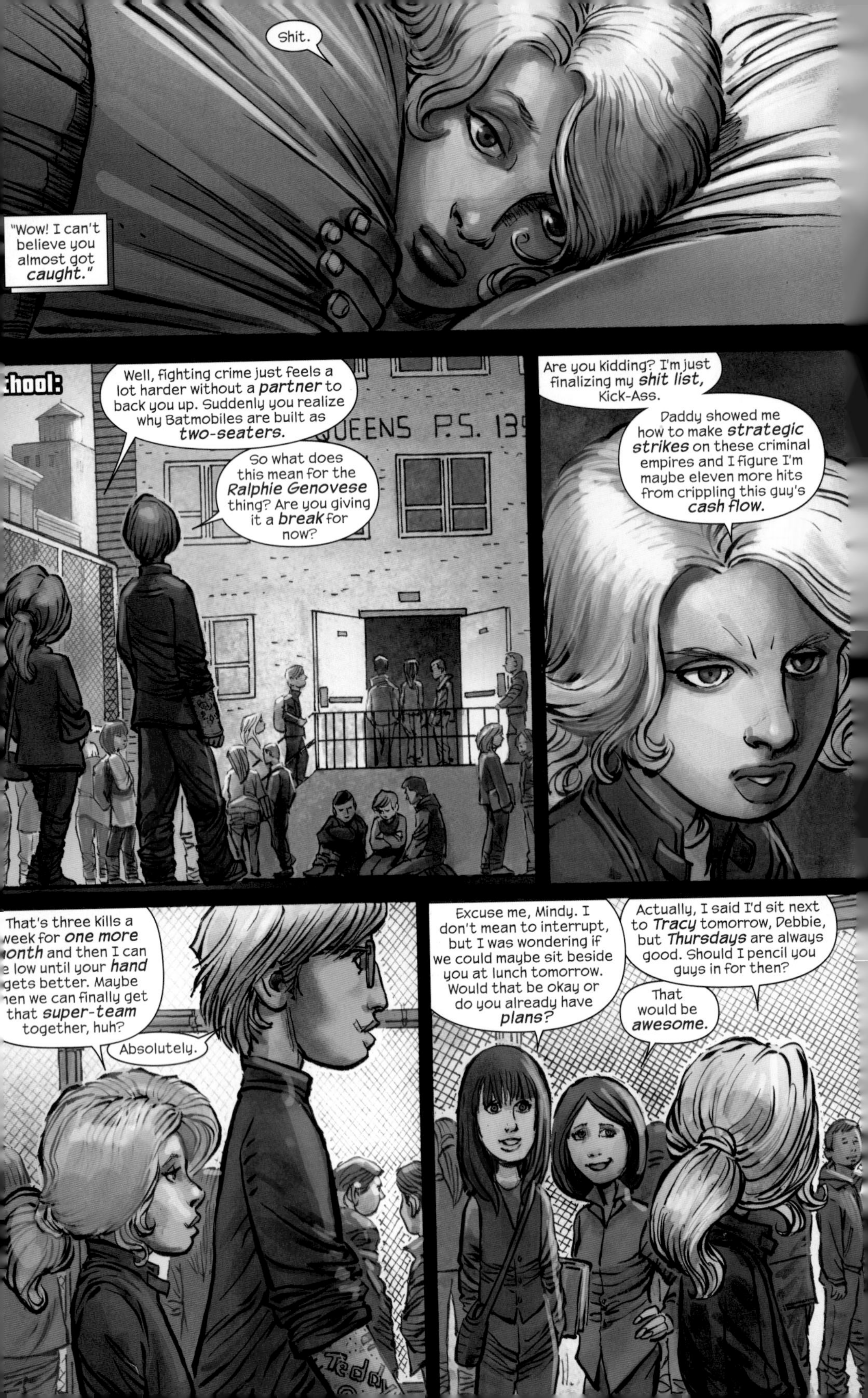
Shit.
"Wow! I can't believe you almost got *caught.*"
hool:
Well, fighting crime just feels a lot harder without a *partner* to back you up. Suddenly you realize why Batmobiles are built as *two-seaters.*
QUEENS P.S. 13
So what does this mean for the *Ralphie Genovese* thing? Are you giving it a *break* for now?
Are you kidding? I'm just finalizing my *shit list,* Kick-Ass.
Daddy showed me how to make *strategic strikes* on these criminal empires and I figure I'm maybe eleven more hits from crippling this guy's *cash flow.*
That's three kills a week for *one more* onth and then I can e low until your *hand* gets better. Maybe en we can finally get that *super-team* together, huh?
Absolutely.
Excuse me, Mindy. I don't mean to interrupt, but I was wondering if we could maybe sit beside you at lunch tomorrow. Would that be okay or do you already have *plans?*
Actually, I said I'd sit next to *Tracy* tomorrow, Debbie, but *Thursdays* are always good. Should I pencil you guys in for then?
That would be *awesome.*

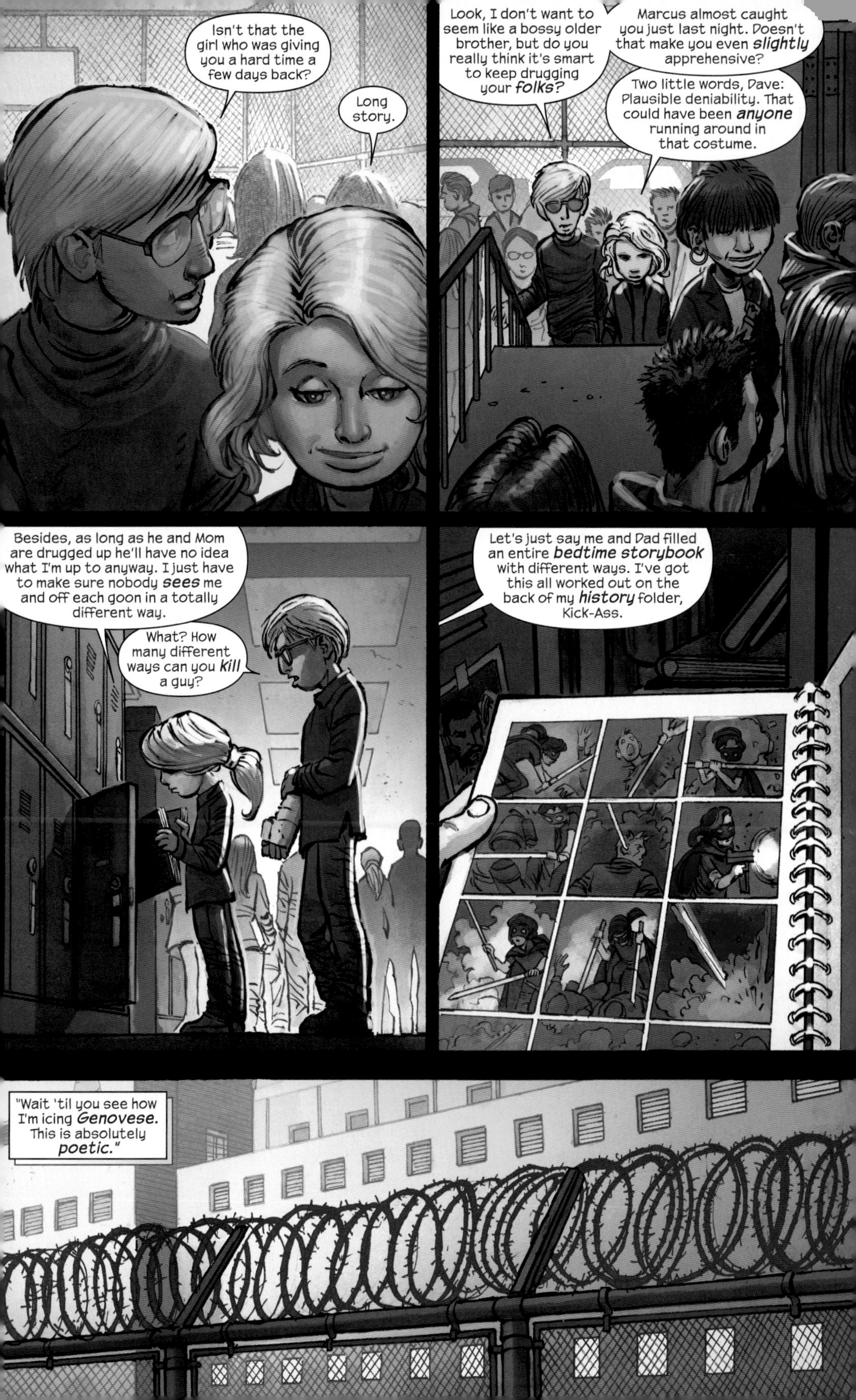
Isn't that the girl who was giving you a hard time a few days back?
Long story.
Look, I don't want to seem like a bossy older brother, but do you really think it's smart to keep drugging your *folks?*
Marcus almost caught you just last night. Doesn't that make you even *slightly* apprehensive?
Two little words, Dave: Plausible deniability. That could have been *anyone* running around in that costume.
Besides, as long as he and Mom are drugged up he'll have no idea what I'm up to anyway. I just have to make sure nobody *sees* me and off each goon in a totally different way.
What? How many different ways can you *kill* a guy?
Let's just say me and Dad filled an entire *bedtime storybook* with different ways. I've got this all worked out on the back of my *history* folder, Kick-Ass.
"Wait 'til you see how I'm icing *Genovese.* This is absolutely *poetic."*

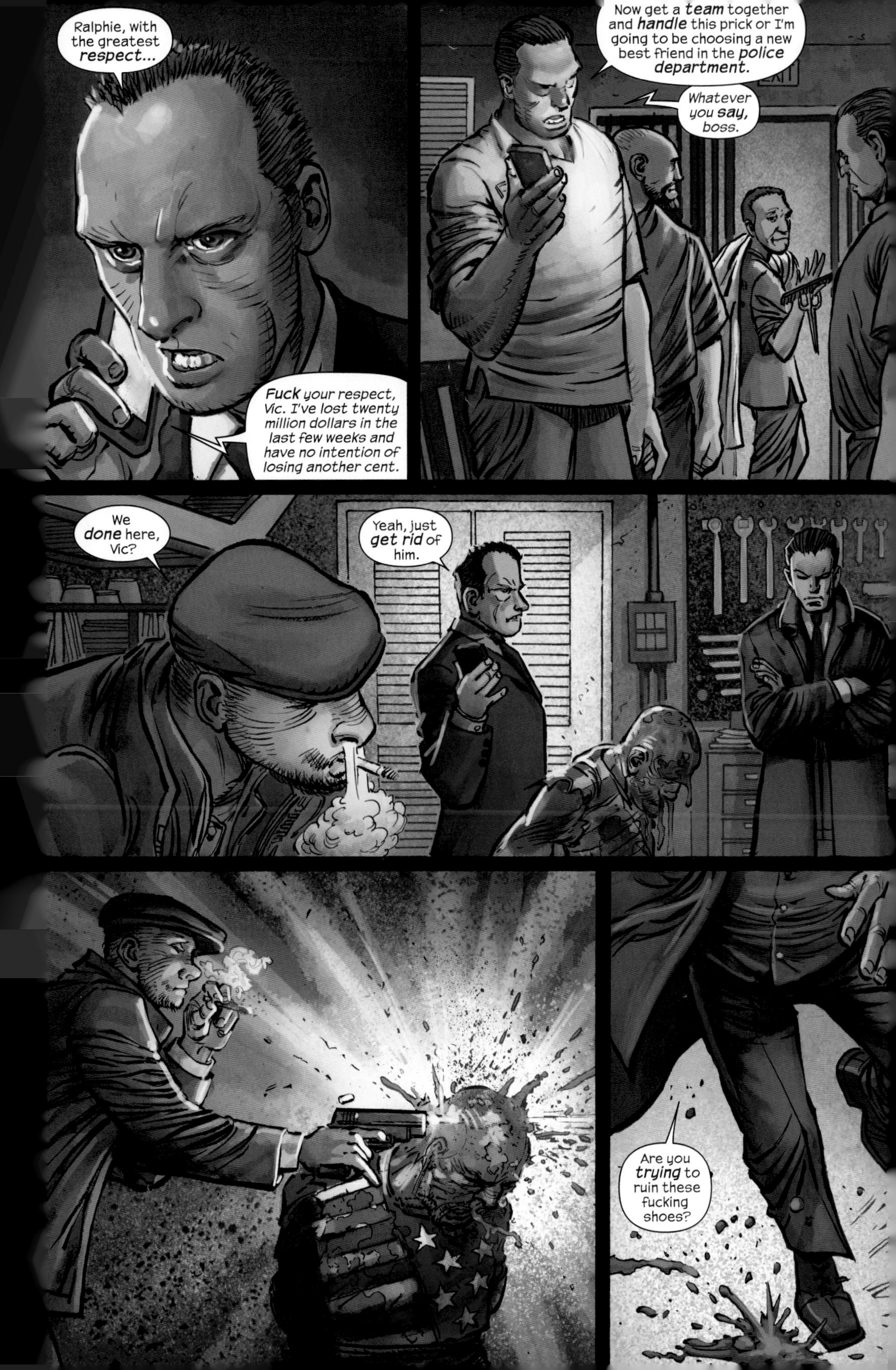

Ralphie, with the greatest respect...
Fuck your respect, Vic. I've lost twenty million dollars in the last few weeks and have no intention of losing another cent.
Now get a team together and handle this prick or I'm going to be choosing a new best friend in the police department.
Whatever you say, boss.
We done here, Vic?
Yeah, just get rid of him.
Are you trying to ruin these fucking shoes?

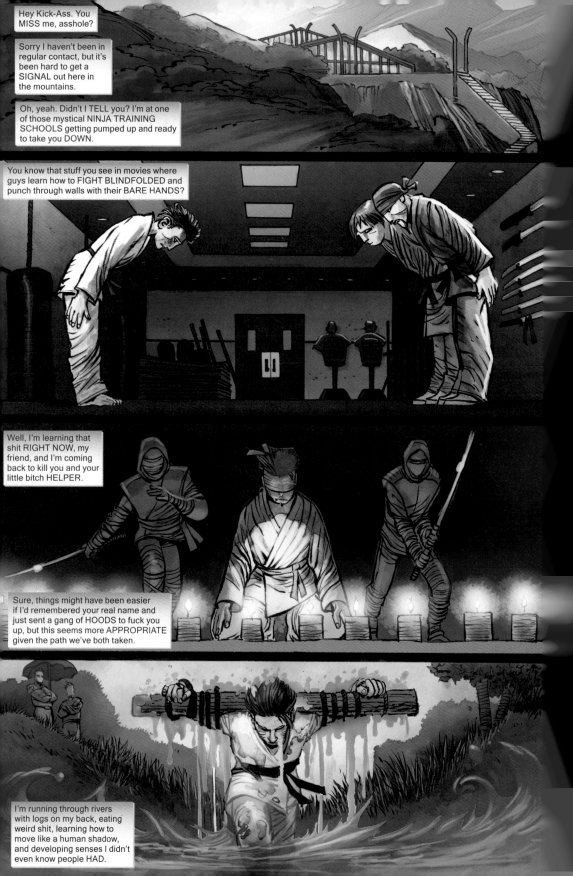

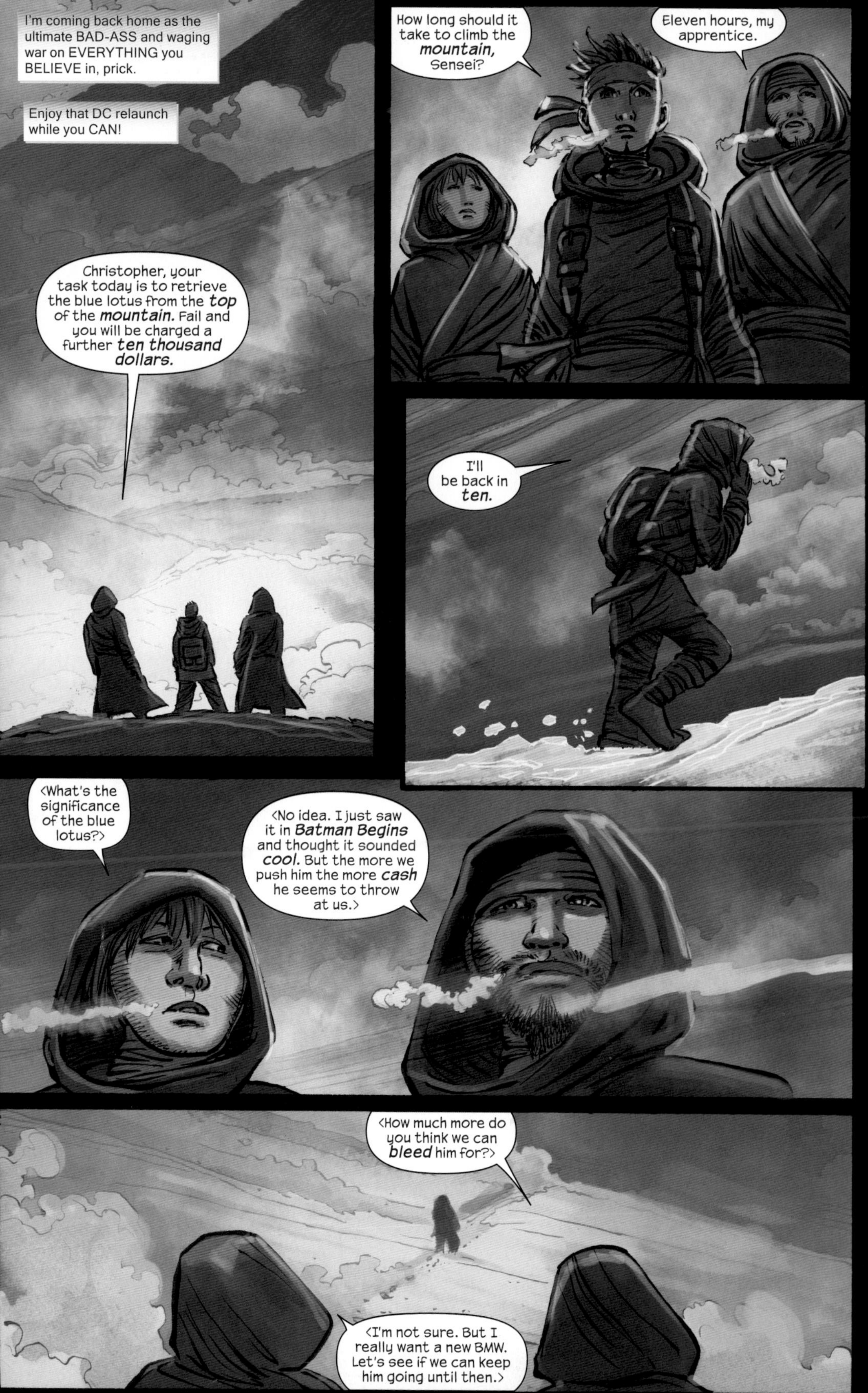
I'm coming back home as the ultimate BAD-ASS and waging war on EVERYTHING you BELIEVE in, prick.
Enjoy that DC relaunch while you CAN!
Christopher, your task today is to retrieve the blue lotus from the *top* of the *mountain.* Fail and you will be charged a further *ten thousand dollars.*
How long should it take to climb the *mountain,* Sensei?
Eleven hours, my apprentice.
I'll be back in *ten.*
<What's the significance of the blue lotus?>
<No idea. I just saw it in *Batman Begins* and thought it sounded *cool.* But the more we push him the more *cash* he seems to throw at us.>
<How much more do you think we can *bleed* him for?>
<I'm not sure. But I really want a new BMW. Let's see if we can keep him going until then.>

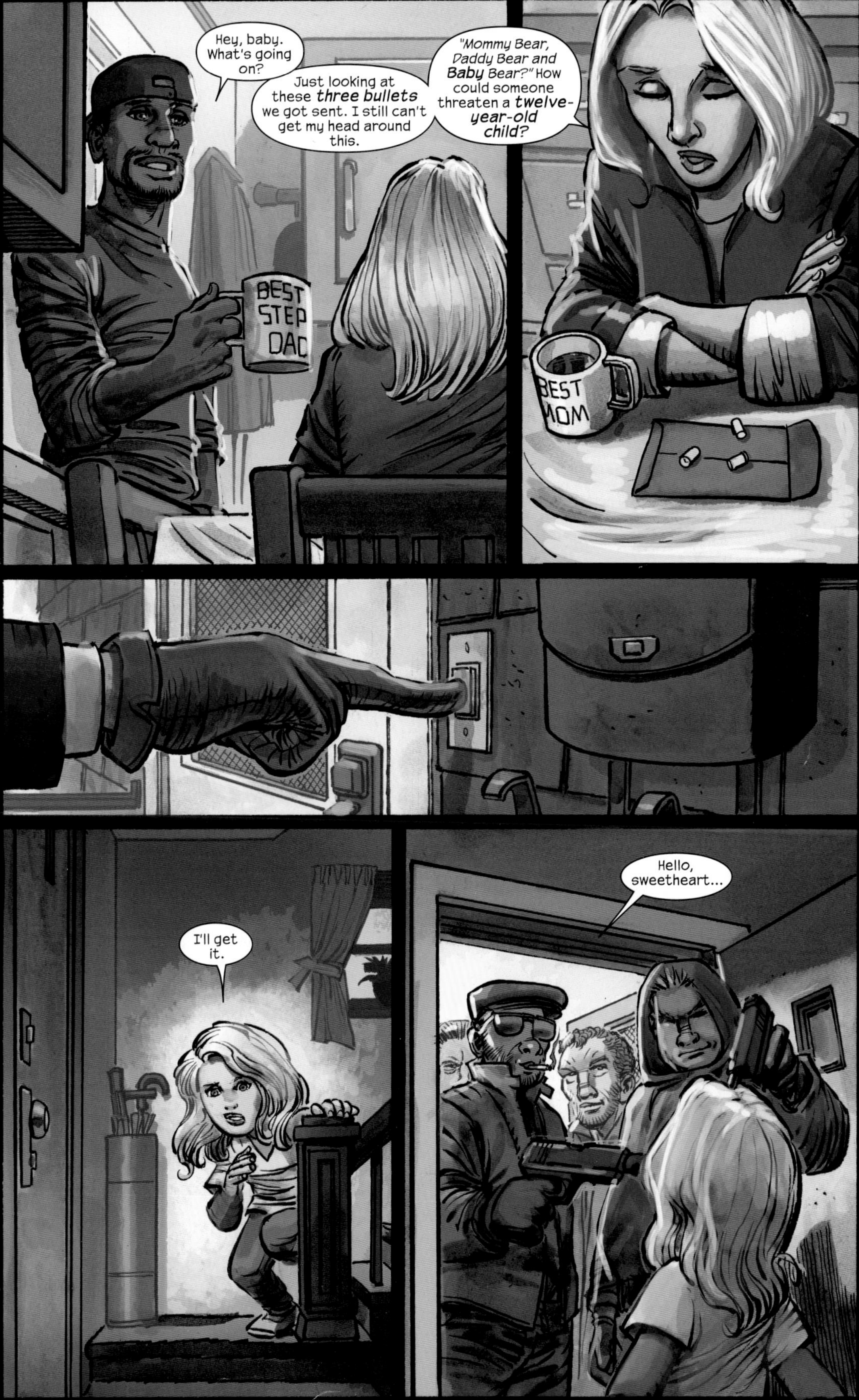

Hey, baby. What's going on?
Just looking at these three bullets we got sent. I still can't get my head around this.
"Mommy Bear, Daddy Bear and Baby Bear?" How could someone threaten a twelve-year-old child?
BEST STEP DAD
BEST MOM
I'll get it.
Hello, sweetheart...

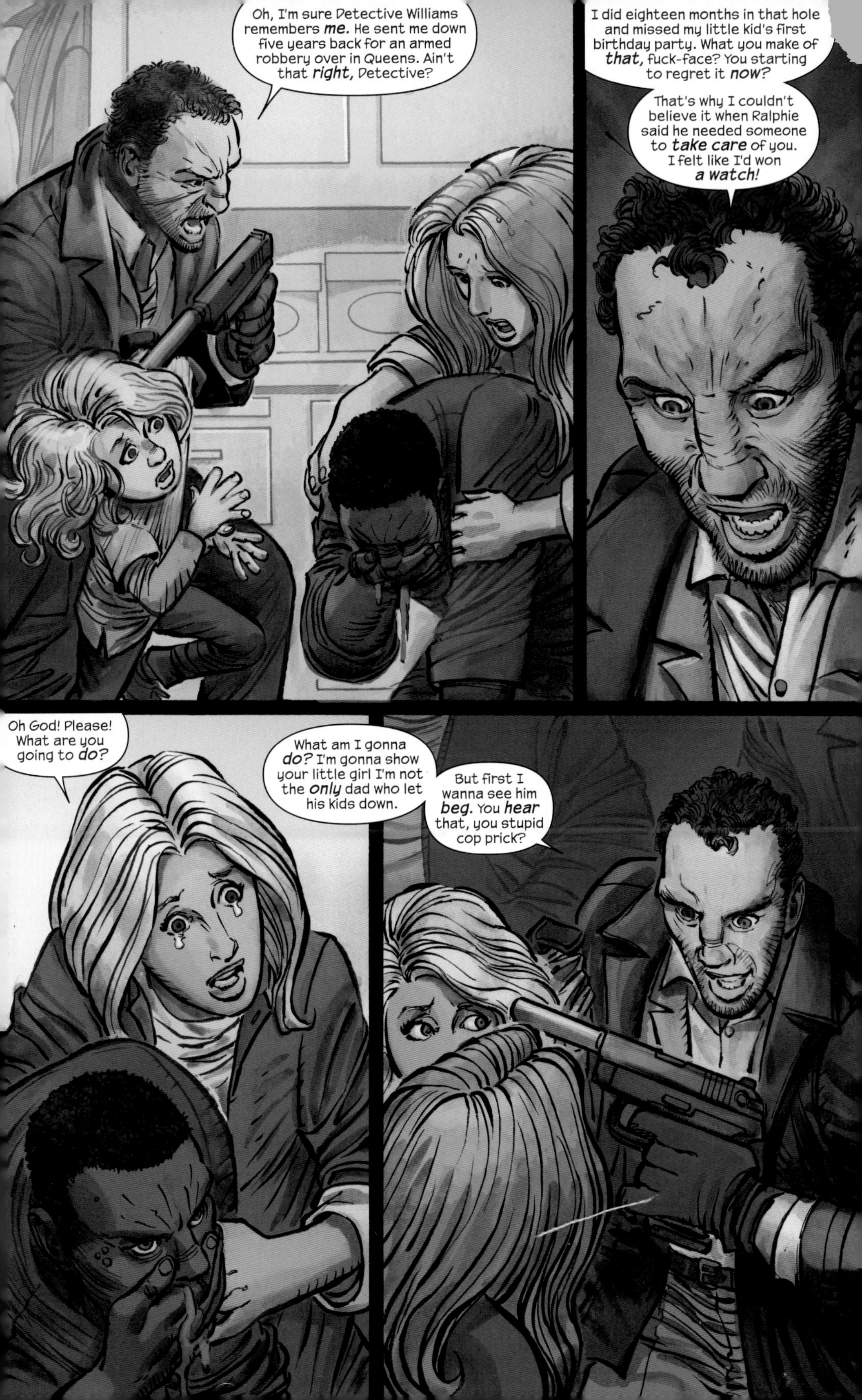
Oh, I'm sure Detective Williams remembers me. He sent me down five years back for an armed robbery over in Queens. Ain't that right, Detective?
I did eighteen months in that hole and missed my little kid's first birthday party. What you make of that, fuck-face? You starting to regret it now?
That's why I couldn't believe it when Ralphie said he needed someone to take care of you. I felt like I'd won a watch!
Oh God! Please! What are you going to do?
What am I gonna do? I'm gonna show your little girl I'm not the only dad who let his kids down.
But first I wanna see him beg. You hear that, you stupid cop prick?

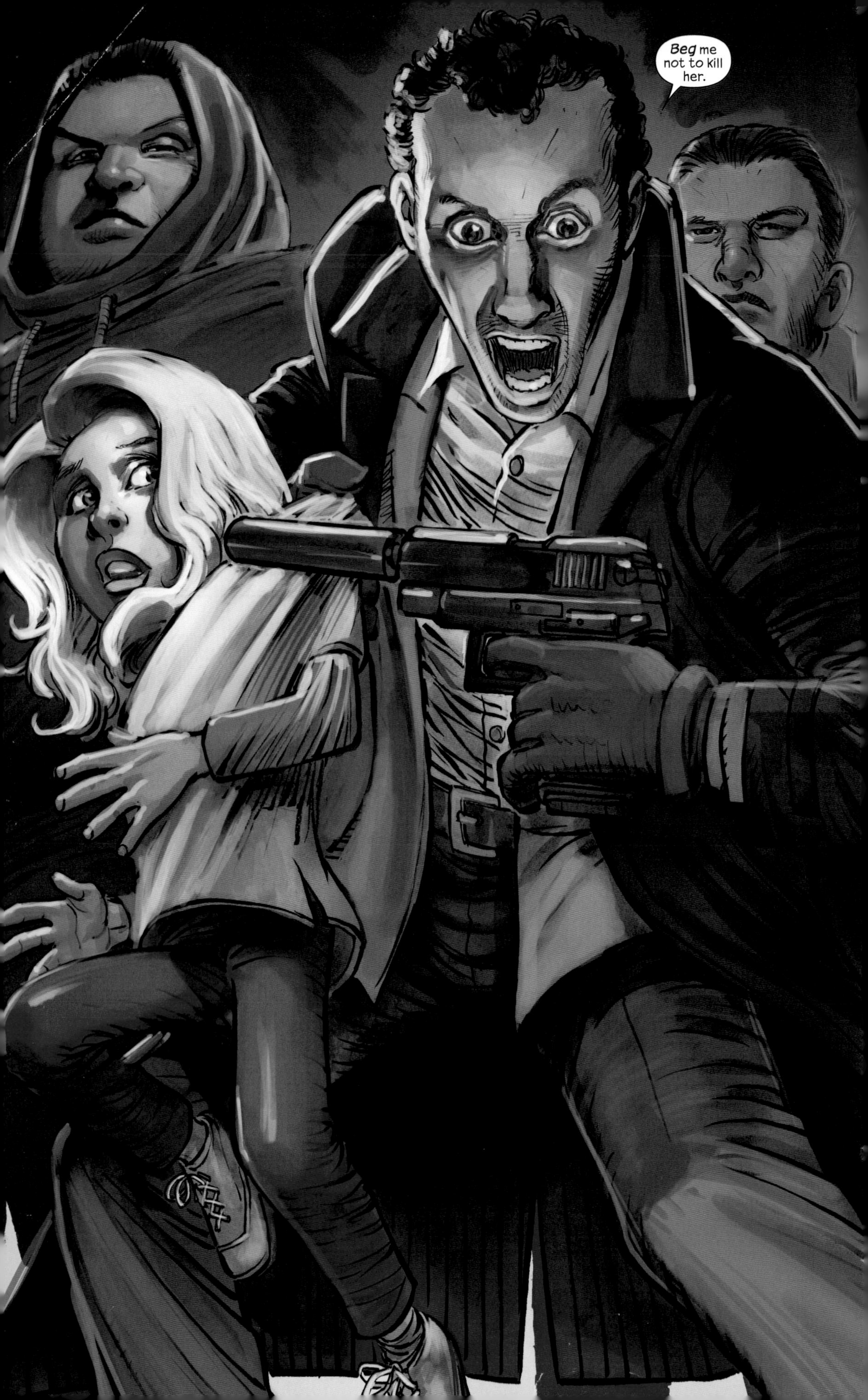
Beg me not to kill her.

FIVE

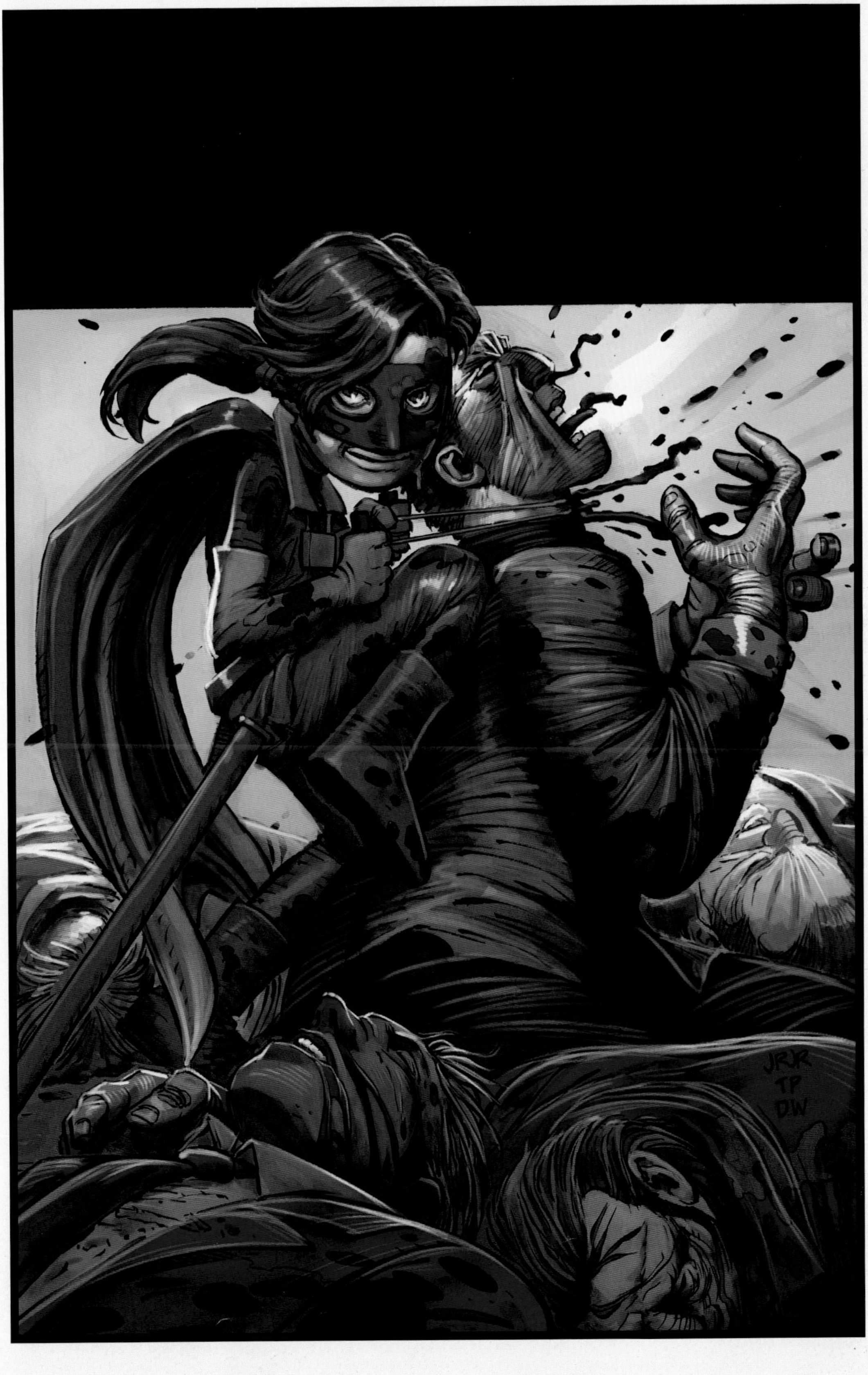
JRJR
TP
D.W

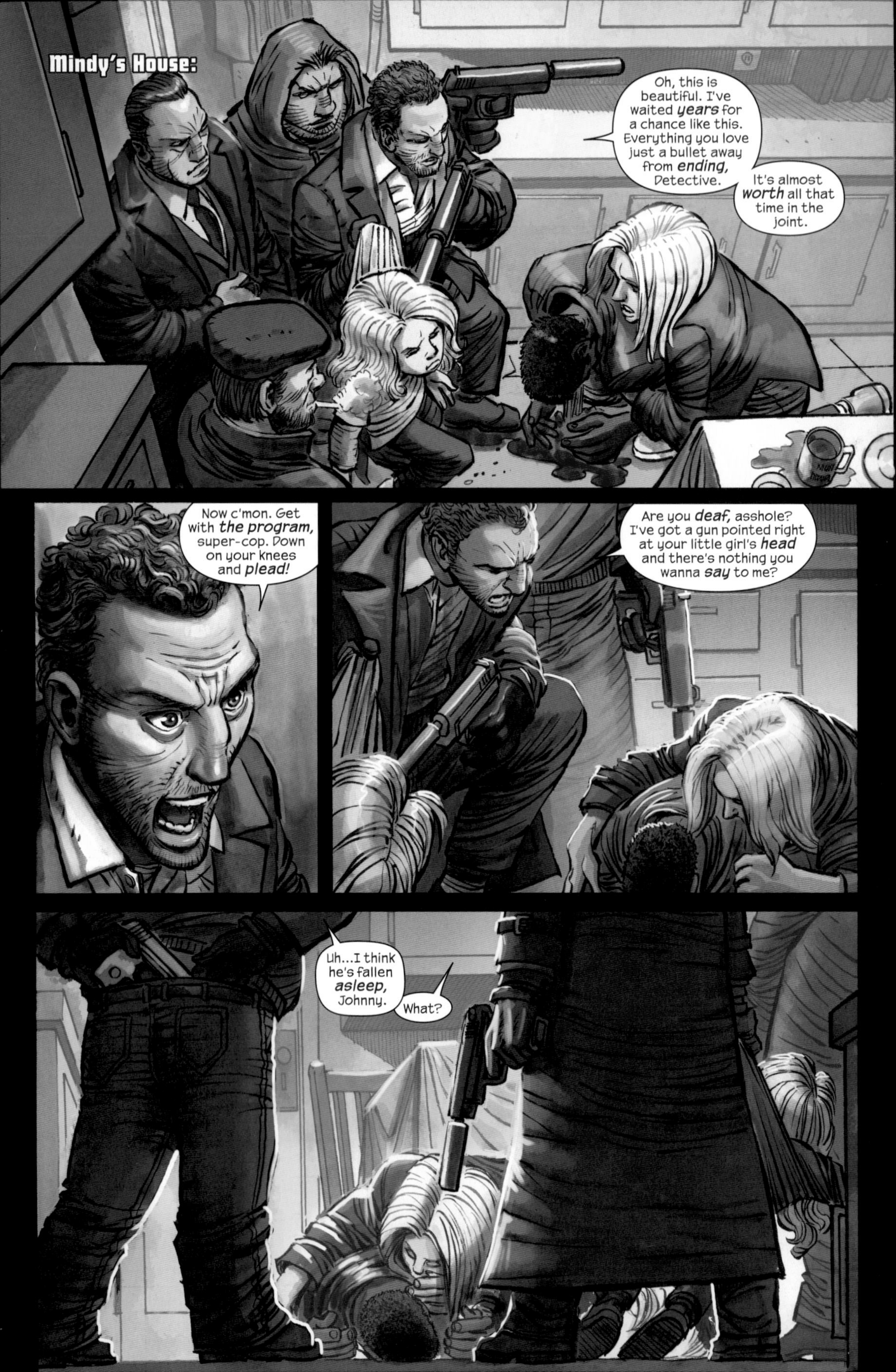
Mindy's House:
Oh, this is beautiful. I've waited years for a chance like this. Everything you love just a bullet away from ending, Detective.
It's almost worth all that time in the joint.
Now c'mon. Get with the program, super-cop. Down on your knees and plead!
Are you deaf, asshole? I've got a gun pointed right at your little girl's head and there's nothing you wanna say to me?
Uh...I think he's fallen asleep, Johnny.
What?

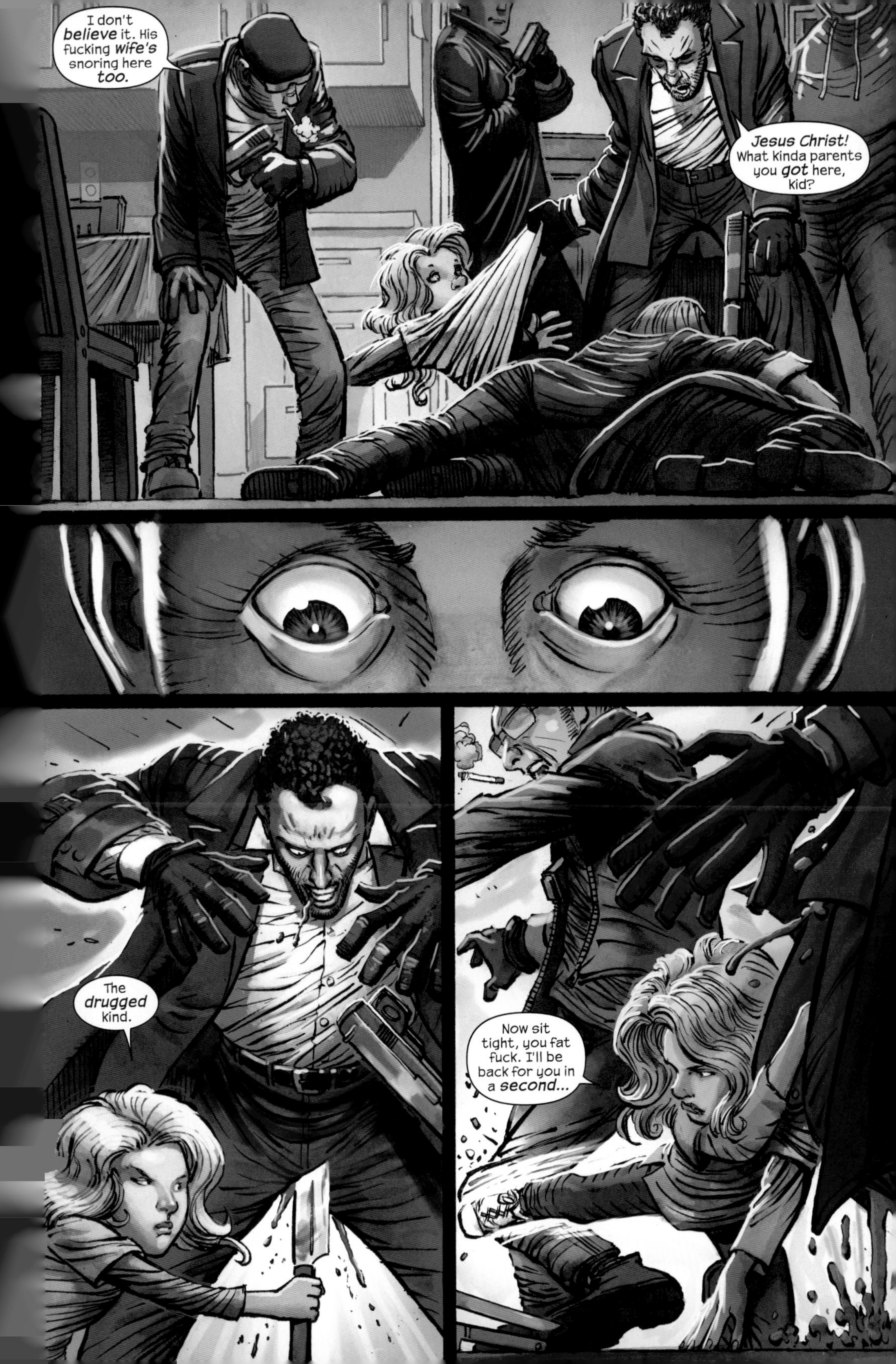
I don't believe it. His fucking wife's snoring here too.
Jesus Christ! What kinda parents you got here, kid?
The drugged kind.
Now sit tight, you fat fuck. I'll be back for you in a second...

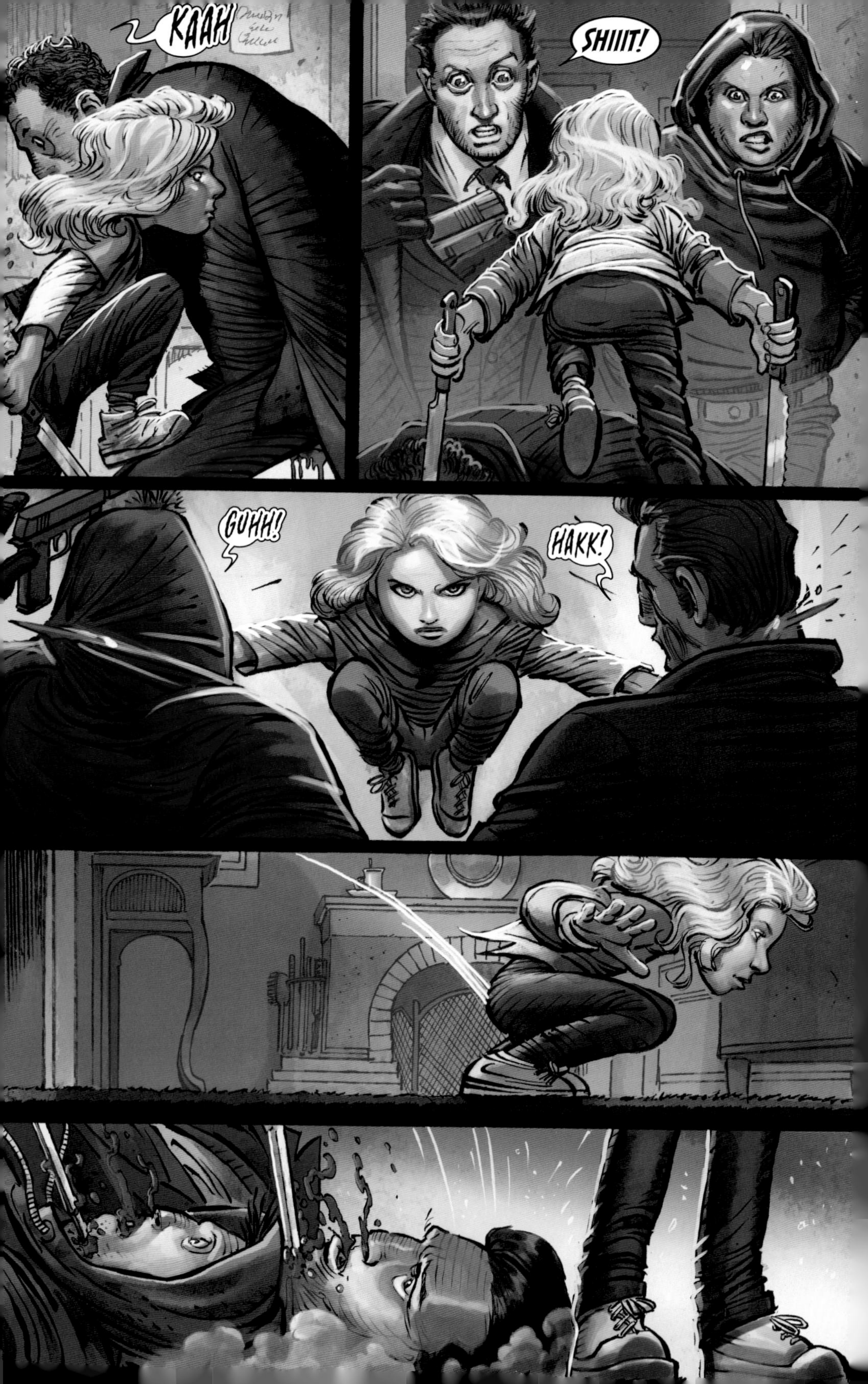
KAAH
SHIIIT!
GUHH!
HAKK!

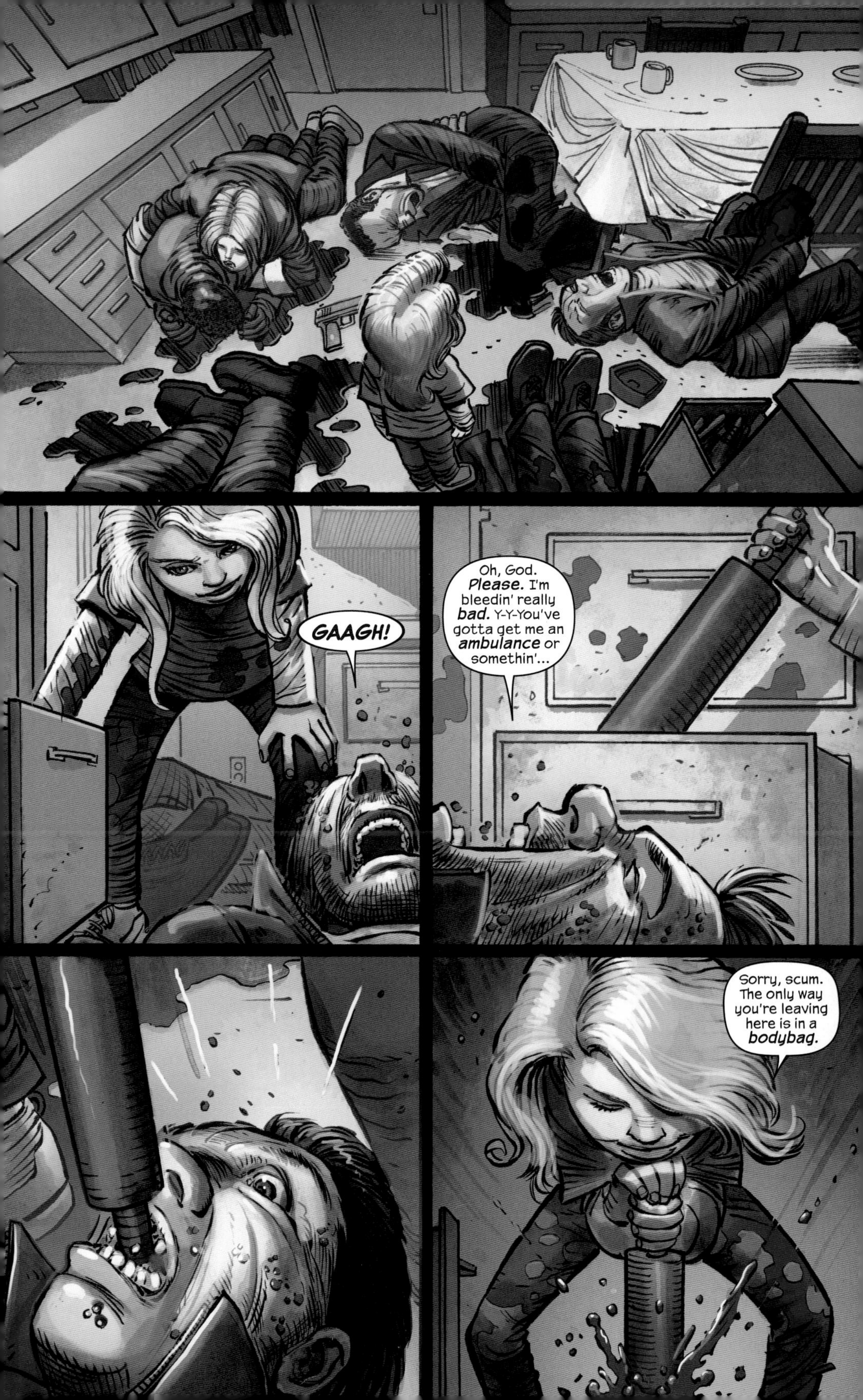
GAAGH!
Oh, God. Please. I'm bleedin' really bad. Y-Y-You've gotta get me an ambulance or somethin'...
Sorry, scum. The only way you're leaving here is in a bodybag.

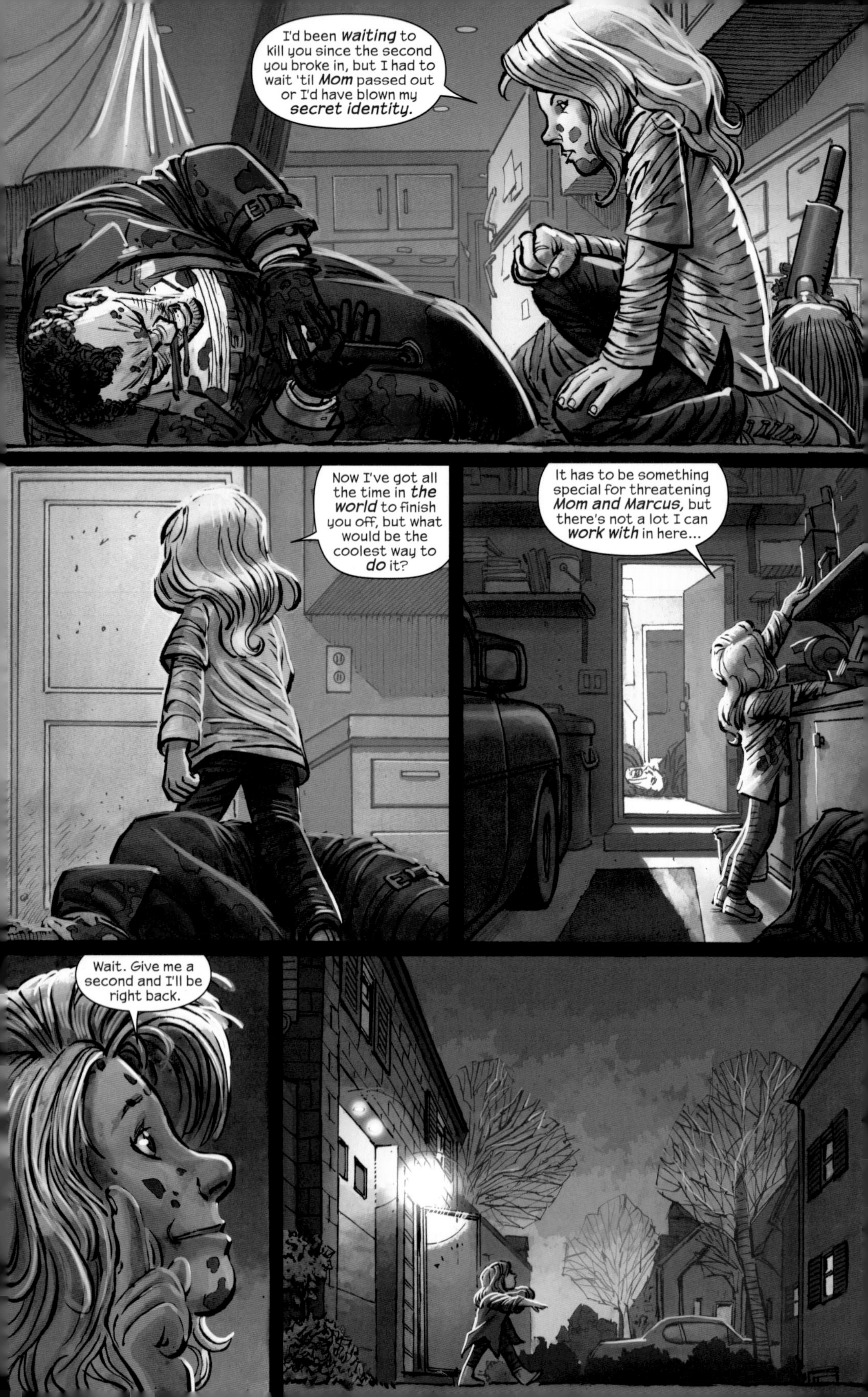
I'd been *waiting* to kill you since the second you broke in, but I had to wait 'til *Mom* passed out or I'd have blown my *secret identity*.
Now I've got all the time in *the world* to finish you off, but what would be the coolest way to *do* it?
It has to be something special for threatening *Mom and Marcus,* but there's not a lot I can *work with* in here...
Wait. Give me a second and I'll be right back.

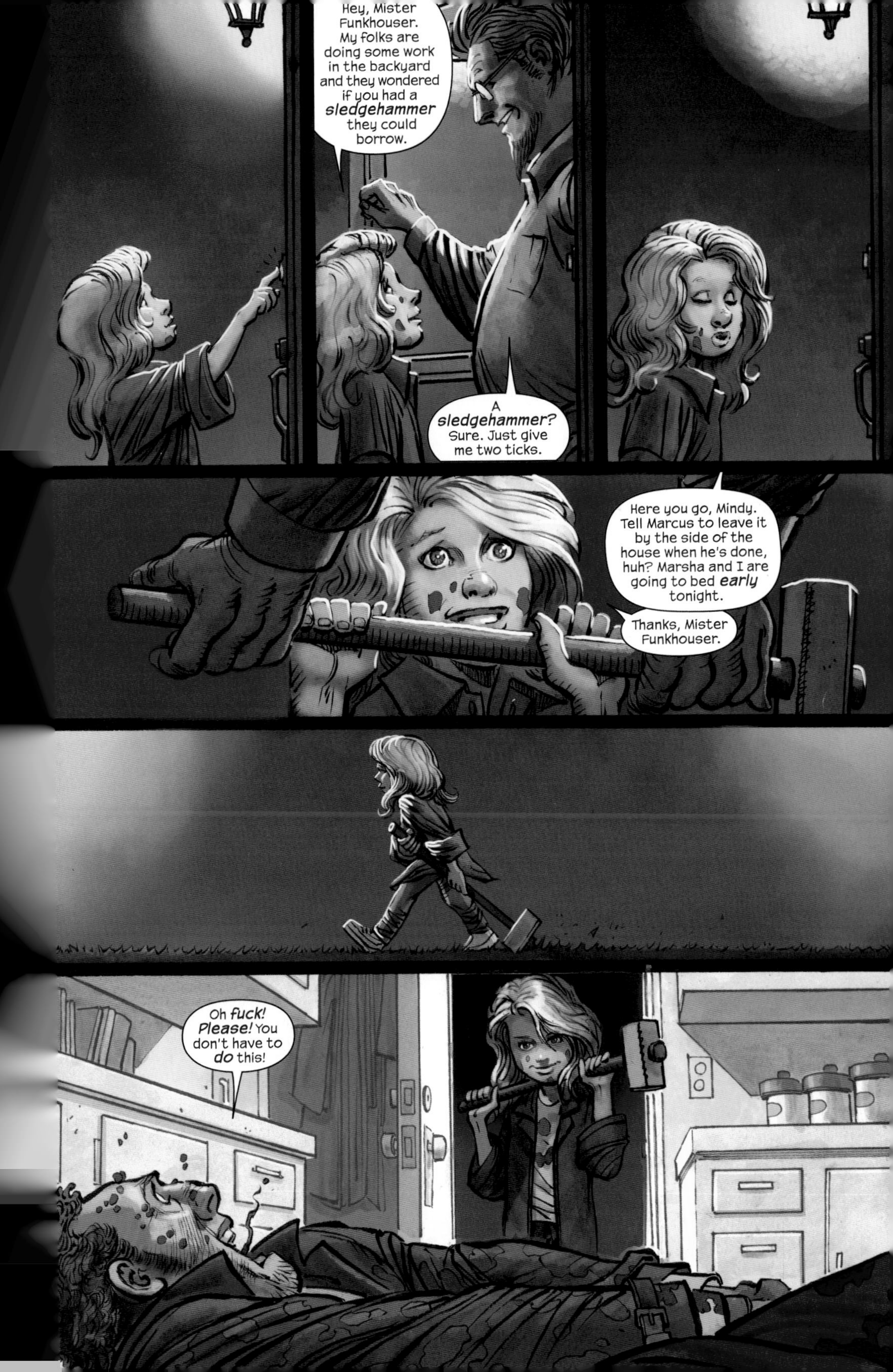
Hey, Mister Funkhouser. My folks are doing some work in the backyard and they wondered if you had a *sledgehammer* they could borrow.
A *sledgehammer?* Sure. Just give me two ticks.
Here you go, Mindy. Tell Marcus to leave it by the side of the house when he's done, huh? Marsha and I are going to bed *early* tonight.
Thanks, Mister Funkhouser.
Oh *fuck! Please!* You don't have to *do* this!

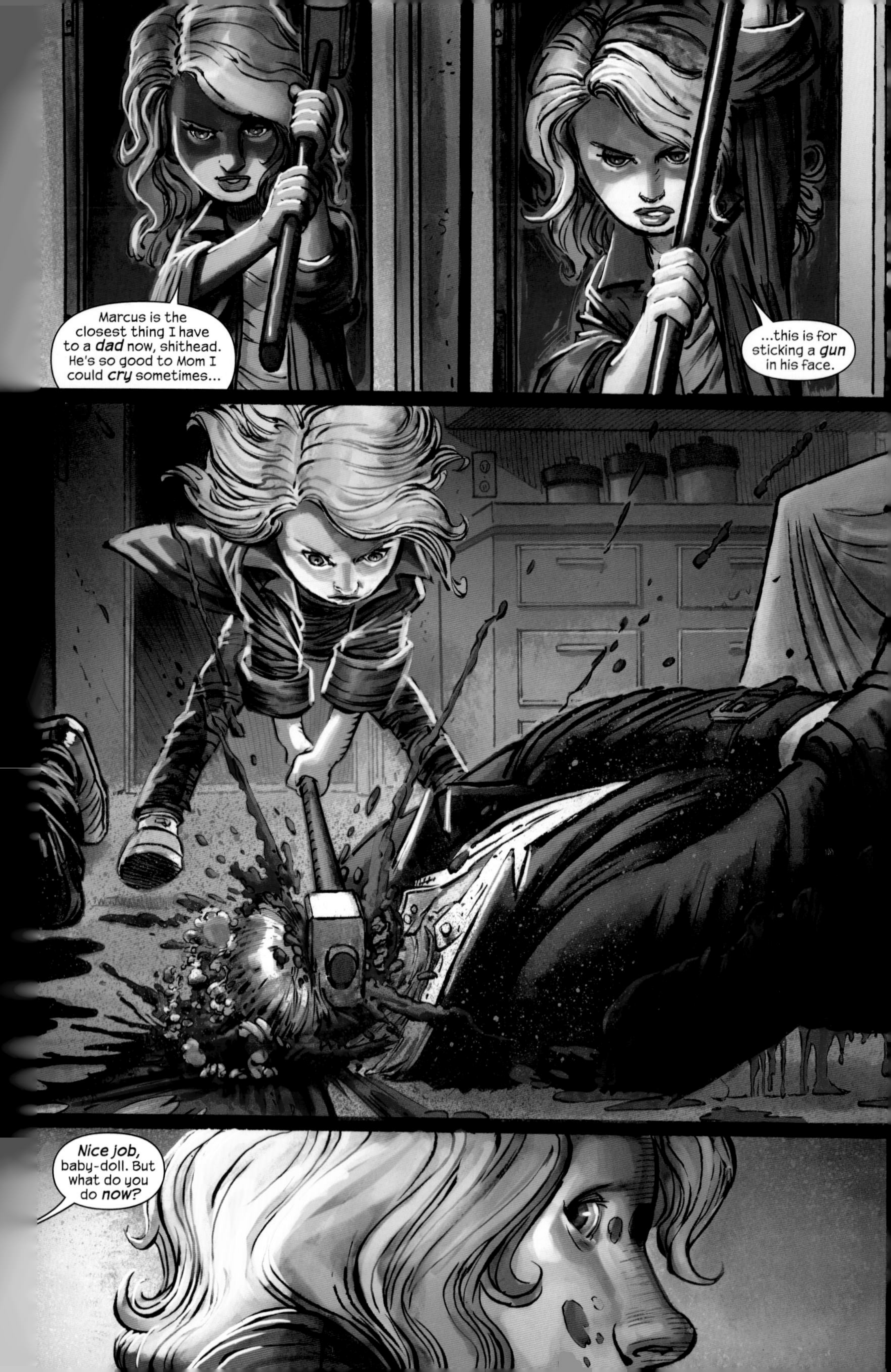
Marcus is the closest thing I have to a *dad* now, shithead. He's so good to Mom I could *cry* sometimes...
...this is for sticking a *gun* in his face.
Nice job, baby-doll. But what do you do *now?*

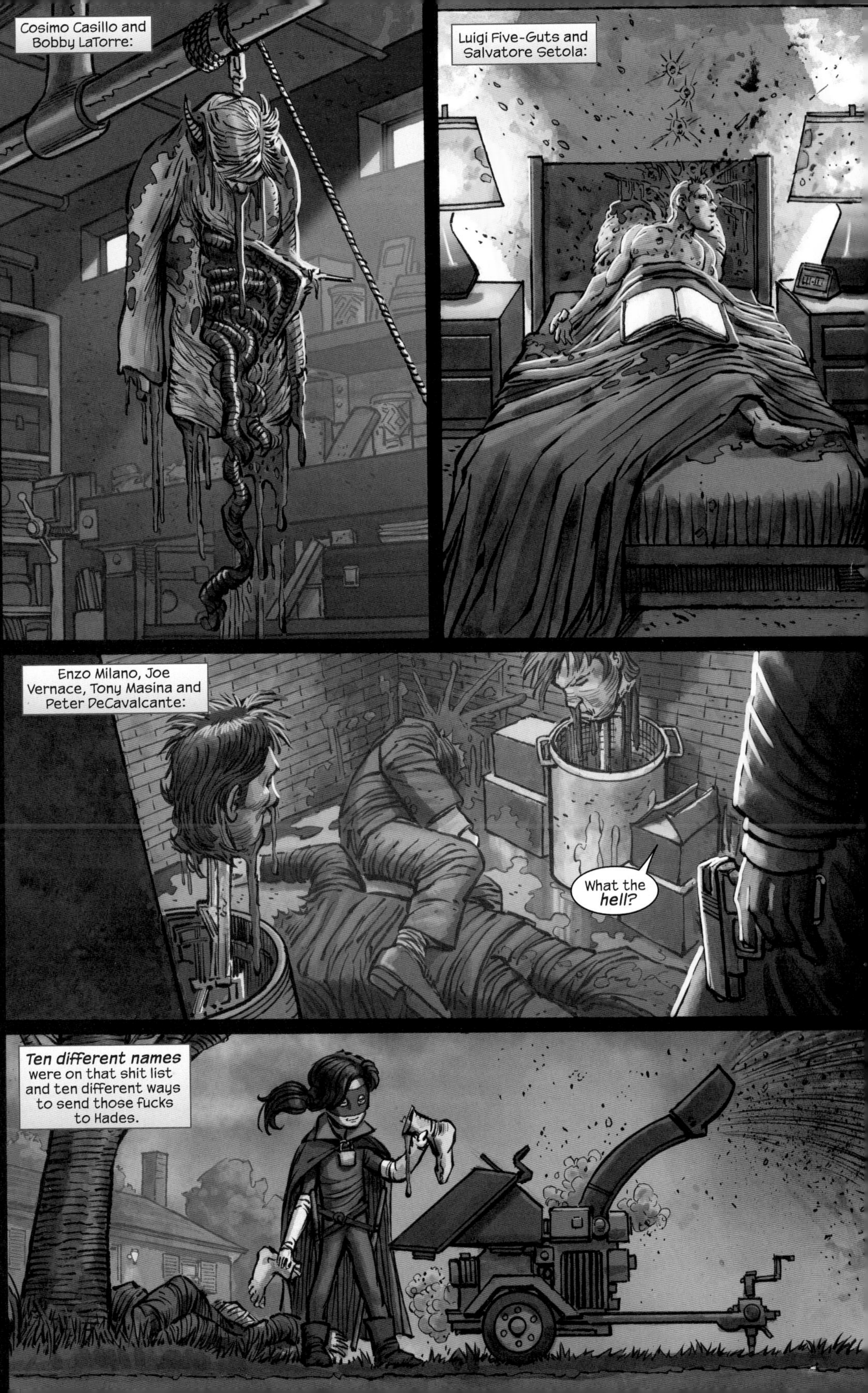
Cosimo Casillo and Bobby LaTorre:
Luigi Five-Guts and Salvatore Setola:
Enzo Milano, Joe Vernace, Tony Masina and Peter DeCavalcante:
What the *hell?*
Ten different names were on that shit list and ten different ways to send those fucks to Hades.

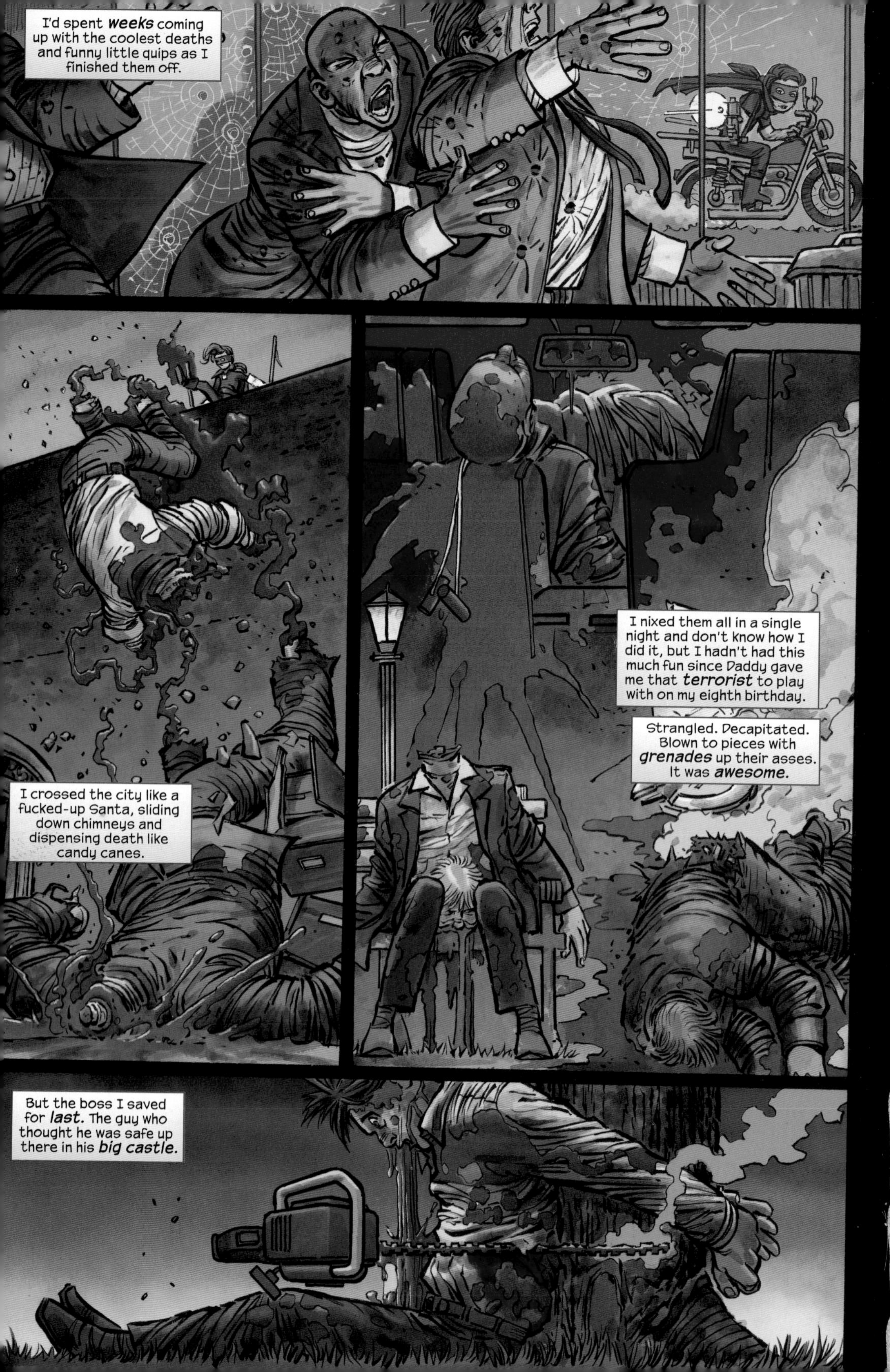
I'd spent *weeks* coming up with the coolest deaths and funny little quips as I finished them off.
I crossed the city like a fucked-up Santa, sliding down chimneys and dispensing death like candy canes.
I nixed them all in a single night and don't know how I did it, but I hadn't had this much fun since Daddy gave me that *terrorist* to play with on my eighth birthday.
Strangled. Decapitated. Blown to pieces with *grenades* up their asses. It was *awesome.*
But the boss I saved for *last.* The guy who thought he was safe up there in his *big castle.*

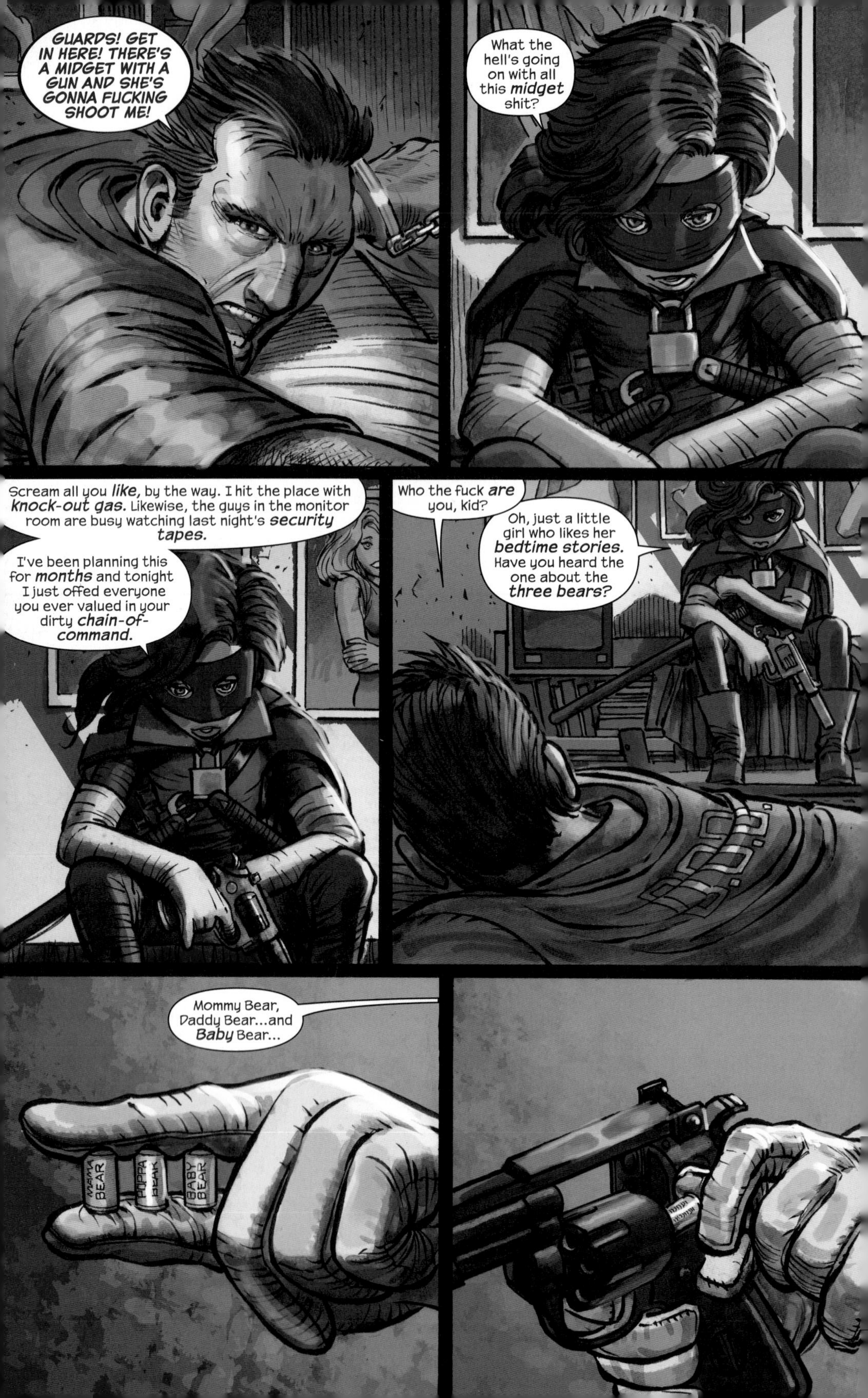
GUARDS! GET IN HERE! THERE'S A MIDGET WITH A GUN AND SHE'S GONNA FUCKING SHOOT ME!
What the hell's going on with all this midget shit?
Scream all you like, by the way. I hit the place with knock-out gas. Likewise, the guys in the monitor room are busy watching last night's security tapes.
I've been planning this for months and tonight I just offed everyone you ever valued in your dirty chain-of-command.
Who the fuck are you, kid?
Oh, just a little girl who likes her bedtime stories. Have you heard the one about the three bears?
Mommy Bear, Daddy Bear...and Baby Bear...
MAMA BEAR
POPPA BEAR
BABY BEAR

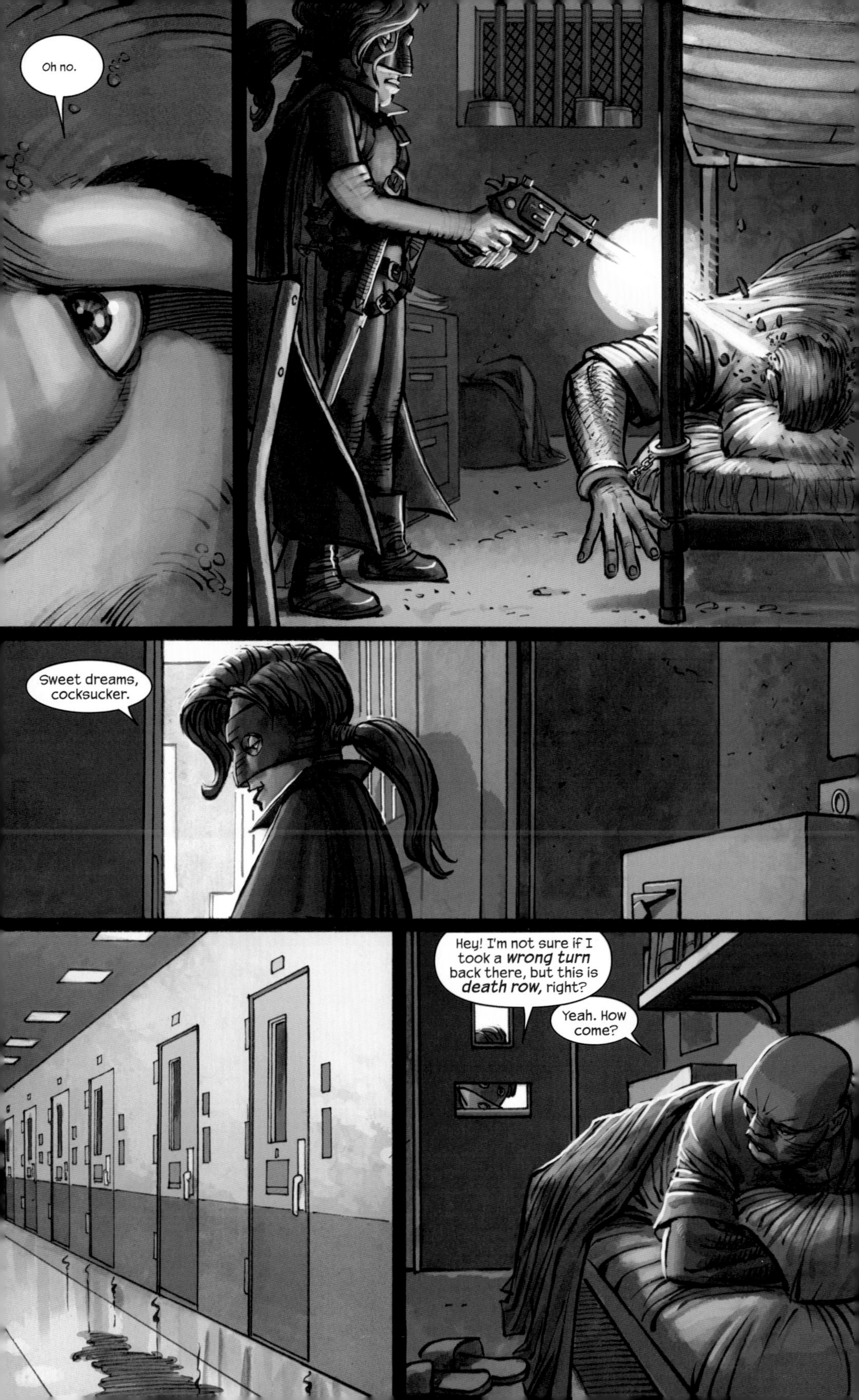
Oh no.
Sweet dreams, cocksucker.
Hey! I'm not sure if I took a wrong turn back there, but this is death row, right?
Yeah. How come?

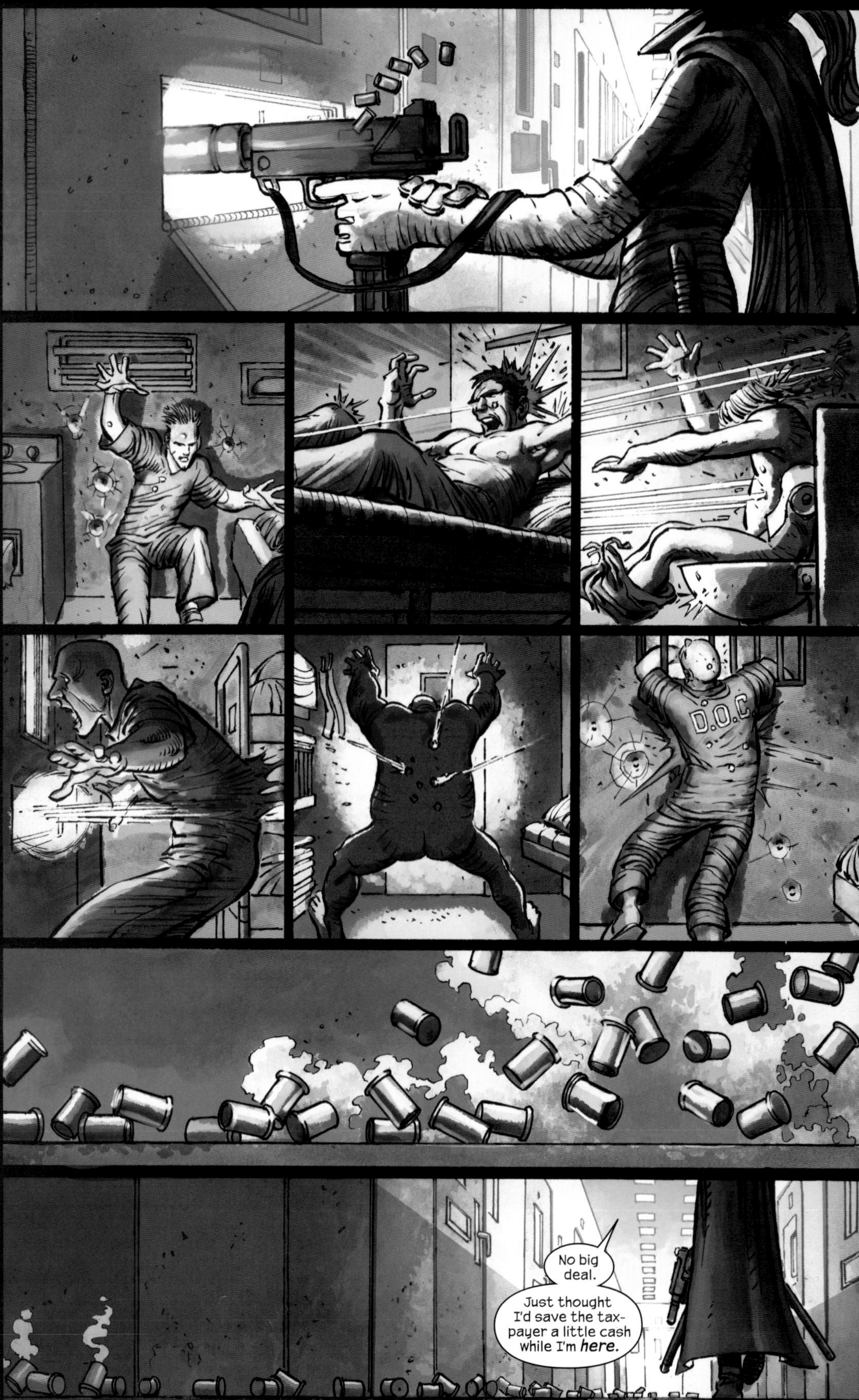
D.O.C.
No big deal.
Just thought I'd save the tax-payer a little cash while I'm *here.*

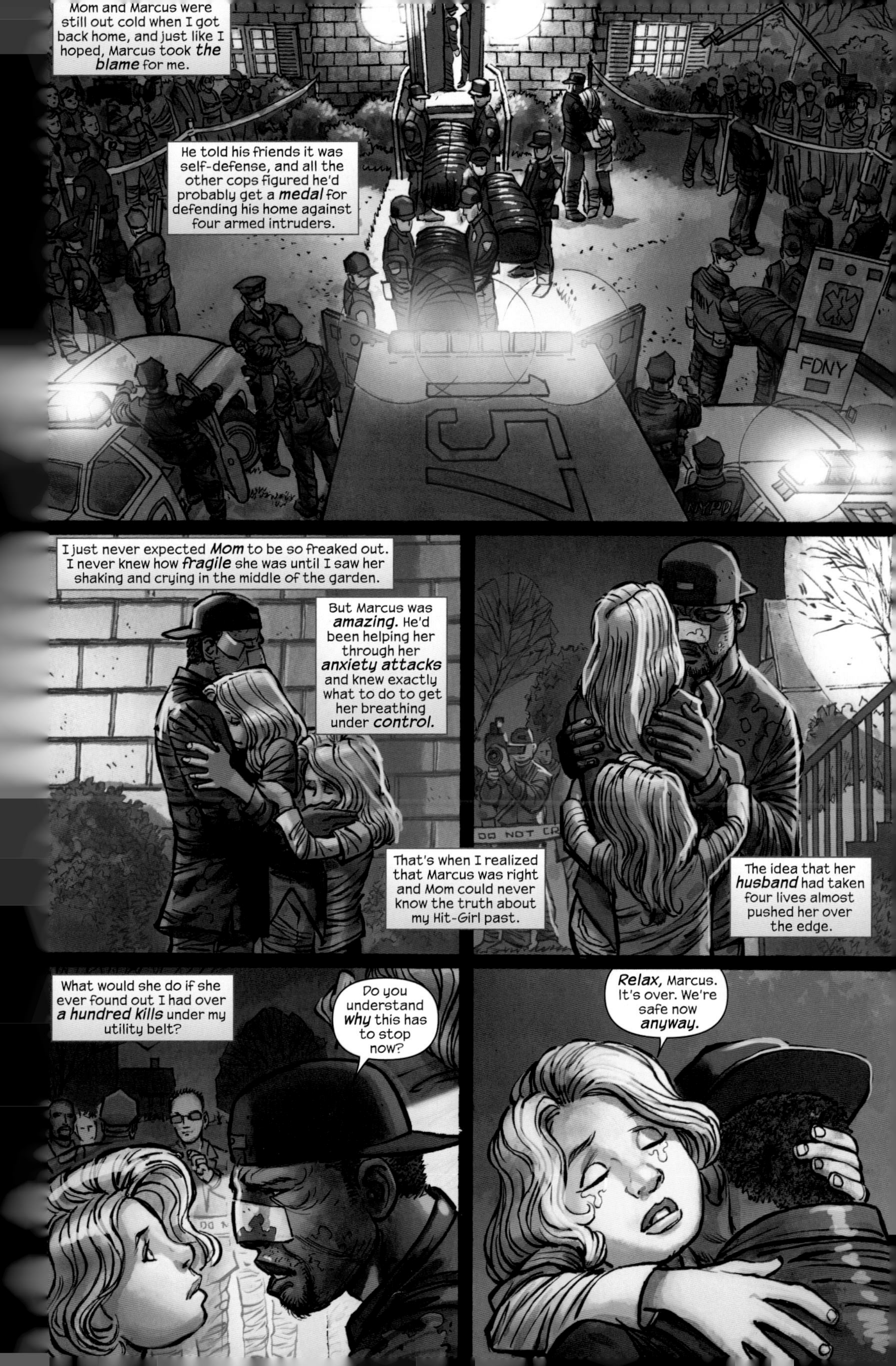
Mom and Marcus were still out cold when I got back home, and just like I hoped, Marcus took *the blame* for me.
He told his friends it was self-defense, and all the other cops figured he'd probably get a *medal* for defending his home against four armed intruders.
FDNY
I just never expected *Mom* to be so freaked out. I never knew how *fragile* she was until I saw her shaking and crying in the middle of the garden.
But Marcus was *amazing.* He'd been helping her through her *anxiety attacks* and knew exactly what to do to get her breathing under *control.*
That's when I realized that Marcus was right and Mom could never know the truth about my Hit-Girl past.
The idea that her *husband* had taken four lives almost pushed her over the edge.
What would she do if she ever found out I had over *a hundred kills* under my utility belt?
Do you understand *why* this has to stop now?
Relax, Marcus. It's over. We're safe now *anyway.*

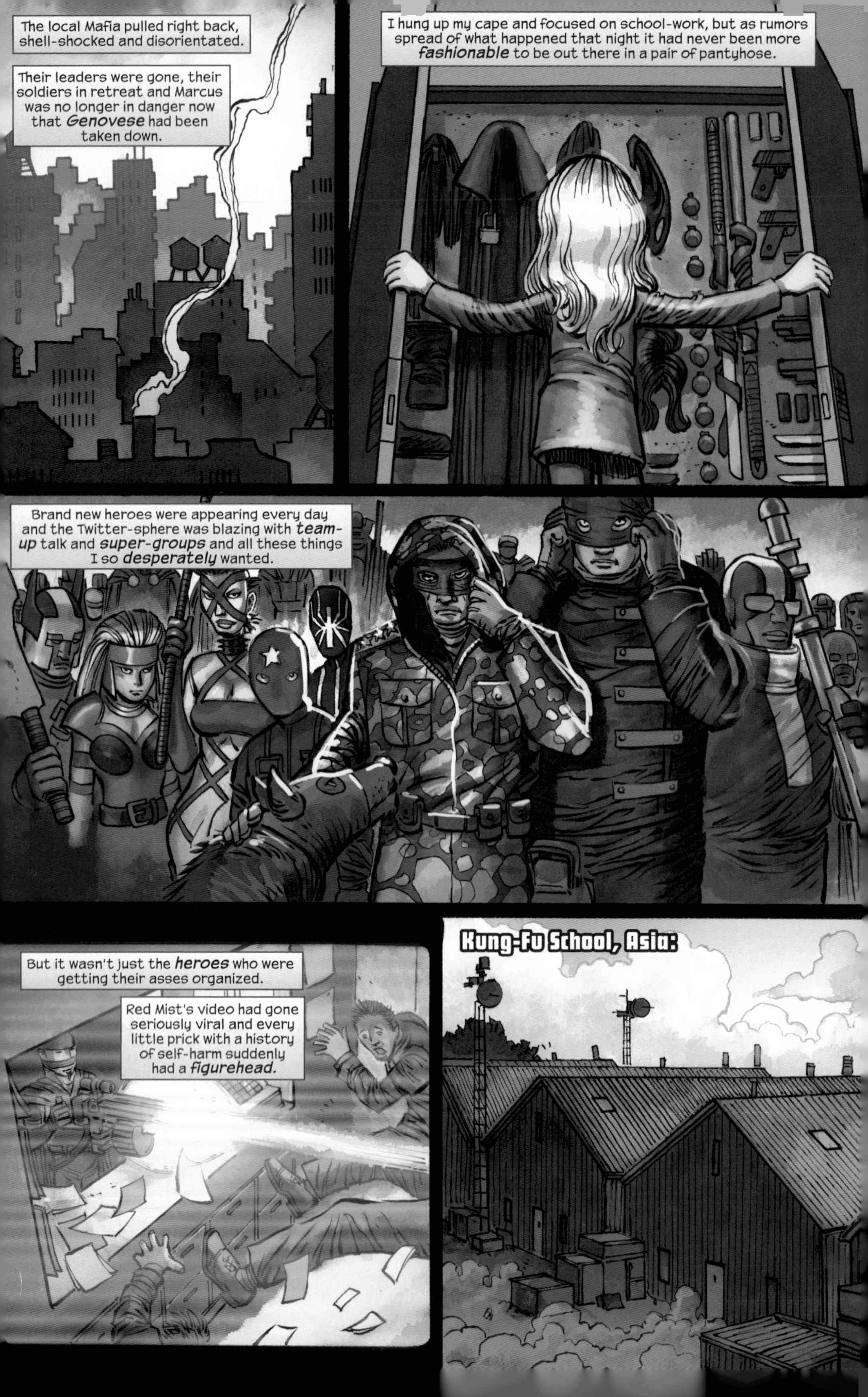

The local Mafia pulled right back, shell-shocked and disorientated.
Their leaders were gone, their soldiers in retreat and Marcus was no longer in danger now that *Genovese* had been taken down.
I hung up my cape and focused on school-work, but as rumors spread of what happened that night it had never been more *fashionable* to be out there in a pair of pantyhose.
Brand new heroes were appearing every day and the Twitter-sphere was blazing with *team-up* talk and *super-groups* and all these things I so *desperately* wanted.
But it wasn't just the *heroes* who were getting their asses organized.
Red Mist's video had gone seriously viral and every little prick with a history of self-harm suddenly had a *figurehead.*
Kung-Fu School, Asia:

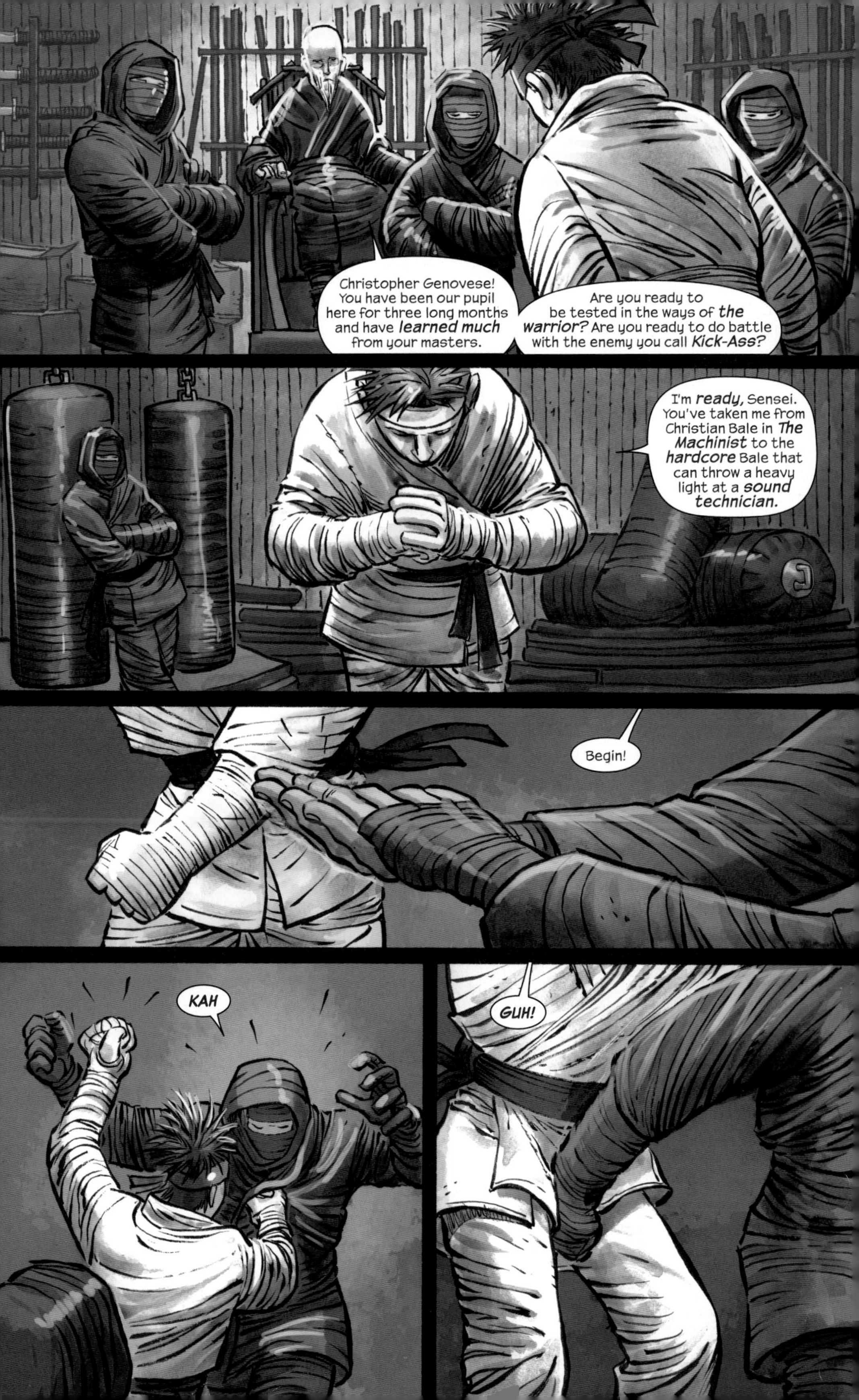
Christopher Genovese! You have been our pupil here for three long months and have *learned much* from your masters.
Are you ready to be tested in the ways of *the warrior?* Are you ready to do battle with the enemy you call *Kick-Ass?*
I'm *ready,* Sensei. You've taken me from Christian Bale in *The Machinist* to the *hardcore* Bale that can throw a heavy light at a *sound technician.*
Begin!
KAH
GUH!

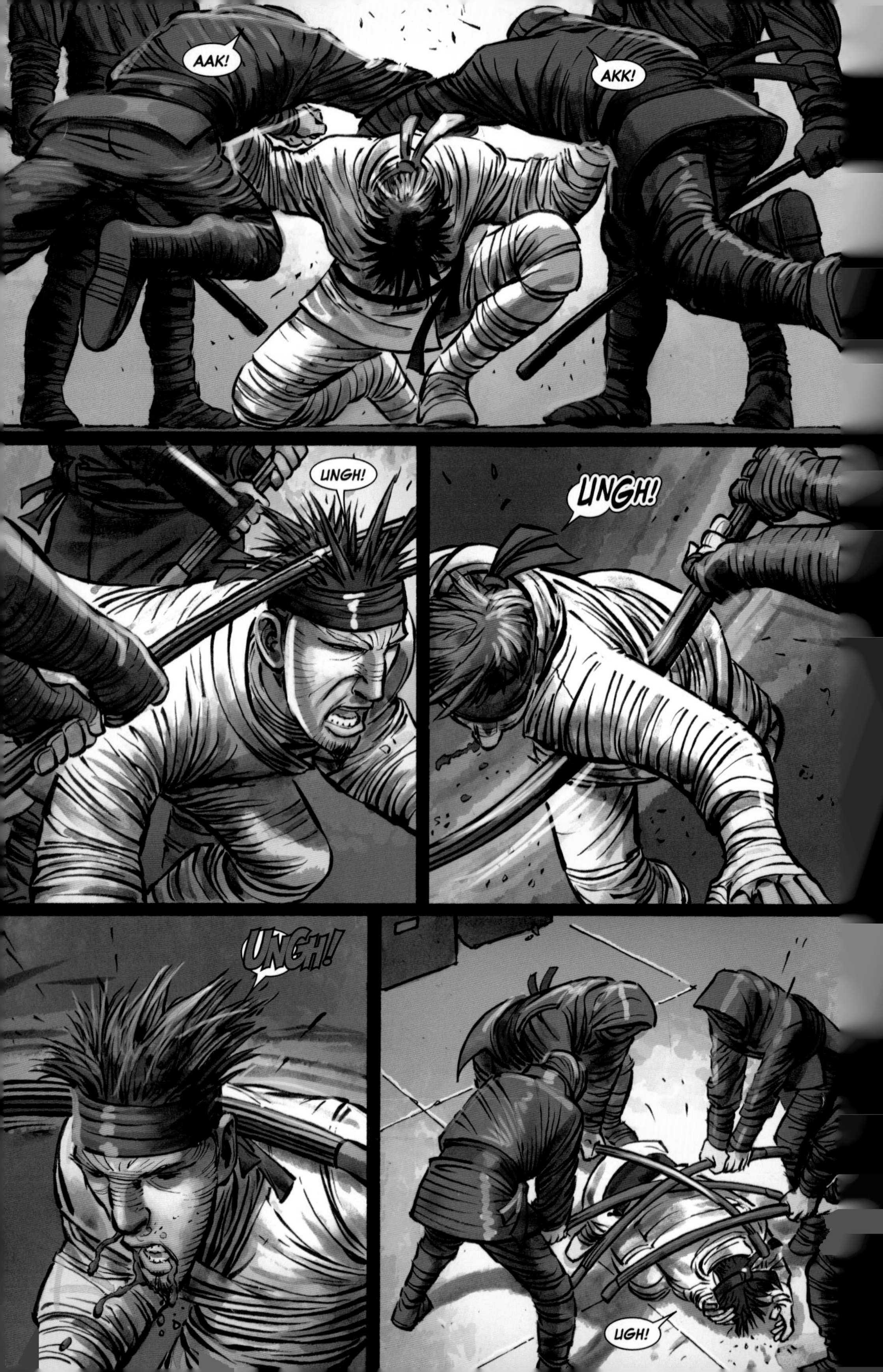
AAK!
AKK!
UNGH!
UNGH!
UNGH!
UGH!

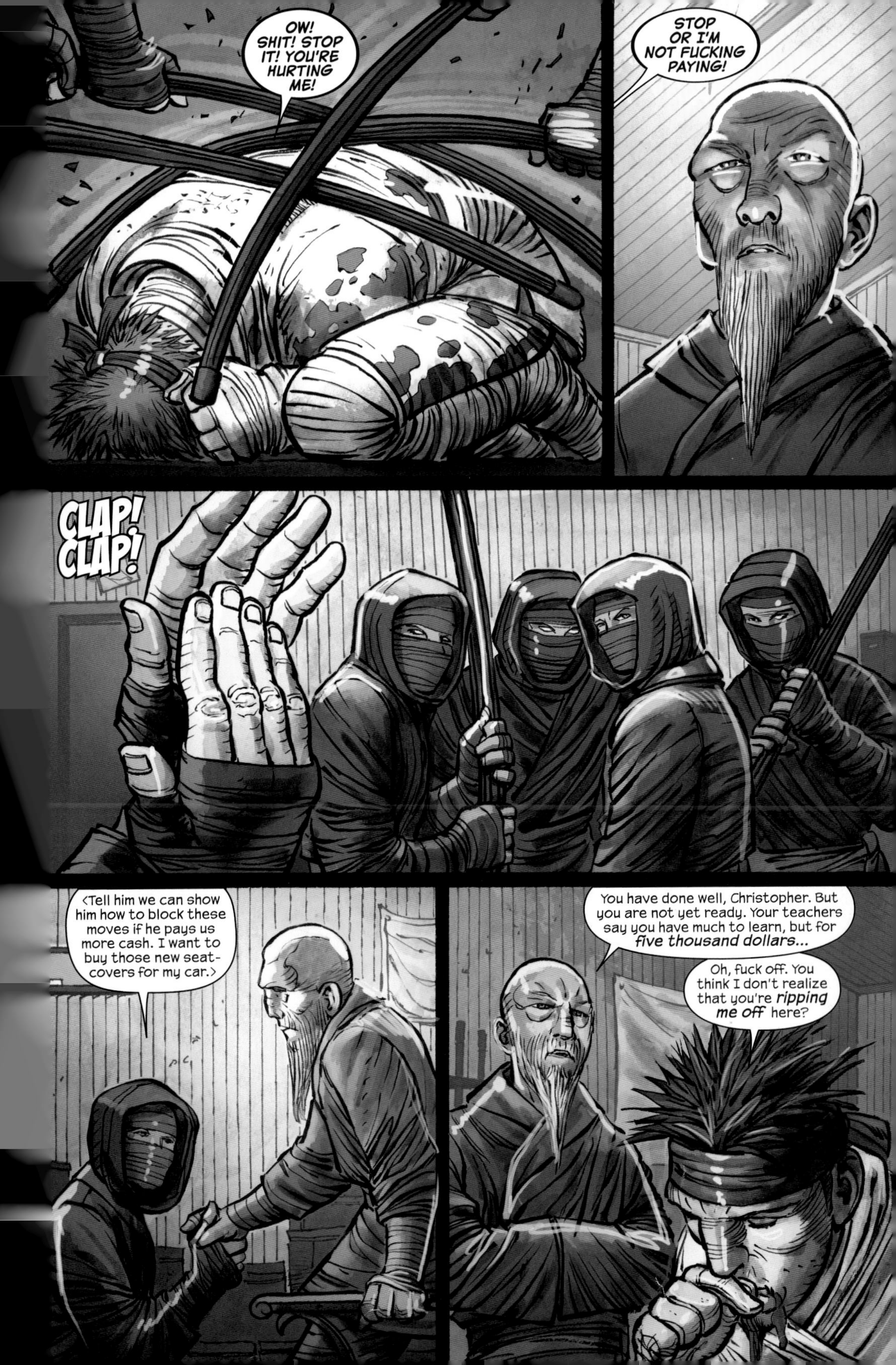
OW! SHIT! STOP IT! YOU'RE HURTING ME!
STOP OR I'M NOT FUCKING PAYING!
CLAP! CLAP!
<Tell him we can show him how to block these moves if he pays us more cash. I want to buy those new seat-covers for my car.>
You have done well, Christopher. But you are not yet ready. Your teachers say you have much to learn, but for *five thousand dollars...*
Oh, fuck off. You think I don't realize that you're *ripping me off* here?

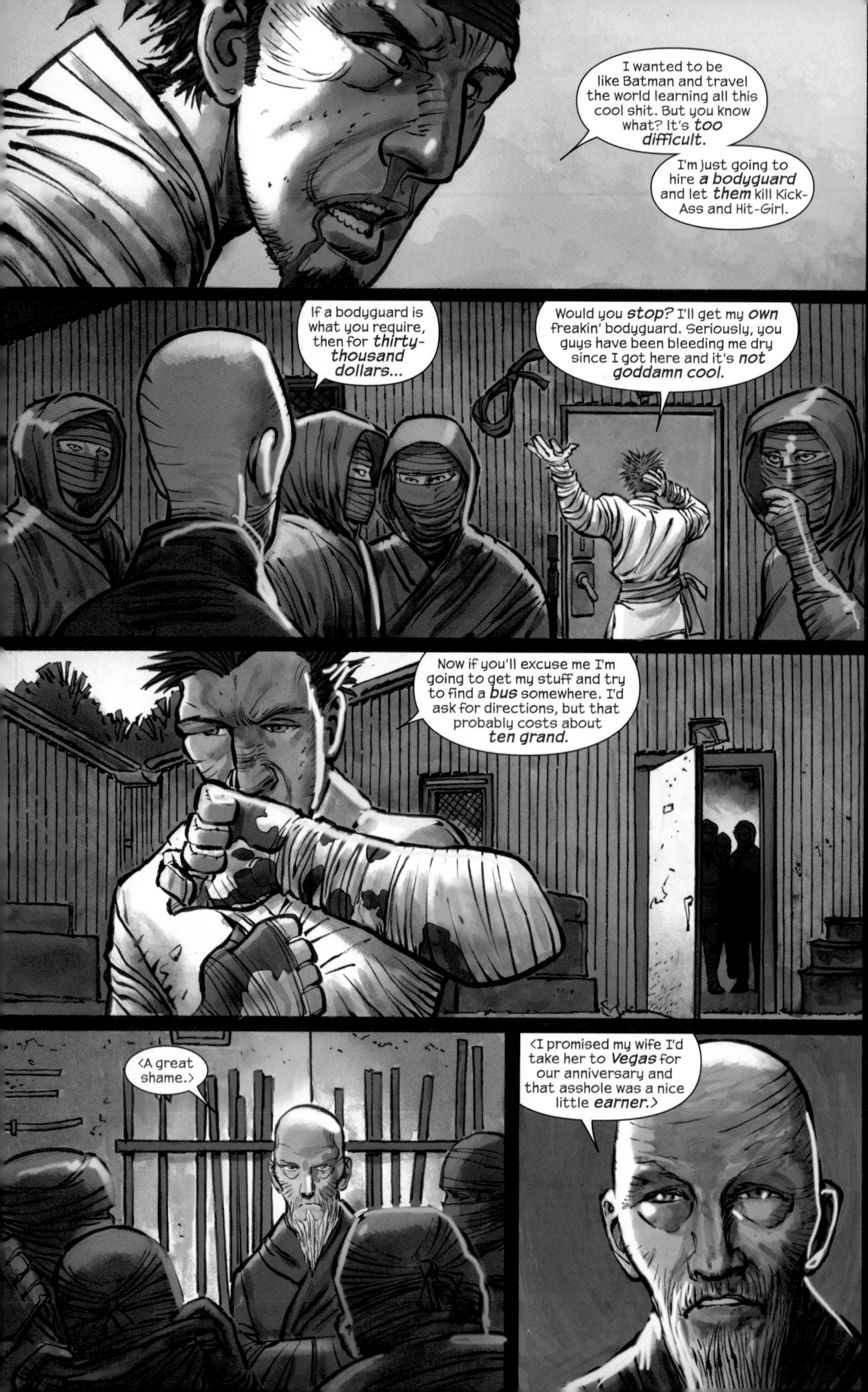
I wanted to be like Batman and travel the world learning all this cool shit. But you know what? It's too difficult.
I'm just going to hire a bodyguard and let them kill Kick-Ass and Hit-Girl.
If a bodyguard is what you require, then for thirty-thousand dollars...
Would you stop? I'll get my own freakin' bodyguard. Seriously, you guys have been bleeding me dry since I got here and it's not goddamn cool.
Now if you'll excuse me I'm going to get my stuff and try to find a bus somewhere. I'd ask for directions, but that probably costs about ten grand.
<A great shame.>
<I promised my wife I'd take her to Vegas for our anniversary and that asshole was a nice little earner.>

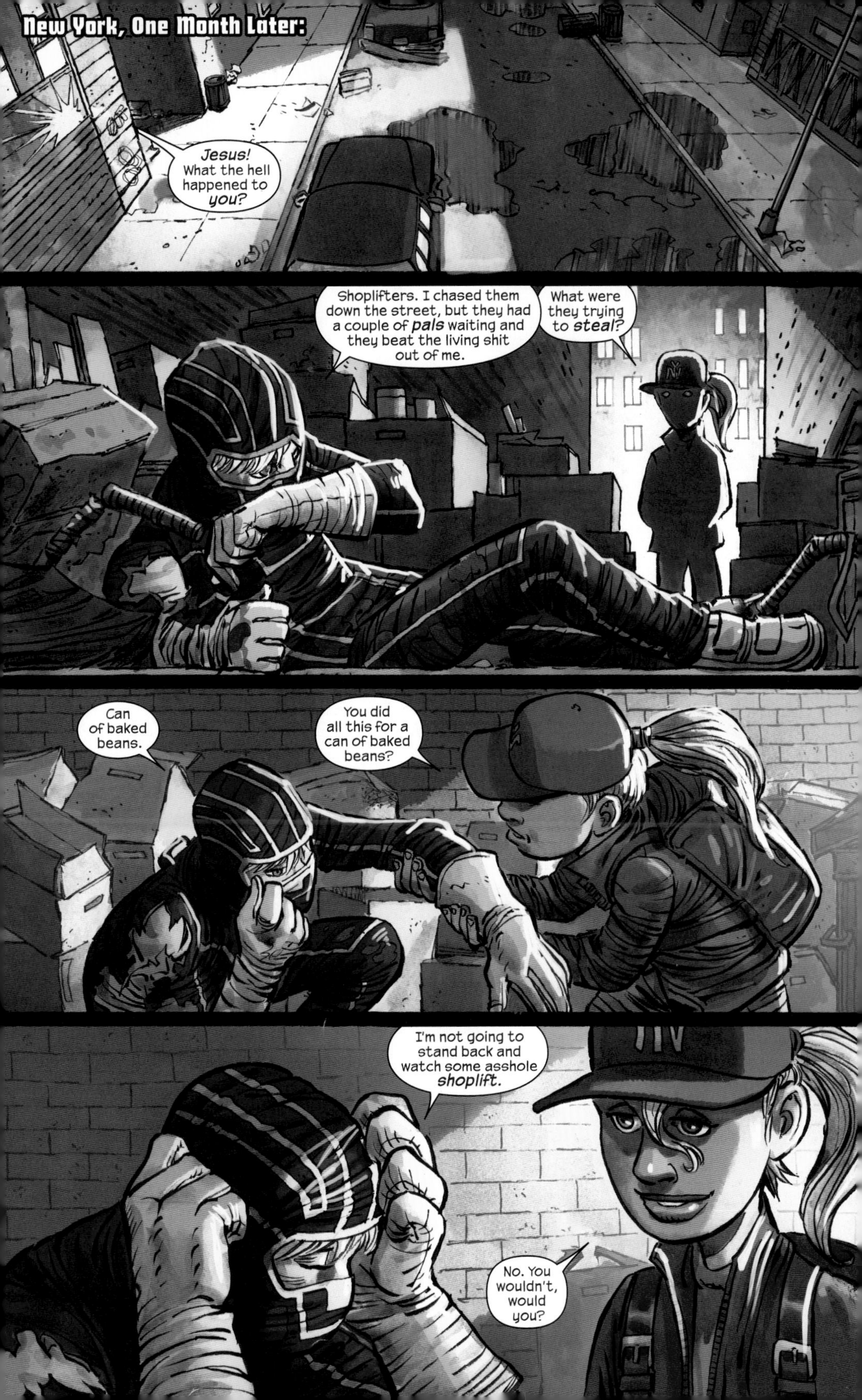
New York, One Month Later:
Jesus! What the hell happened to you?
Shoplifters. I chased them down the street, but they had a couple of pals waiting and they beat the living shit out of me.
What were they trying to steal?
Can of baked beans.
You did all this for a can of baked beans?
I'm not going to stand back and watch some asshole shoplift.
No. You wouldn't, would you?

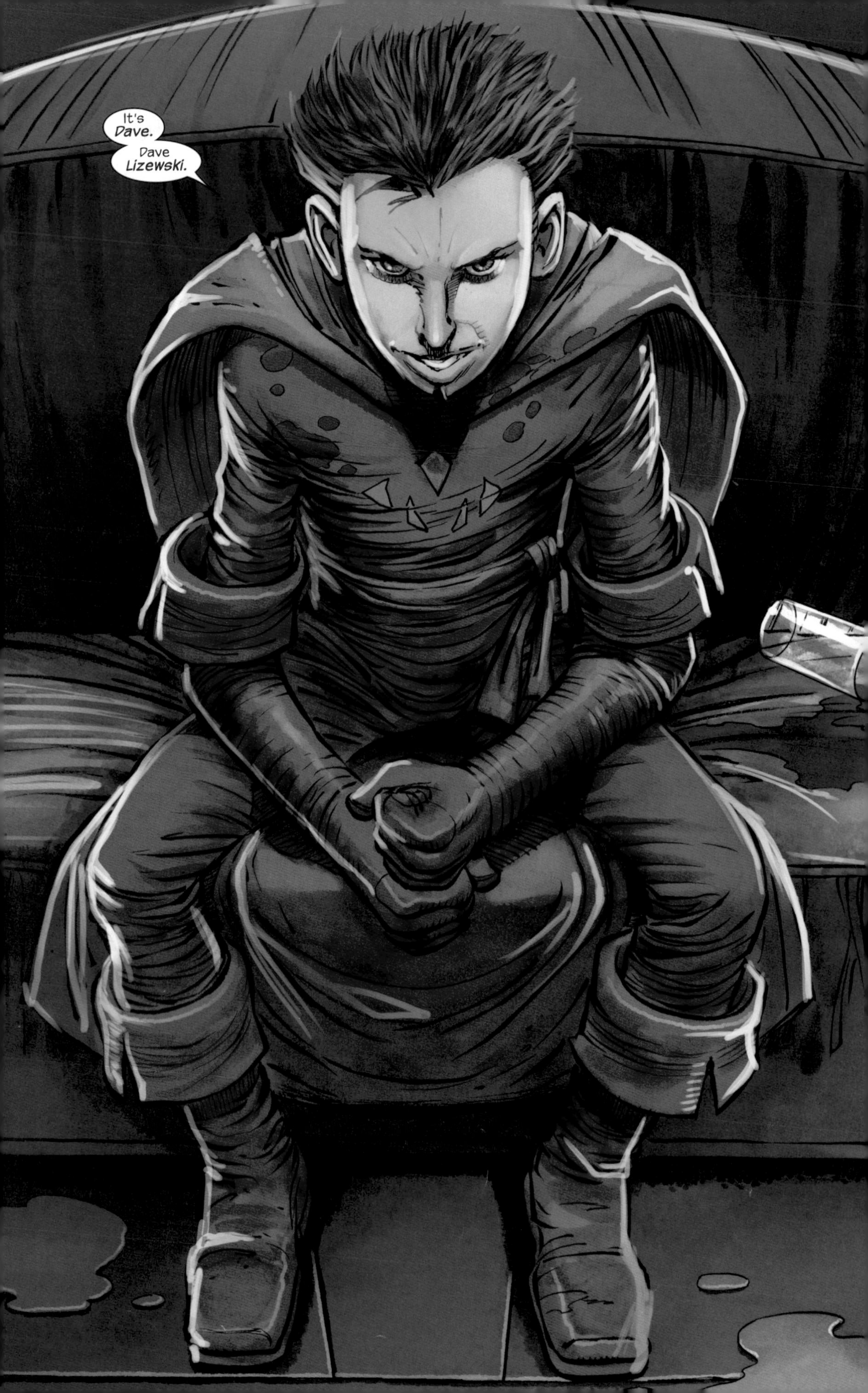
It's *Dave.*
Dave *Lizewski.*

END OF BOOK TWO

MARK MILLAR has written some of Marvel's greatest modern hits including *The Ultimates*, *Ultimate X-Men*, *Spider-Man*, *Wolverine: Old Man Logan,* and *Civil War*, the industry's biggest-selling series of the last decade. His Millarworld line boasts a roster of creator-owned smashes such as *Wanted*, turned into a blockbuster movie starring Angelina Jolie; *Kick-Ass*, which starred Nicolas Cage; and *Kick-Ass 2*, starring Jim Carrey. Millar is currently working on *Kick-Ass 3*, *Jupiter's Legacy*, and *Nemesis Returns*. In his native UK, he's the editor of *CLiNT* magazine, an advisor on film to the Scottish government, and CEO of film and TV company Millarworld Productions. He also serves as Creative Consultant on Fox's Marvel movies in Los Angeles.

JOHN ROMITA JR is a modern-day comic-art master, following in his legendary father's footsteps. Timeless runs on *Iron Man*, *Uncanny X-Men*, *Amazing Spider-Man,* and *Daredevil* helped establish him as his own man artistically, and his work on *Wolverine* and *World War Hulk* is arguably the most explosive comic art of the last decade. In addition to *Eternals* with writer Neil Gaiman, JRJR teamed with Mark Millar on the creator-owned *Kick-Ass*, later developed into a blockbuster feature film starring Nicolas Cage. Avid Spider-Man fans rejoiced at the artist's return to *Amazing Spider-Man* with the Brand New Day storylines "New Ways To Die" and "Character Assassination." He later joined writer Brian Michael Bendis on the relaunched *Avengers*. Recent titles include the blockbuster crossover *Avengers vs X-Men* and the relaunch of *Captain America*.

TOM PALMER has worked as an illustrator in the advertising and editorial fields, but has spent the majority of his career in comic books. His first assignment, fresh out of art school, was on *Doctor Strange*. He has since gone on to lend his inking talents to many of Marvel's top titles, including *X-Men*, *The Avengers*, *Tomb of Dracula*, and more recently *Punisher*, *Hulk,* and *Ghost Rider*. He lives and works in New Jersey.

DEAN WHITE is one of the comic industry's best and most sought-after color artists. Well-known for his work on titles such as *The Amazing Spider-Man*, *Punisher*, *Dark Avengers*, *Captain America*, *Black Panther*, *Wolverine*, and countless more, Dean's envelope-pushing rendering and color palette bring a sense of urgency and power to every page he touches.

CHRIS ELIOPOULOS is a multiple award-winner for his lettering, having worked on dozens of books during the twenty years he's been in the industry — including Erik Larsen's *Savage Dragon*, for which he hand-lettered the first 100 issues. Adding to his success as a letterer, he also publishes his own strip *Misery Loves Sherman*, wrote and illustrated the popular *Franklin Richards: Son of a Genius* one-shots, and wrote Marvel's *Lockjaw and the Pet Avengers* series.

JENNIFER LEE is a story editor and producer working across film, comics, and prose. She's edited for both Marvel and DC Comics, and her books include *Daredevil*, *Black Widow*, *100 Bullets*, *Transmetropolitan*, and the award-winning illustrated prose novel *The Sandman: The Dream Hunters*. *Hit-Girl* marks Jenny's reunion with Mark Millar and John Romita Jr, whom she edited during their seminal run on *Wolverine*. Film credits include *True Adolescents* starring Mark Duplass and Melissa Leo; *Small, Beautifully Moving Parts*; *Union Square* starring Mira Sorvino and Tammy Blanchard; *Arcadia* starring John Hawkes; and *The Skeleton Twins* starring Kristen Wiig and Bill Hader. She lives in New York with her husband, comics illustrator Cliff Chiang.

VARIANT COVERS

ONE

(VARIANT BY PHIL NOTO)

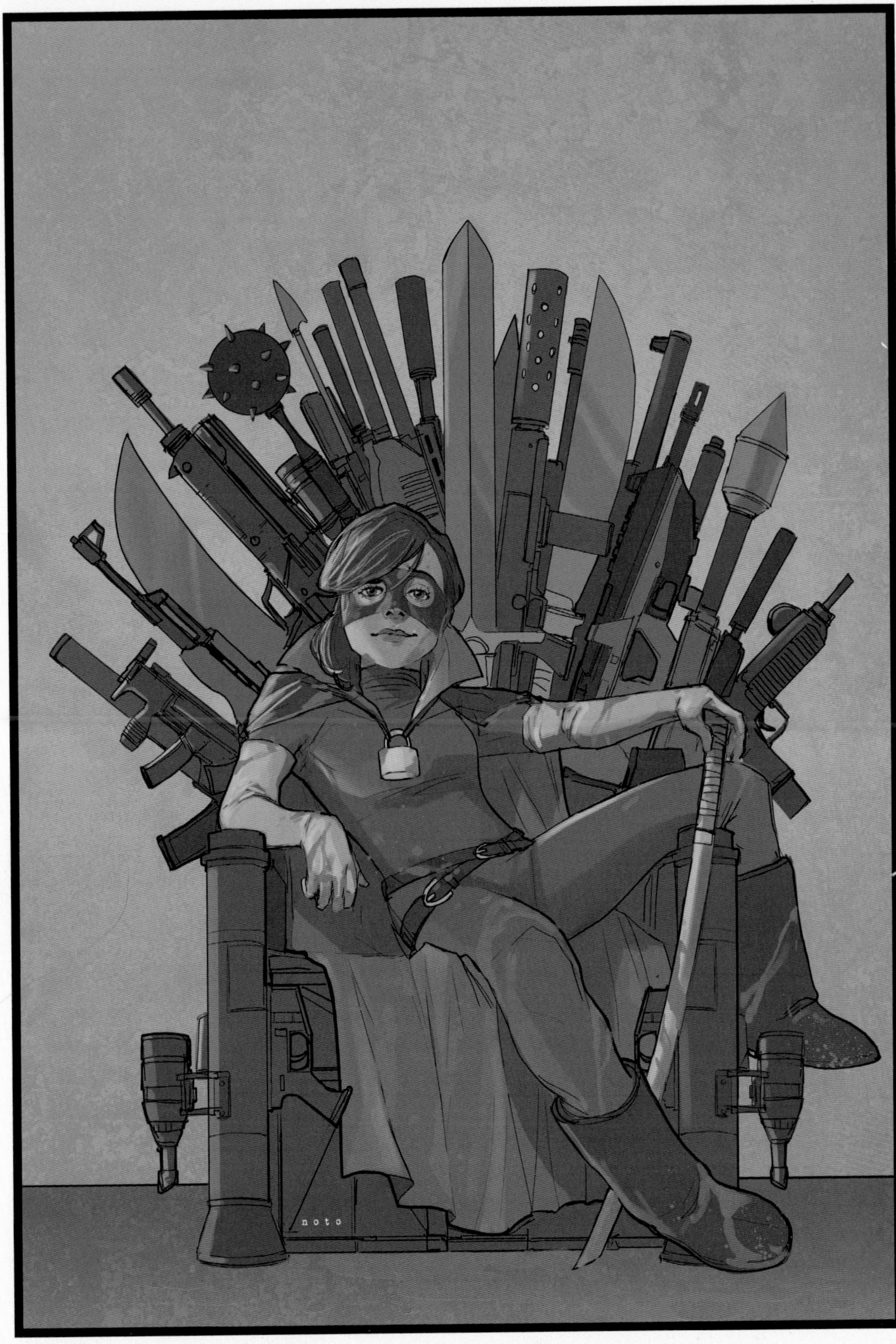
noto

ONE

(SKETCH VARIANT BY JOHN ROMITA JR. & TOM PALMER)

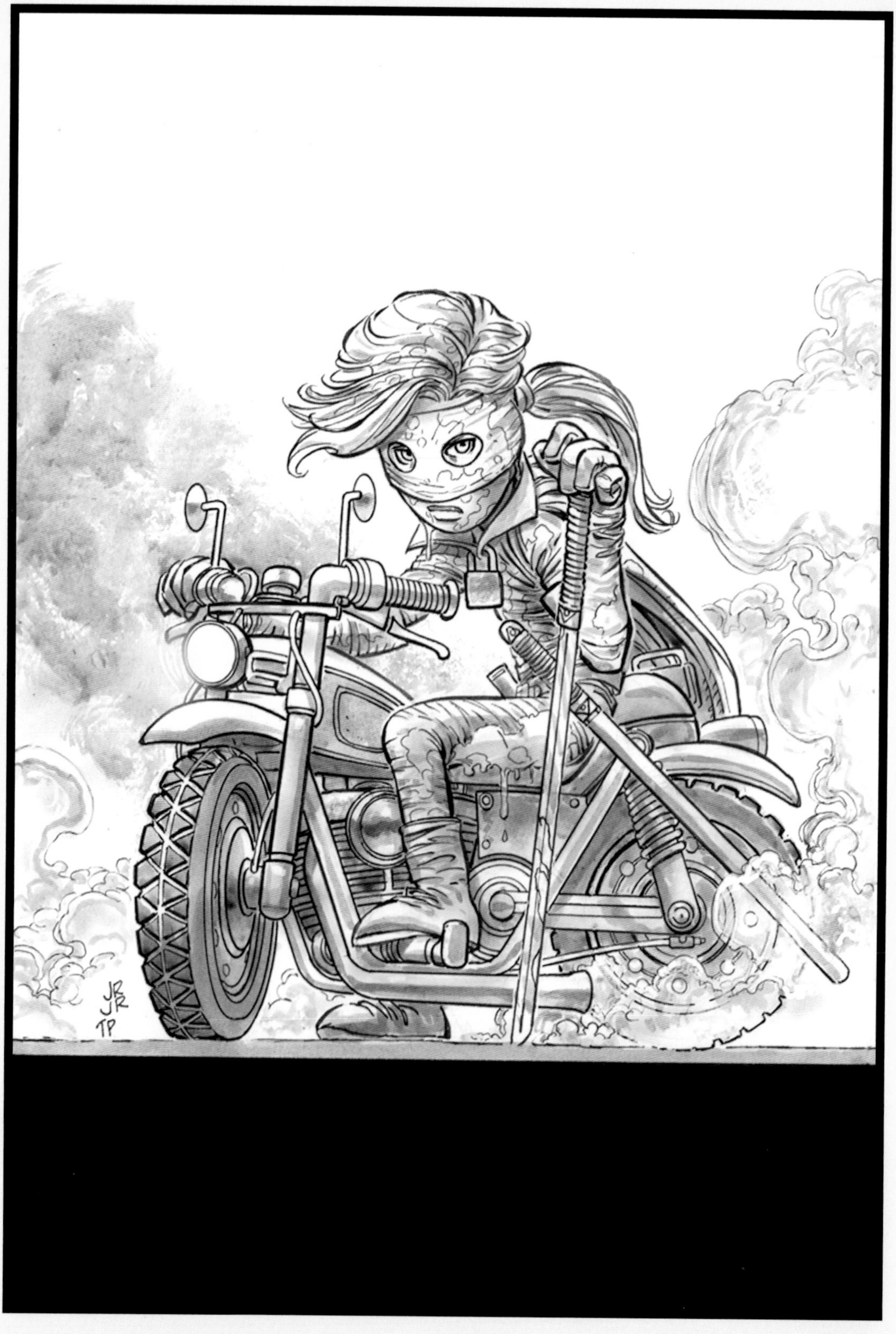
JR JR TP

ONE

(VARIANT BY LEANDRO FERNANDEZ & ILEANA MONTECHIARINI)

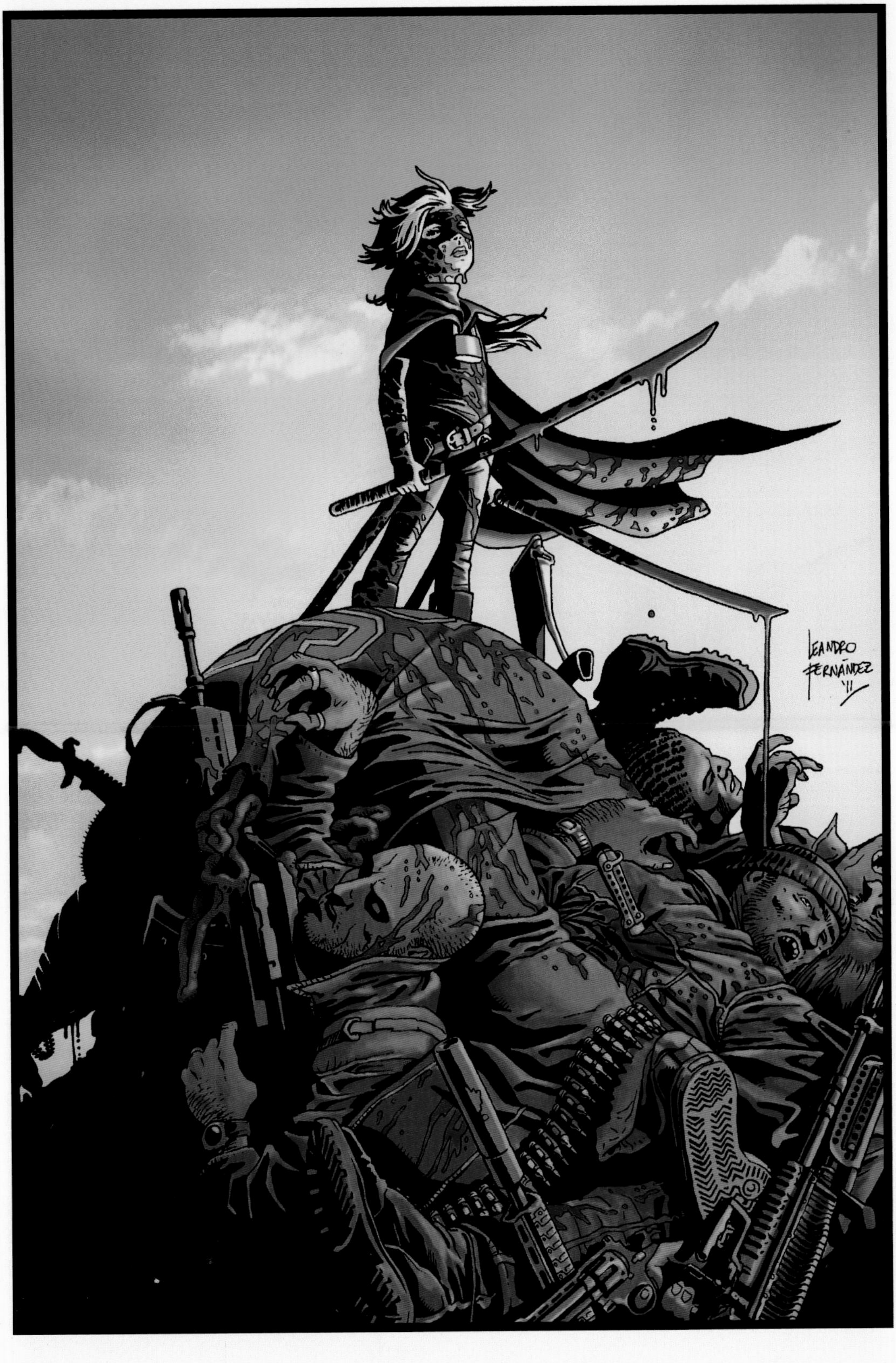
LEANDRO
FERNÁNDEZ
'11

TWO

(SKETCH VARIANT BY JOHN ROMITA JR. & TOM PALMER)

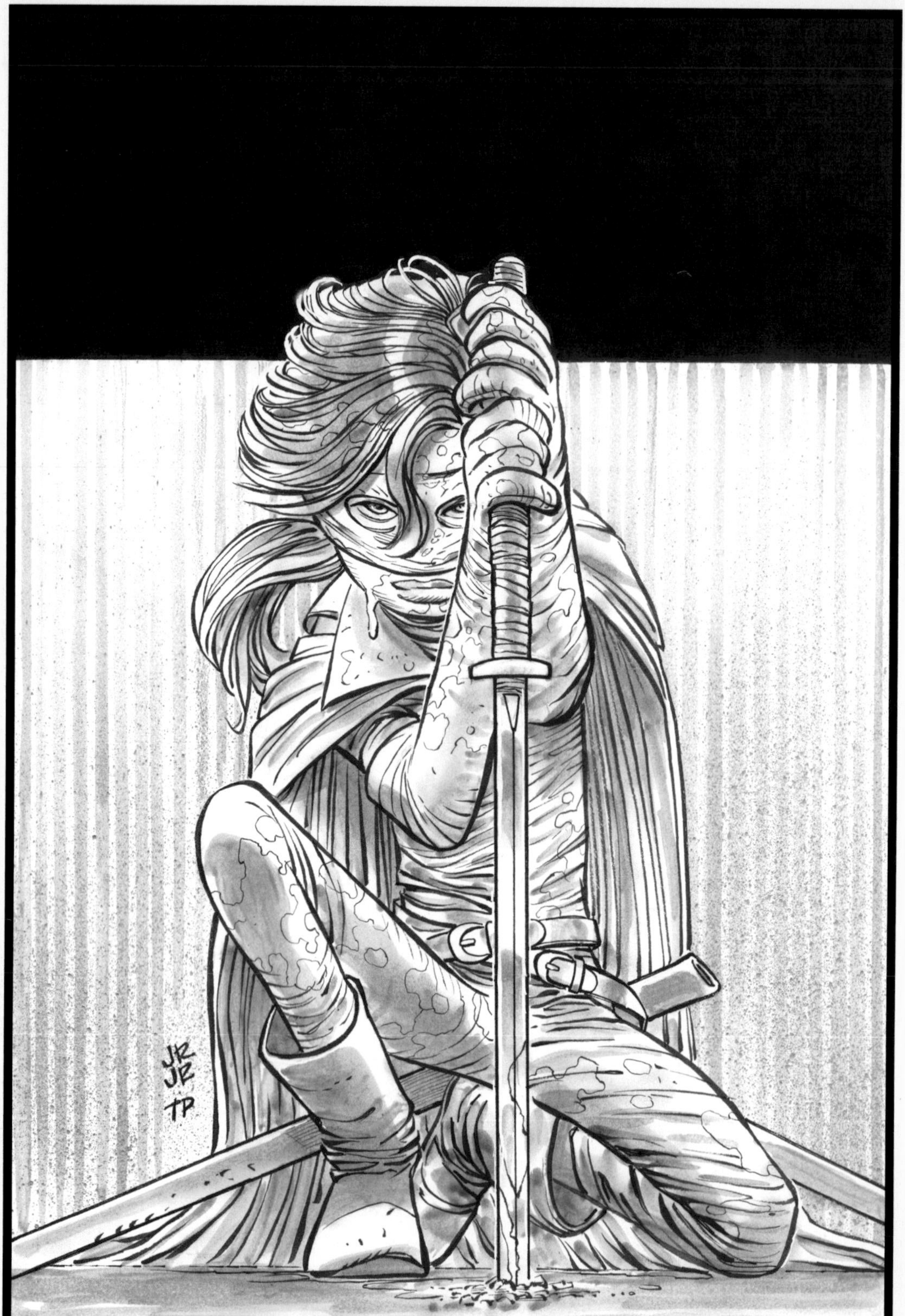
JR JR TP

TWO

(VARIANT BY DAVE JOHNSON)

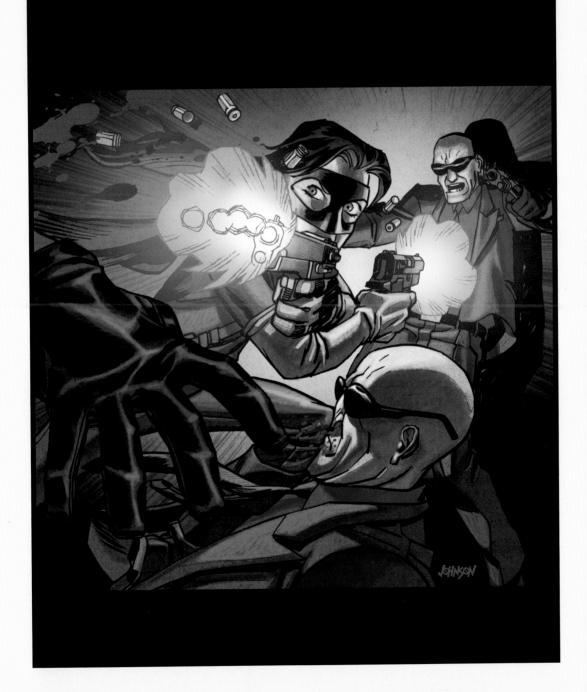

THREE

(SKETCH VARIANT BY JOHN ROMITA JR. & TOM PALMER)

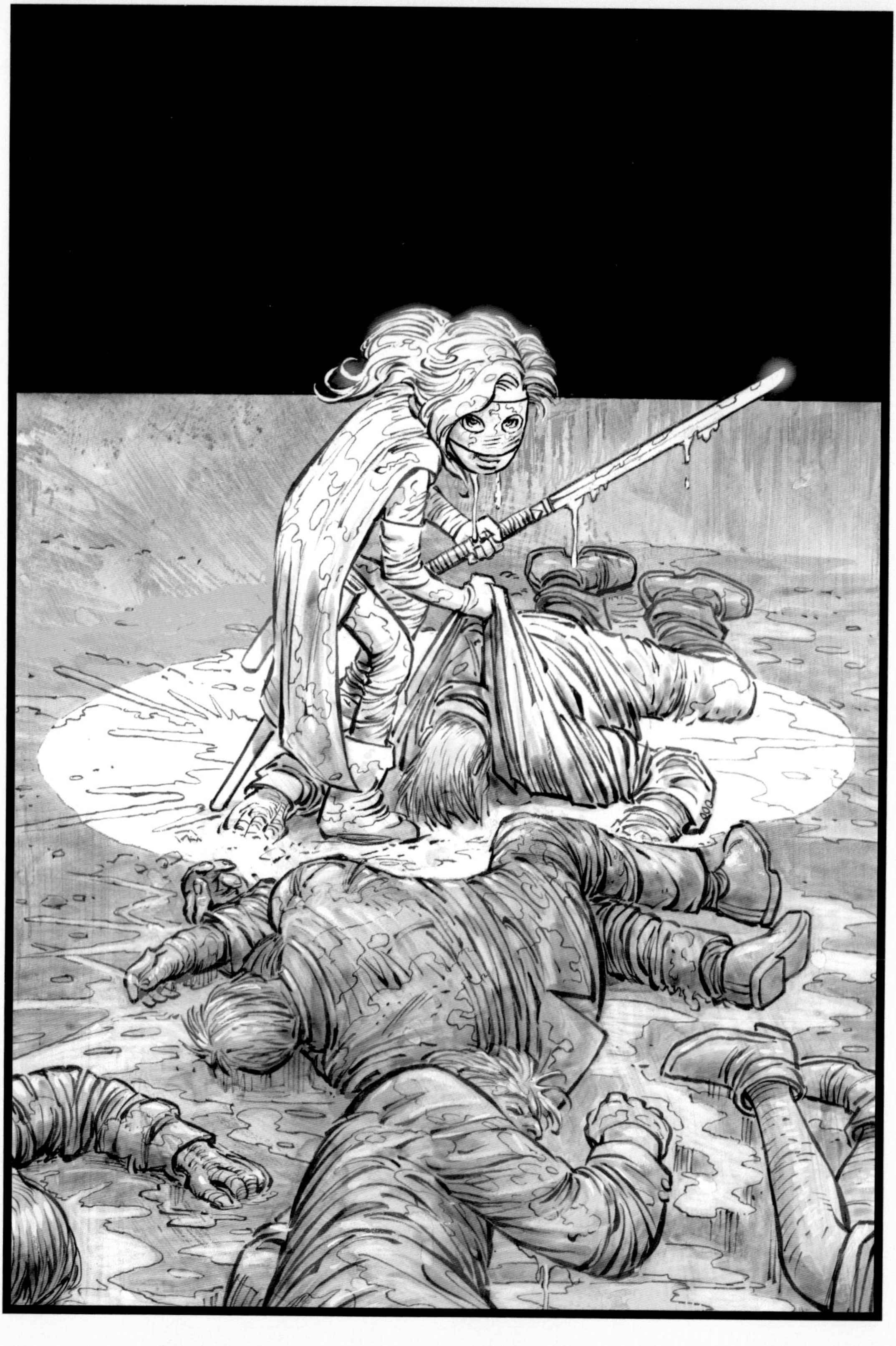

THREE
(VARIANT BY JOCK)

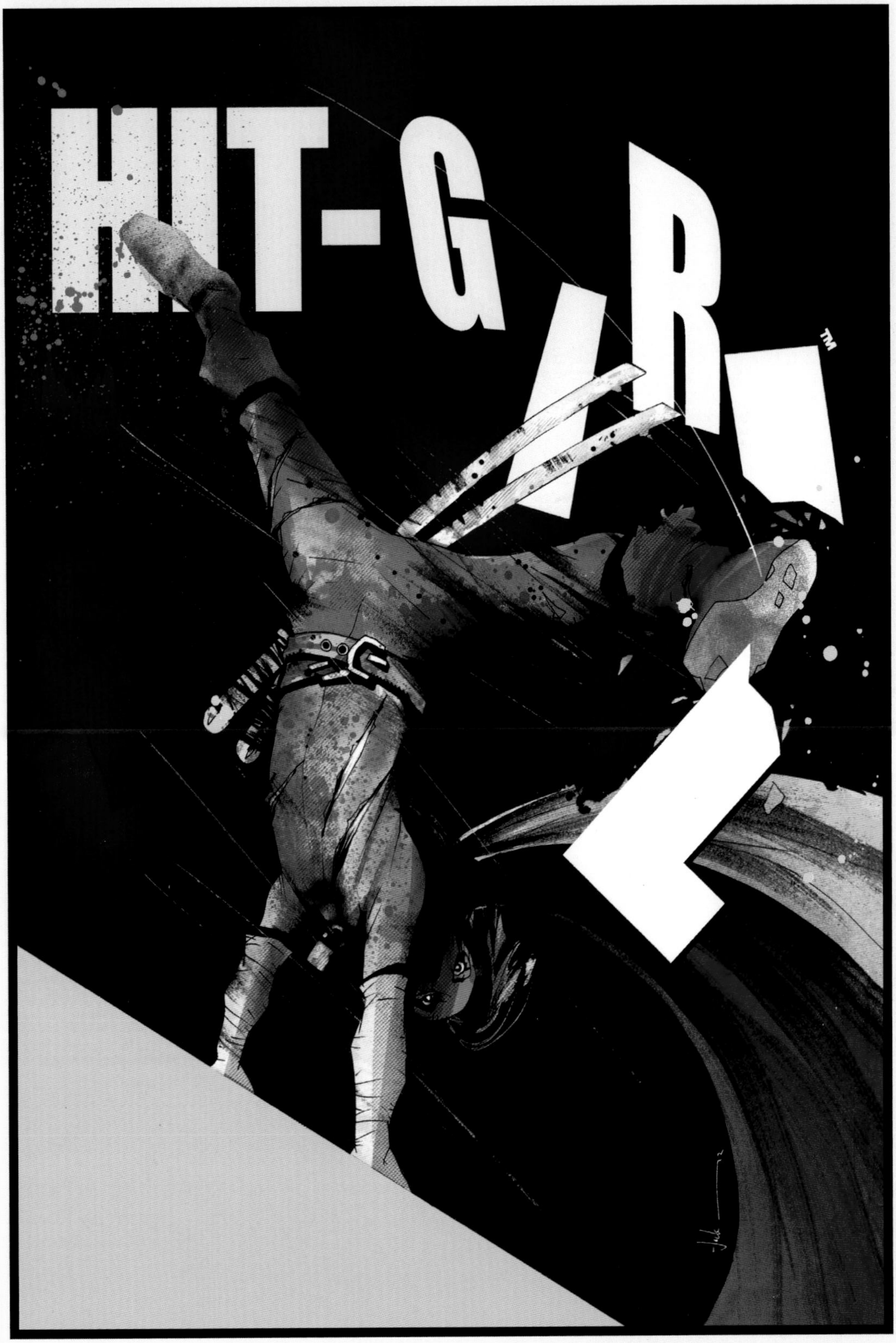
HIT-GIRL™

FOUR

(SKETCH VARIANT BY JOHN ROMITA JR. & TOM PALMER)

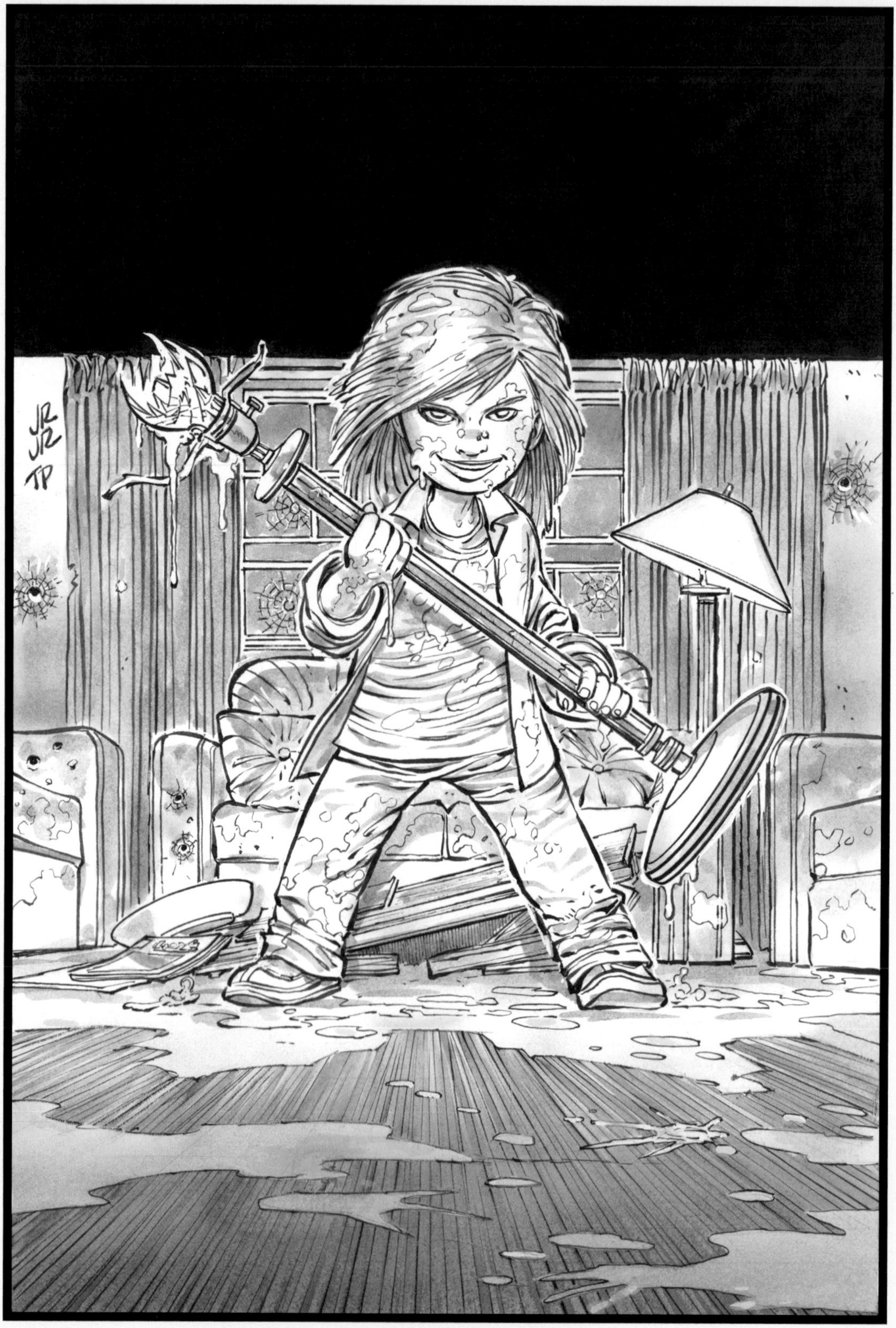
JR
JR
TP

FOUR

(VARIANT BY GEOF DARROW & PETER DOHERTY)

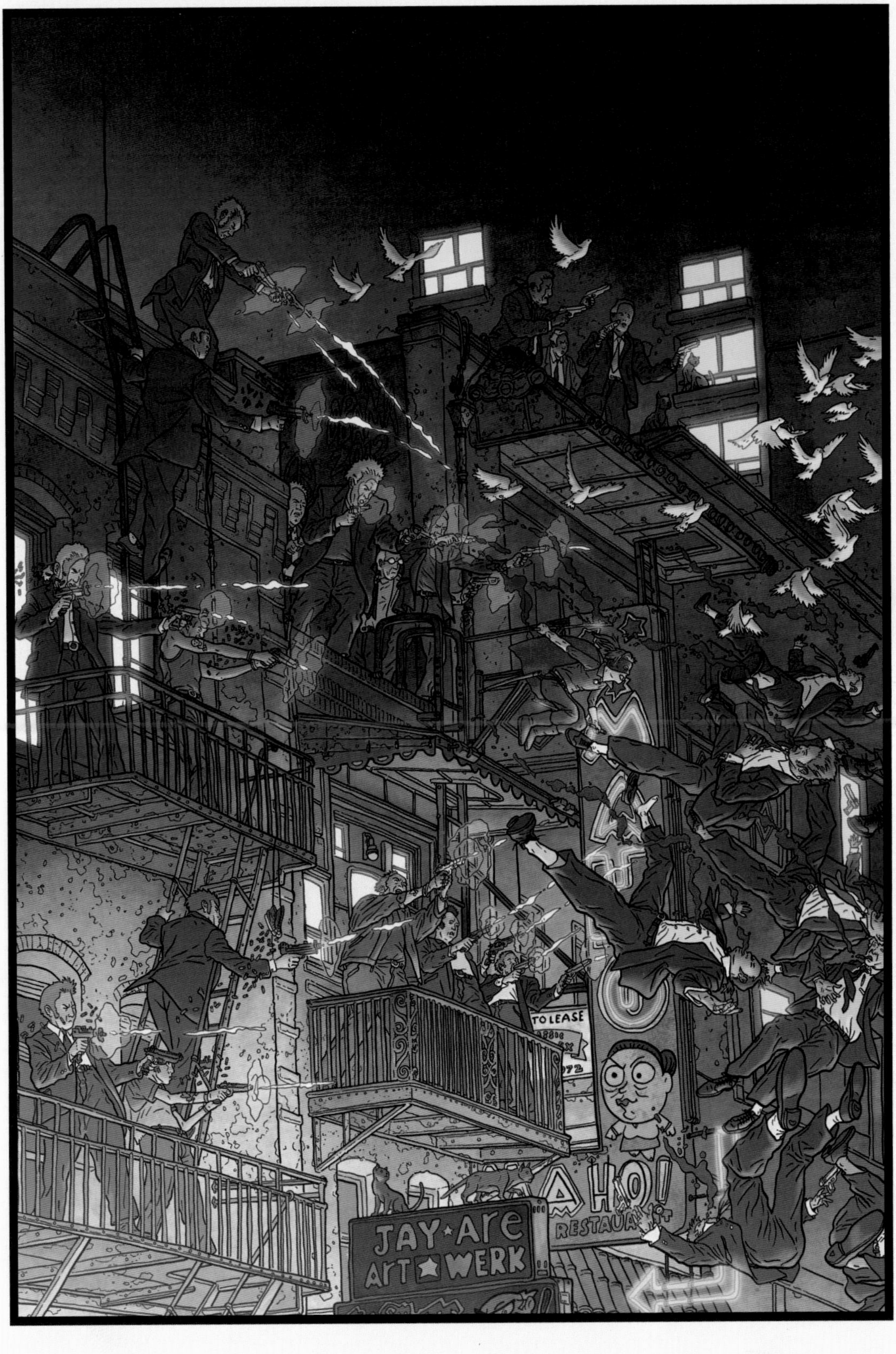
TO LEASE
HO!
RESTAU
JAY ARE
ART WERK

FIVE

(SKETCH VARIANT BY JOHN ROMITA JR. & TOM PALMER)

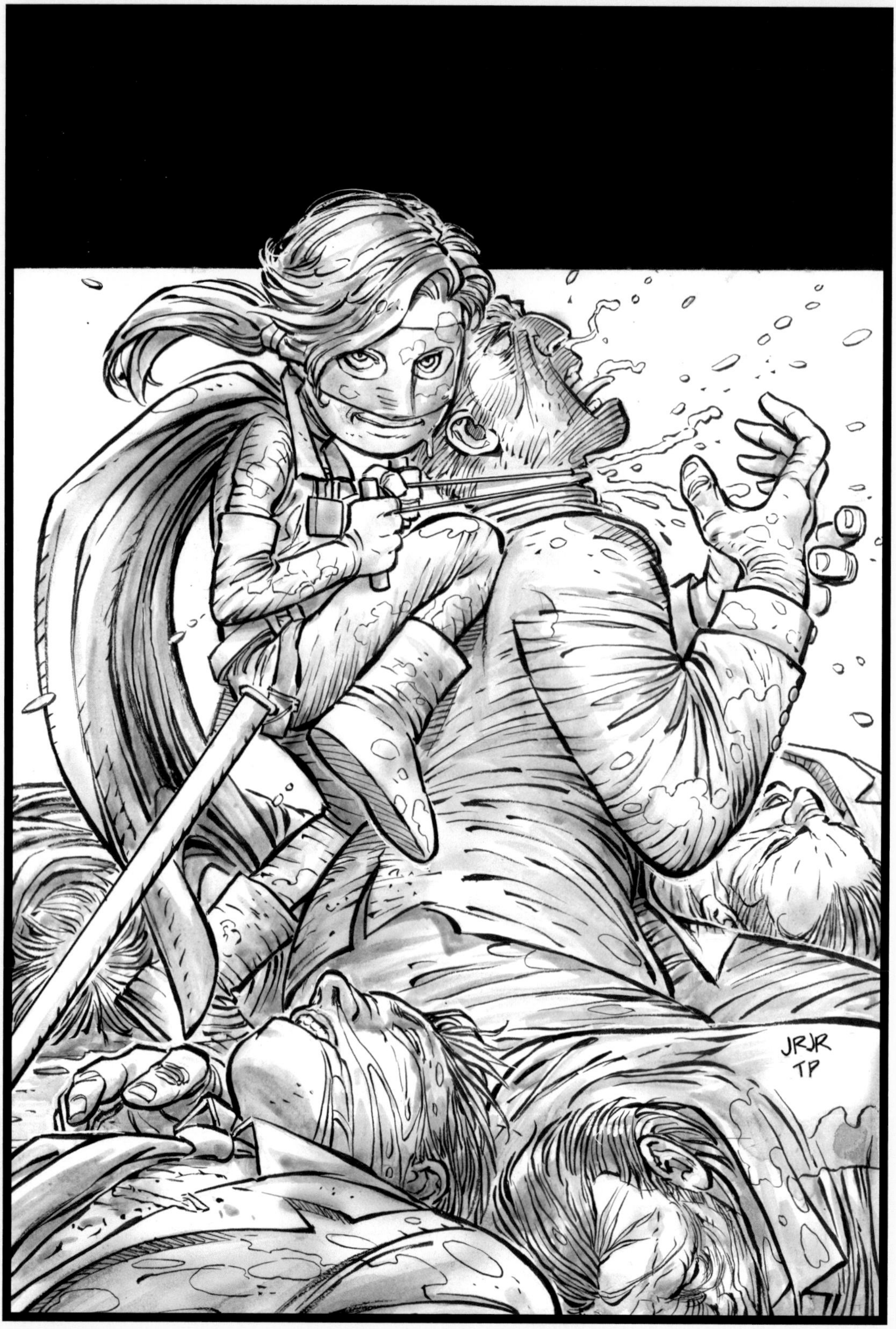

JRJR
TP

FIVE

(VARIANT BY BILL SIENKIEWICZ)

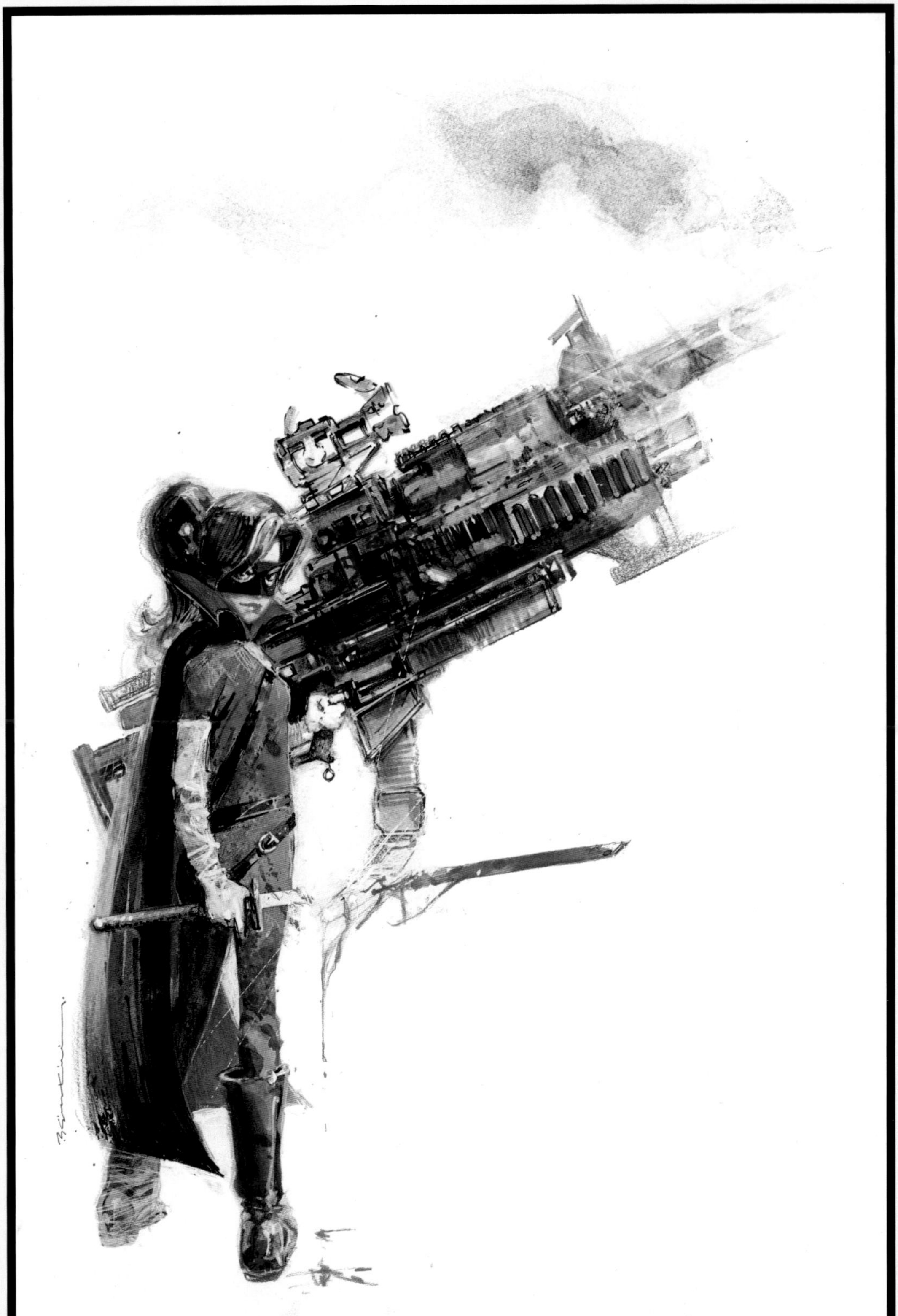

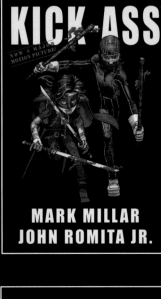

KICK-ASS
NOW A MAJOR MOTION PICTURE!
MARK MILLAR
JOHN ROMITA JR.

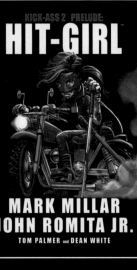

KICK-ASS 2 PRELUDE:
HIT-GIRL
MARK MILLAR
JOHN ROMITA JR.
TOM PALMER and DEAN WHITE

THE MILLAR

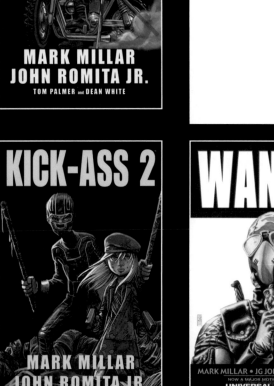

KICK-ASS 2
MARK MILLAR
JOHN ROMITA JR.

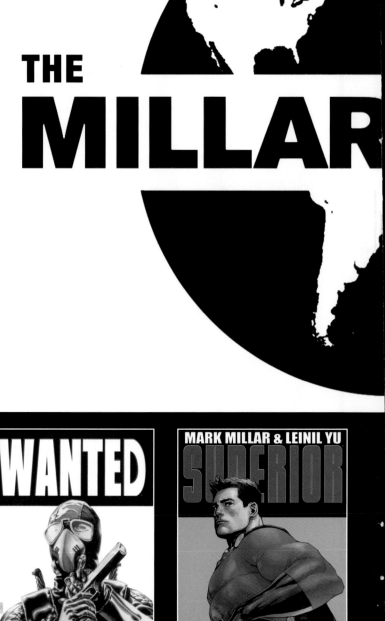

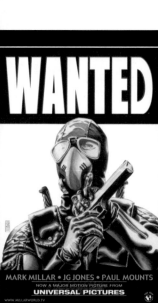

WANTED
MARK MILLAR • JG JONES • PAUL MOUNTS
NOW A MAJOR MOTION PICTURE FROM
UNIVERSAL PICTURES
WWW.MILLARWORLD.TV

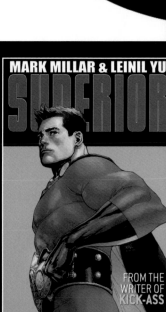

MARK MILLAR & LEINIL YU
SUPERIOR
FROM THE
WRITER OF
KICK-ASS

WORLD™
COLLECTION

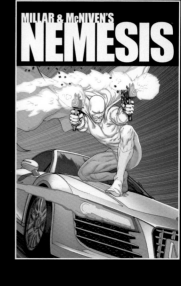

MILLAR & McNIVEN'S
NEMESIS

MARK MILLAR   DAVE GIBBONS
the
SECRET SERVICE

6
$2.99

MARK MILLAR · FRANK QUITELY
JUPITER'S LEGACY

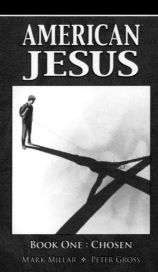

AMERICAN JESUS

BOOK ONE : CHOSEN
MARK MILLAR ✦ PETER GROSS

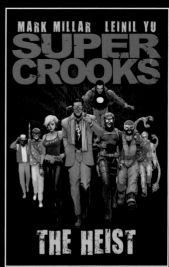

MARK MILLAR   LEINIL YU
SUPER CROOKS

THE HEIST

KICK-ASS READING ORDER

PART ONE

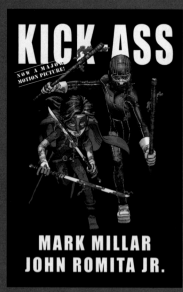

KICK-ASS
NOW A MAJOR MOTION PICTURE!
MARK MILLAR
JOHN ROMITA JR.

PART TWO

KICK-ASS 2 PRELUDE:
HIT-GIRL
MARK MILLAR
JOHN ROMITA JR.
TOM PALMER and DEAN WHITE

PART THREE

KICK-ASS 2
MARK MILLAR
JOHN ROMITA JR.

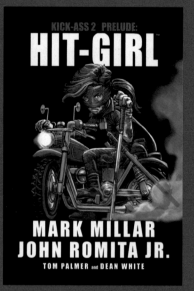

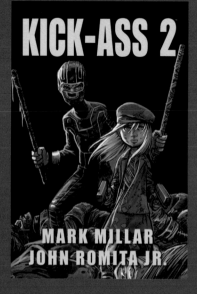

PART FOUR

KICK-ASS 3

THE GRAND FINALE

MAY 2013